HEROES OF THE TWENTIETH CENTURY

HEROES OF THE TWENTIETH CENTURY

IAN FELLOWES-GORDON

HAWTHORN BOOKS, INC.
PUBLISHERS NEW YORK

Manufactured in Great Britain
4525

920
F33

CONTENTS

ACKNOWLEDGEMENTS

We should like to express our indebtedness to the following publishers for permission to quote extracts from books published by them as follows: Hodder and Stoughton Ltd., *Three Lives of Helen Keller* by Harrity and Martin; Hodder and Stoughton Ltd. for an extract from *High Adventure* by Sir Edmund Hillary, Copyright 1955 by author; George Allen and Unwin Ltd., *Alone Across the Tasman Sea* by Francis Chichester (referred to in the text as *Seaplane Solo*, the title under which it was first published); John Murray Ltd., *Unflinching* by Edgar Christian; Peter Davies Ltd., *Determined to Live* by Brian Hession; The Hutchinson Publishing Group, *The Face of Victory* by Leonard Cheshire; Macmillan and Co. Ltd. and Richard Hillary's literary executors, *The Last Enemy* by Richard Hillary; Macmillan and Co. Ltd. and Mr. Lovat Dickson, *Richard Hillary* by Lovat Dickson; Macmillan and Co. Ltd., *The Art of Adventure* by Eric Linklater; Vallentine, Mitchell and Co. Ltd., *The Diary of Anne Frank*.

ILLUSTRATIONS

Introduction

This book, in a way, is a personal one. It has to be. For to select twenty or so heroes, a list that will enrage no one by its omissions or its entries, is an impossible task. Comparisons are futile, and until someone devises a computer programme which will feed in all the relevant—and irrelevant—details, and abstract a score at the other end, we will have no reasonable method of lining up our heroes, biggest on the right, littlest on the left, and awarding prizes.

Yet this happens. In wartime, for instance, when big medals, little medals, and tiny ones are handed out to those who have served their country. Well-deserved rewards—but how many others are there—men and women, unsung, unmentioned, unrewarded and probably dead—who deserve them?

Think, too, of the thousands—but why limit ourselves to thousands?—who are heroes nowhere near the battlefield. The givers of kidneys, rescuers of the sick and maimed, pushers-back of frontiers—and simply those who, by their example, lead the rest of us.

Military heroes are a minority in this book, but their views on the matter, just because they are the only heroes officially recognized outside the Soviet Union, are of value. They agree on two things. First, that there are others who deserved the same recognition and didn't get it: second, that none of them is, habitually, a "brave" man. No one is. "If you've got any imagination at all," says one V.C., "you find yourself thinking, why did they choose me?" "Why," asks another, "should how I behave for five minutes of my life count for anything?"

My aim in these chapters is to write of a few men and women who in some way or other have particularly influenced me, including one or two of whom I disapprove. For this is

9

another aspect of heroism: if a man can rally six hundred million people behind him on the basis of his example, like Mao Tse-tung, then he is a hero even if—well, even if. Richard Hillary is a hero in that he inspired countless young men to give their all: but he is one not so much because of what he did, but because of what happened to him.

None of our heroes—none of them in this book—is perfect, any more than the rest of us. Some have moments of cowardice to set against deeds of valour; some, ignoble acts against a background of self-effacing courage. A deed of heroism may be a lifetime, like that of Albert Schweitzer. But more likely it is one single, startling action. Scientists tell us each cell in our bodies is replaced regularly; that the man of today is, quite literally and in every part, not what he was a year ago. So it is irrelevant that a man called Edmund Hillary appeared to indulge in an unsporting and selfish dash to the South Pole ahead of his partner—for a man with the same name got to the top of Everest and inspired millions. And that is all that need concern us. To downgrade a hero for something he subsequently does is as muddled and pointless as renaming Stalingrad.

As Madame de Sevigné is supposed to have said, "No man is a hero to his *valet de chambre*". Whether she said it or no, the point is made: no man is a hero to all the rest of us. Antigonus of Sparta put it the same way: when Herodotus wrote verses likening him to the sun, he studied them for a moment, then laughed. "This will be news—surprising news—to my body-servant."

And so to our heroes. But not quite yet—for, as we said at the start, this is—has to be—a personal book. The deeds and the people who performed them will not be every man's choice —but they are mine. At least one of my heroes will be unknown to almost everyone who reads this. But they are people who have impressed and influenced me, one way or the other, and for this, in the age of the anti-hero, I am profoundly grateful. There is a bit of Walter Mitty in all of us and perhaps more in me than in most. I have dreamed, like Walter, of doing heroic things, sailing or flying single-handed across the Atlantic, shooting down squadrons of enemy aircraft, leading people, thousands of them, on some crusade. Like Walter Mitty, I have done none of it. But knowing about those who have, has not only inspired me: it has, on more than one occasion, changed the course of my life.

And so—very briefly—a little about me, to explain why this oddly assorted group of men and women has been brought together.

The very first English I spoke was "I do not spik English because I am ver' stupeed." I was four at the time, in Paris, and my bilingual parents, to whom I was devoted, had instructed me in this as my party piece. They spoke to me only in French because, with a French nanny, it was the only language I knew. And at the slightest overture from an English-speaking guest, I went into my act, my English sentence. I was terribly proud of it—and in total ignorance of what it meant. I was already, at four, a happy misfit, ripe for the attentions of Thurber and his Mitty.

Two years later the family was in New York, and there we stayed ten years. My English at first was pitiful, my American non-existent, and soon my incoherence, my un-American clothes, made me enemies. My obvious resentment egged them on to worse, and for my first year or so in the U.S.A. I was a solitary, bravely bearing my cross, composing poetry under the bed and deciding at an early age to be a hero. Like Lindbergh. He—though he is not in these pages—was my first one: his face was suddenly on the cover of every boy's magazine, he was the biggest hero the world had ever known, to me and millions more. It was spring and I was an incoherent foreigner of six when he performed the feat which touched off this huge explosion of hero worship. I read in the *New York Evening World* that this was "The Greatest Feat of a Solitary Man in the Records of the Human Race", and I went right along with the view. I followed the flight of this awkward, likeable, man, his descent on Paris, France, and his return to America in a cruiser, thoughtfully despatched by President Coolidge. I went into town with my father and helped drop ticker-tape from an office window as he drove in triumph up Broadway. After I'd left, the Street Cleaning Department picked up eighteen hundred tons of the stuff.

11

During these childhood years in America I developed an admiration, growing ever deeper, for someone else I regarded as a hero, who happened to be a cousin as well. He was much older than me, with children of his own, but he took an interest in the doings, the problems of the young people in the whole of our large family. He was a busy man, yet he was always able to answer a letter from a garrulous child.

He had already, by the time I was seven, made a name for himself in politics, but this meant, at the time, precisely nothing to me: what inspired and fascinated me was that he had been, in the year I was born, struck down with an illness which had suddenly and dramatically deprived him of the use of both legs—and he had fought back. He seemed to have an energy, a sense of humour and, above all, a courage, denied to the rest of us. He also had a car, the controls of which, grouped round the steering wheel so his hands could operate brake, throttle, clutch and the rest of it, fascinated me when I was allowed to fiddle with them.

His name was Franklin Delano Roosevelt and, though he impressed himself on me at my most impressionable, he would be in this book if I had never met him. In fact, until he died, we kept up a correspondence. Obviously the President of the United States had no time to initiate a correspondence with an adolescent cousin, but this one unfailingly replied to every one of the letters, hopeful, boastful, miserable or just stupid, with which I bombarded him.

The start of war found me in Britain and a new-joined, ill-fitting member of her Regular Army. On the face of it, I seemed unlikely to distinguish myself. A whole host of heroes began to parade themselves before me, daring me to do likewise. Richard Hillary's book *The Last Enemy* made me apply for transfer to the R.A.F. Luckily for myself and for the Air Force I was refused. The tale of Gandhi ,part-myth, part-fact, had something to do with my volunteering to serve in the East and indirectly altered my life.

And so on. *My* list of heroes may not be *your* list of heroes. But here it is.

IAN FELLOWES-GORDON,

January, 1966.

Chapter 1

Emmeline Pankhurst

As we said at the beginning, your hero may not be my hero, mine may not be yours, and we both may disapprove of the other man's. But a man who can rally thousands, even millions, behind him, a hero in their eyes if not in ours, is still a hero.

By this criterion, Hitler was a hero. All the raised hands and expostulation that a statement like that brings forth cannot cancel out the fact that, had we lost the war, as we so nearly did, Adolf Hitler, now a benign, silver-haired old murderer, much as lovable old Uncle Joe Stalin was becoming when fate pulled him into the wings, would be a hero over half the world.

And that includes the English-speaking part of it. There were quite enough people in Britain, applauding carefully when victory came, whose views had approximated sufficiently to Hitler's own—on the Jews, on industrial discipline, on a hundred other matters—to have formed a nucleus for the loyal Germanic province we would have become. To say nothing of

13

those whose views were different but who would have changed them.

We cannot afford to be smug about France—or Holland, or Denmark, or any other of the occupied countries. We won—partly because we had a Churchill and they did not, partly through our own efforts, largely through the most outrageous good luck. We were never tested.

I think it is important to be clear in one's mind about this. Heroes are, they arise, and for the most part there is nothing you or I can do about it. And let no one doubt that if Hitler, or Stalin, or Mussolini or Genghis Khan, were suddenly to re-appear, then literally millions of people would be out in the streets, applauding.

All of which is an inappropriate start to a chapter on Emmeline Pankhurst. That this brave woman should be mentioned on the same page as Hitler seems utterly outrageous. But one does so only to point out, again, that we all have different ideas of heroes. Mrs. Pankhurst was undeniably a hero, and to millions: I find her, as an historical character, quite insufferable.

She was born on 14 July, anniversary of that Quatorze Juillet, Bastille Day—and perhaps that had something to do with it. Her Quatorze Juillet was in 1858, and in Manchester. Her father, Robert Goulden, was an admirably self-made man, who had begun his working life as errand boy and risen to be partner in a prosperous cotton firm, finding time as well to rear no less than ten children. He and his wife were devout liberals, with a small "l", espousing every cause that came their way, from the emanicipation of the slaves which had already made Mr. Goulden's fortune, to women's suffrage. By 1867, when his daughter Emmeline was nine years old, there was a flourishing "Suffrage Committee" in Manchester (indeed, that town was the centre of the movement) and it looked, for a moment, as if women might be given the vote that year. John Stuart Mill had moved an amendment to the Reform Act, putting "person" in place of "man" as a thing entitled to vote, but it failed.

One of the most ardent supporters of female suffrage was Dr. Richard Pankhurst, a man who had graduated from London University in the year Emmeline was born. His name was much in the news when Emmeline left Manchester, aged fourteen, to go to school in Paris. He was also a good friend of her father.

At the Ecole Normale, in the Avenue de Neuilly, she immediately made a firm friend of a girl, Noémie, whose father, the Communist Marquis de Rochefort-Luçay, refused his title and styled himself "Henri Rochefort". He had been sentenced—but not for this—to life transportation to New Caledonia. Then, while the two girls were at school together, he had escaped in a small boat, been picked up by an American liner and taken to safety in the New World. This made, as naturally it would, a deep impression on the young English girl. It also equated a defiance of the law with heroism.

And Henri Rochefort, quite apart from his courage, was an aristocrat, a man of importance, whose denial of his proper title served, as it usually does, merely to pinpoint him as a member of the nobility.

Already, the boys of her own age had begun to seem, to quote her daughter's revealing biography of the future Mrs. Pankhurst, "insignificant". So much so that Emmeline had already decided she "would only give herself to an important man". School over, and with this in mind, she returned to Manchester. By now she was an attractive and graceful young woman.

Almost immediately, she went back to Paris: her younger sister Mary was also to go to the Ecole Normale, and Emmeline had permission to accompany her.

This time in Paris, her closest friend was an American girl, daughter of the American socialist, Albert Brisbane. She and Mary and Miss Brisbane now took up the cause of Socialism as ardently as Emmeline had supported the adventures of the Marquis de Rochefort-Luçay.

It was in Paris that another influential happening took place. Noémie, now married to her rich man, urged Emmeline to do the same as soon as possible. Preferably to a Frenchman, so they might continue to live near each other, be friends. And of course the man to marry must be successful, one with whom she would find opportunity for her "gifts as hostess, influencing a brilliant circle".

The idea appealed and, in no time at all, Noémie discovered

a suitor. He was a man who had already made his mark in the world, who would be only too happy to marry the attractive English girl. Provided, of course, that an adequate dowry was forthcoming.

This, old Mr. Goulden back in Manchester stoutly refused to do. He was damned if he would have his daughter going off with a man who wanted her for her money—for his, Goulden's, money.

To a girl of Emmeline's temperament, nothing could have made a more lasting or vivid impression. Here she was, caught between the greed, as she saw it, of two men: one who would marry her if it were made worth his while; another who refused the money to which, by the custom of her day and class, she was fully entitled.

But in Richard Marsden Pankhurst, a little later, she found the man she had been looking for. Twenty years her senior, already a success, not demanding a dowry, and with views on practically everything which were identical with her own. They married in 1879, and had four children within six years. She grew ever more devoted to her restless, middle-aged husband, who now prepared to stand for election to Parliament as an Independent Radical. He failed to be elected in 1883 and again in 1885, which is perhaps hardly surprising in view of his platform, which even in these days might be considered a little daring. The Doctor was going to abolish the Monarchy as well as the House of Lords, disestablish the Church of England, nationalize land, grant Home Rule to Ireland. In the intervals of implementing all this, he would found a "United States of Europe" and ultimately an "International Commonwealth".

Despite the efforts of his wife and her father, who was his election agent, Dr. Pankhurst failed on both occasions. In many ways it is a great pity Pankhurst never seemed to have realized that politics is the pursuit of the possible and been content to bide his time for some of his reforms. He was a wise, kind, and good man, who would have been a valuable addition to the House of Commons. But he went back to his work as barrister, dealing with cases in Manchester and London, while his wife, enraged by a second defeat at the hustings, attacked every target within range, from the Irish who had perversely voted against the Doctor, to the judge who summed up against him in a case he unsuccessfully brought for slander. ("It is to be regretted that there should be found on the English bench a judge who will lend his aid to a disreputable section of the Tory Party in doing their dirty work; but for what other reason were you ever placed where you are? I have, my Lord, the honour to be, Your obedient servant——.")

In search of that financial independence which, ever since the disappointment of the refused dowry, she had demanded for herself, she and her sister Mary opened a small shop in London, in the Hampstead Road, where they sold an odd assortment of "fancy goods" which ran from milking stools to photo frames, most of it painted and decorated by themselves. Emmeline moved her family in with her, and although the shop made little money, life was pleasant.

Then, when she was away in Manchester, her little son Frank sickened and suddenly died.

Emmeline, heartbroken—for she loved, and continued to love, her family more than each cause she espoused—decided the damp house had been responsible, and immediately sold it. The shop she transferred to Berners Street, off Oxford Street, and for the family she bought a house in Russell Square.

And now it seemed as if fortune would smile on her at last. Within a year of little Frank's death, another boy was born: at the same time she found herself the political hostess of which she had dreamed. There were two big intercommunicating rooms at 8 Russell Square, and soon these became the centre for meetings of practically every sort of "advanced"—or as we would style them in the jargon of today, "progressive"— thinkers. Agnostics sipping sherry cannoned off Fabians munching cucumber sandwiches, trade unionists drinking tea: there were Socialists, atheists, free-thinkers, free-lovers, the advanced of every shade and inclination. There were even opportunities to take part in Trafalgar Square meetings and rallies, to join her husband in supporting his various causes and hectoring the police.

But slowly this widely disseminated moral energy was being canalized into a worthwhile cause—though one wonders whether Emmeline, in her restless urge to do something for

17

someone, as long as authority was on the other side, realized this was happening. Had the wheel of chance stopped at Theosophy, Anti-vivisection, Agnosticism or Yoga, her extraordinary energies and abilities might well have been used for one or other of these causes.

Fortunately for the world, it was Votes for Women which attracted Emmeline Pankhurst. One of the most worthwhile of causes, it had been successfully blocked for years by interests which varied from casual men-about-town to brewers, who feared that giving the vote to women would result in large-scale social reform. No longer would a man be allowed to get drunk, or commit any of the other countless offences he regularly did, without restraint, in what was, very literally, a man's world.

The women's cause was hardly helped by some of their number. Lydia Becker led a section which was all for votes, as long as *only single women got them*, for, as Miss Becker put it to Emmeline, "married women have all the plums of life". Perhaps it is hardly surprising that Gladstone, confronted by a mob of mutually antagonistic women, should have contemptuously thrown the cause of Women's Suffrage back at them and turned his mind to weightier subjects. Fortunately Emmeline was already Mrs. Pankhurst and came down heavily against such splitting of the movement. She went further to press for a Married Women's Property Act. Up to this time, married women legally owned nothing: their property, any earnings they might have, belonged automatically to their husbands. The Bill became law and a few years later the agitation of Emmeline Pankhurst was responsible for passing an Infants Act, which gave mothers the right of custody and guardianship of their children.

Already, Emmeline Pankhurst's energies had been canalized. Between her successive agitations for better conditions for women, she devoted tireless energy to succouring the poor. In 1893 the family had moved back to Manchester (and Dr. Pankhurst failed yet again in an election) and now, with huge numbers of unemployed around her, she formed a Relief Committee. Always a woman who *did* things, rather than one who sat back and complained, she collected food, begged it from stall-holders in the market, and distributed it every day to

thousands of cold and hungry people in Stevenson Square.
She coupled this with violent and successful agitation for
reform of the workhouses where these wretched people were
sent when no longer able to resist. There they were fed, in
dirt and disgrace, on, for the most part, bread and water. The
City Council, in one of the many restrictive edicts they tailored
over the years for Emmeline Pankhurst, prohibited her from
addressing public gatherings—but she was able to persuade
a few Members of Parliament to force the Council to change
its mind.

In the summer of 1898, Emmeline took her eldest daughter
Christabel to stay in Geneva for a year with her own old friend
Noémie. It was marvellous to be back with Noémie—even
though she had grown startlingly fat, no doubt from not doing
all the things Emmeline did—and they went for long, soul-
searching walks together in the few days Emmeline had allotted
herself in Switzerland.

The holiday was interrupted by a telegram from Dr. Pankhurst. "Please come home. I am not well."

Mindful of the tragedy of her little son who had died in
London while she was away, Emmeline dropped everything,
rushed to England. It was in the train which was taking her
from London to Manchester that she saw the news in the
evening paper, "Dr. Pankhurst Dies".

The blow was a cruel one, for she had been devoted to her
husband. From this moment in the train, she resolved to achieve
all those things he had worked for. At the same time, she would
stand firmly on her own two feet and support her four children;
not for her the temptations of a second marriage. She persuaded people to get her the job of local Registrar of Births and
Deaths: this would at least keep them.

And she opened another shop.

But it was in the Registrarship that she was brought into
closer contact with the miseries of human life. Mothers came
to register yet another—a tenth, a twelfth—unwanted birth:
unmarried mothers—most of them mere children—registered
their own and were only too eager to pour out their pitiful
tales to the kindly, helpful, woman who wrote down their name
and address. She discovered that it was almost impossible to

19

force the father of an illegitimate child to contribute to the child's upkeep. (She found, with deep shock, that the child's father and grandfather were sometimes one and the same person.) A court might impose a maintenance of five shillings a week—often less—but until this was thirteen weeks in arrears the young mother had no redress. Then, if the father were able to produce another man who would swear on oath that he, too, had had sexual relations with the girl, her claim was automatically set aside.

By now the cause of women's rights had become for Emmeline Pankhurst the only one in the world. This sort of thing could not be allowed to go on: men had proved themselve incapable of running a decent world by themselves. With her three daughters, Christabel, Sylvia and Adela, and a few women members of the Independent Labour Party, she assembled a "Women's Social and Political Union" on 10 October, 1903. Its members, soon to be dubbed "Suffragettes" by the *Daily Mail*, would very soon become a major force in the country.

The great reformer and agitator, Keir Hardie, strongly approved of the new movement and the way they were setting about it. Their motto, "Votes for Women", particularly appealed to him, as it made their campaign straightforward and understandable to the electorate: other questions of franchise, the giving of votes to poor as well as rich, simple as well as clever, young as well as old, could be dealt with separately.

The movement spread like wildfire. The most unlikely-seeming, the meekest, women suddenly appeared as Suffragettes to storm political meetings and demand loudly from each candidate, "If returned to power at the next election, will your Party give us the vote?" Those—like the unfortunate Winston Churchill, who had the misfortune to contest an election in Manchester itself, the Pankhurst stronghold—who were unable to agree, were howled down, their meetings wrecked. Women of all ages and shapes, displaying an agility which no man would have believed possible, appeared from underneath platforms, down ventilation shafts, through windows, to shout down the speakers. Every one of Winston Churchill's meetings was wrecked in this way, and he lost the election.

In 1905 Emmeline and her W.S.P.U. managed to persuade an M.P. to introduce a bill for Votes for Women, in Parliament. On 12 May, when the Bill was set down for debate, the lobbies of the House of Commons, the streets outside, were jammed with women—Lancashire cotton workers, members of the Co-operative Women's Guild, rich and poor—who had come from all over England to give support to this Bill.

If ever a last straw had been needed to break the restraint of Mrs. Pankhurst, this was it. The Bill was deliberately "talked out". Speaker after speaker in the House got up and wasted time on the First Order of the day, which provided for a rear light on road vehicles, grinning, looking at the clock, chattering on, until it was too late to introduce the Second Order—Votes for Women.

Enraged, Mrs. Pankhurst held, or tried to hold, a meeting of protest outside the very door of Parliament. The police, not too gently, moved them on, while women screamed, demanded Government intervention to pass the Bill.

And on this day, 12 May, 1905, the Suffrage Movement took a new and decisive turn. It became militant. From now on, no Suffragette would leave a meeting unless carried out by force. Christabel, Mrs. Pankhurst's daughter, was one of the first to implement the decision. She set off for a meeting in the Manchester Free Trade Hall announcing, "I shall sleep in prison tonight"—and did.

But this was only the start. Violent, militant, action was needed. The Pankhursts had seen, in the House of Commons, the complacent faces of the men who represented them in the Mother of Parliaments. Obviously, they were worse than useless: if Votes for Women were to be achieved, they would have to be achieved by women.

The new Liberal Government, outlining its programme in the King's Speech in February, 1906, made no mention of Votes for Women, and now Emmeline realized she could no longer operate her movement from as far away as Manchester. Helped by a sympathetic and wealthy lawyer, Frederick Pethick-Lawrence, and his wife, she set up her H.Q. off the Strand in London. From this new centre she toured the country, making speeches, distributing handbills, lobbying M.P.s.

"We shall not rest or falter until the long, weary struggle for enfranchisement is won. For the vote we are prepared to give life itself—or, what is perhaps even harder, the means by which we live——"

And she meant it. The number of arrests mounted. She organized regular demonstrations outside the House of Commons, interrupted every political meeting, instituted a rival "Women's Parliament" in the nearby Caxton Hall. No Suffragette would pay a fine, so all had to go to prison. She went to prison (on one of many occasions) and Suffragettes grew still more violent on her behalf. The windows of 10 Downing Street were smashed, in an effort to attract attention to the movement and to those of its members who were in prison.

By now Suffragettes (and who could tell which woman was a Suffragette, which rose-lipped, almond-eyed, little thing, might not suddenly produce a brick from under her petticoat and hurl it; might not burst out at a meeting with words no woman was supposed to know, far less use?)—by now Suffragettes, and any who might turn out to be, were banned from most political meetings. But women were appearing at them on the end of ropes from the ceiling, popping up from under the furniture. No holds were barred, so long as the nuisance drew attention to the cause. Women chained themselves to railings, had to be released by sweating policemen with hacksaws. One threw herself in front of the King's horse at the Derby and was killed.

Women imprisoned now hit upon the idea of the hunger-strike and refused to eat. They were fed by force, but when the details came out there was an upsurge of public protest. In despair the Home Secretary pushed through a Bill, soon dubbed "The Cat and Mouse Act", which permitted the authorities to discharge a prisoner temporarily on medical grounds if she began a hunger-strike. As she was unlikely to continue this at home, the authorities waited until she seemed recovered, and arrested her again. This Act was used against Mrs. Pankhurst no less than eight times.

Mercifully, perhaps, for the movement, a World War began, in August, 1914. The Suffragettes had certainly drawn attention to a disgraceful state of affairs, but they had alienated a great

deal of support. But with the coming of war, Emmeline Pankhurst was able to urge her followers to stop their agitation, get
out and prove themselves the equals of men.

They did so, flooding on to the battlefields as nurses and
ambulance drivers, working long hours—and often more
efficiently than men—in the vital work of making weapons of
war. By the time war was half over, "Votes for Women" were
inevitable.

In the war's last bloody year, the Bill was passed. But it was
inadequate: women were still disenfranchised for various
reasons, such as being under the age of thirty. Emmeline went
on fighting. Comically enough, her agitation was responsible for
pushing through a Bill which allowed women to be elected to
Parliament—at 21, though they could only vote from the age
of thirty.

The final Bill, extending the vote to all over 21, male and
female, irrespective of means, property and education, was
passed in June, 1928.

On the day it passed, Emmeline Pankhurst, a month short
of seventy-one, died peacefully in London.

Female suffrage was long overdue and had to come—and
Mrs. Pankhurst made it come sooner than it might have. But
probably her greatest contribution lies in the attention she
focused on the cruel position of so many women in the world.

She was a strange person, and her motives for much of what
she did seem somehow obscure. But she succeeded in lighting
a flame in women's hearts, in urging literally millions of
women—and a good few men—into a universal frenzy of
activity such as England had never known.

Chapter 2

Edith Cavell

Edith Cavell—Nurse Edith Cavell—is a controversial figure, and though it would have been high treason to say so half a century ago, you may like her or dislike her intensely. But the fact remains that she inspired people, multitudes of them, in a more all-embracing—blunderbuss—way, than most other popular heroes. People were inspired to fight harder for their country; to rush—if they were not already in uniform—to the nearest recruiting station; to hate Germany with a pathological, quite unreasoning, hate; to strive to become better nurses, doctors, Christians. They were inspired, in short, to avenge Nurse Cavell.

America came into the war.

And eighteen months after that war—thanks largely to American intervention—had ended victoriously, Edith Cavell's body was exhumed from its shallow grave in Belgium. Four years had elapsed since her execution.

Hers was a name at the back of everyone's mind : suddenly

it was again on everyone's lips. For the mortal remains of Edith Cavell were found—miraculously, men said—to be perfectly preserved, her features to be as clear and recognizable as in life. And the body had not been embalmed.

This fact has never been explained—and you may make of it what you wish. But when the little body with its four neat bullet holes, one straight through the heart, was brought back to England by train, by one of His Majesty's destroyers, and by train again—the world burst out in praise. The *New York Times* said, "She had kept the faith, she had not faltered: she had been blessed more than others with opportunity to bear witness. No firing squad could slay these things——." You may find those words meaningless and incomprehensible, but those, and a million more just like them, in every paper in the world, caught at the hearts and imaginations of people and the world went into mourning. Schoolchildren, tears streaming down their faces, strewed flowers in the path of the funeral procession as it approached Westminster Abbey, while their weeping teachers, grief-stricken parents, watched. The orgy of grief and recrimination which had ended halfway through the war began again.

She was born, 4 December, 1865, in the small hamlet of Swardeston in Norfolk, a second daughter of the Rector, the Reverend Frederick Cavell, and his wife Louisa. She grew up as a typical country child, picking blackberries and strawberries in the summer, weighed down by the thickest of flannel in the winter. Life was comfortable and proud, Victoria was a fine queen, lavishing the benefits of peace and a far-flung empire upon the inhabitants of the old country; the Crimea was over, the memory of Miss Nightingale was all that remained, and half the girls in England were being christened Florence. One of these was Edith's older sister.

But in the Cavell household there was the steady, constant reminder of a Being above this, above even Victoria. The Rector had carefully laid out the grounds of his Rectory so that the back garden adjoined the cemetery, and then clinched the matter by building a footpath that ran through both, making them into one. Death, for the Cavell family, was a trusted friend, and only halfway down the garden.

Sundays at the Rectory were devoted to meditation, with all

temptation rigorously excluded. All toys, all secular books, all needlework—practically everything movable, save the Bible—was locked up by Mr. Cavell every Saturday evening, with the same weekly concentration which other householders devote to winding clocks. It stayed under lock and key till Monday morning.

From our freer, laxer, twentieth-century vantage point, it is tempting and easy to dismiss the Reverend Frederick Cavell as a stock Victorian character from the pages of Dickens, dropping to his knees a hundred times a day, probably beating his children, terrorizing his wife and making drudges of the household servants. Perhaps he did all this—but he was a good man, if you could make him out through the gloom of the Swardeston Rectory. He had, for example, a firm and unshakable rule that all luxuries at table be shared with the needy: the family found themselves week after week sharing the Sunday roast, the occasional fowl, with poor people, sometimes beggars from the street.

He was not a rich man himself, and he taught all four of his children to the best of his ability, for there was no money to afford schools for all.

But with Edith an exception was made. She progressed well under her father's teaching, more than did her two sisters and young brother: and so, at considerable personal sacrifice, Mr. and Mrs. Cavell sent her off to a succession of schools, finally to blossom forth as one of the clever Young Ladies leaving Miss Gibson's School for them in Peterborough, hard by the cathedral. She had, from the beginning, shown interest and ability in all the arts, and particularly in the French language. Miss Gibson, for her part, responded to this attractive, hard-working girl, and when the time came for her to leave, arranged what had been her greatest desire—a job in a French-speaking family.

She crossed the Channel, to Brussels, where she became governess to the four children of a lawyer called François. They fell in love with her immediately, and years later were to recall her kindness, her energy, and her French, which she spoke "with a charming English accent".

They also remembered her "veritable horror of lying".

Life in Brussels, gay, cosmopolitan, was indeed different to Swardeston and Peterborough, and she found it all thrilling, a challenge and a delight. The years passed quickly and it seemed she might live the rest of her life in this gay, rewarding atmosphere, surrounded by her delightful pupils, their cheerful parents.

Then it all ended—and Edith Cavell, without a moment's hesitation, accepted the fact. Her father had become ill, and her mother, frail and ailing, was quite unable to look after him. Edith said goodbye to Brussels, went back to Swardeston.

Her touch—and this is another aspect of Edith Cavell which, like the eternal incorruption of her body, has been pondered— literally worked a miracle. The old man had been at death's door: within a few weeks he was on his feet again.

A few weeks more and she felt herself able to leave: her father had made a complete and astonishing recovery, was able to turn the tables, in effect, and look after Edith's mother.

But now she knew she had this power of healing, was it right to go back to being a governess?

It was not. However much she might long for the lights and the gaiety and warmth of Brussels, she must stay in England, develop her God-given gift. Then she would be able to help others.

She joined the London Hospital in Whitechapel Road as student nurse, though she was considerably older than most of the other "probationers". It was in the East End, near the Thames docks, a huddle of sooty, uncared-for buildings, dealing with the poor, the aged, the insane—a very marked transition from the happy work of a governess in a rich Belgian family. And because she was older, more mature than the others, she was able to relate their life, the life and death in the wards, to the world outside—to compare it, consider how much of it was good, how much of it necessary, how much needed improving.

In 1897, when she was thirty-one, she was sent to Maidstone to take charge of emergency measures against an outbreak of typhoid. Her work then, as during her training, was reported on as "outstanding", and her disposition "calm, unruffled, kind".

From the docks and typhoid at Maidstone, she went to the

North St. Pancras Infirmary, which dealt largely with accident cases and was in a neighbourhood as forbidding as that of her student days at the London. But this was not to be for long: soon she had been promoted, was sent as Assistant Matron to the Shoreditch Infirmary, a bleak, enormous, hospital in a squalid neighbourhood, where she had charge of seven hundred and fifty bed patients and a hundred and twenty nurses. Here she seems to have become a real angel of mercy, working tirelessly for the welfare of her patients and her nurses, starting the brand-new innovation of visits to children recently discharged from hospital, lending, to people who had hardly ever seen such things before, hot-water bottles, bedding, chairs.

There is much of Nightingale here, and one sees her as a woman of deep feelings, boundless sympathy and a rare ability to get things done. She was also totally humourless, shocked at the goings-on of the young, and intolerant of anything she felt was inefficient, slovenly, or dishonest.

She was forty-two and it was 1906 when she went back to Brussels. Dr. Antoine Depage had started his clinic, he was determined to improve the low standard of nursing in his country, and he insisted this Englishwoman, who had the twofold advantage of being highly respected in the world of nursing and knowing Brussels and the Belgians, come over and help him run it.

It was a difficult decision. The only nursing in Belgium was done by nuns, absolutely without medical training, whose modesty often prevented them from keeping a patient clean. They were constantly involved in religious debate which had nothing to do with nursing, and yet because of a shortage of doctors all over the country they were indispensable.

And any woman who took up nursing without at the same time taking holy vows was quite likely to be condemned as not only atheist, but prostitute.

Not a very pleasing prospect to the daughter of the Rectory. But Edith Cavell decided it was her duty: yes, she *was* the best person to help them; and help them she would. Soon she was established at Depage's Clinic, training the desperately needed young nurses he was bringing in from all over Europe. Soon she had graduate nurses from England, Holland, France, and other countries to help her in the training and the Clinic had, almost before they had noticed, become a huge and thriving concern.

And now she had a chance, with much of the day-to-day routine taken off her hands, to think of the standard of nursing. For a start, she decided, it must be raised in the Belgian social scale, and she set about this as probably only an Englishwoman could, insisting, demanding, that a nurse called out to do private work in a household be treated not only as a member of the family, but as an honoured one, and of course taking her meals with the rest of them, not in the kitchen. Doctors, too, would treat their nurses with respect: Nurse Cavell had not been impressed with what she had seen of the relationship.

At the same time, she insisted that no nurse leave a case, however disagreeable, until it was over.

She was universally admired and trusted—and as universally found still, solemn, and hard to know. She seemed to think of nothing but her work, of the standard of nursing and teaching at the Clinic, and how it could be improved. She worked her staff—and herself—extremely hard. Then, when the day's work was done—late, very late, at night—she would sit down at her old upright piano and play softly to herself. It was her only relaxation.

By 1914—in fact, well before that—she had proved herself a most remarkably versatile, indispensable woman. She had become much in demand as surgeon's assistant, her absolutely calm, ice-cold reaction to emergency impressed surgeons and she was sent for by practically every hospital in Belgium for their most serious operations. But she refused to specialize in surgery—or in anything else. She insisted that nursing must embrace all illness, that no woman should put all her talent, skill and compassion into just one aspect of it. She made her nurses do likewise, nursing every case, mental patient or contagious illness, just as it came.

On 14 July, Edith Cavell left for her regular summer visit home. Her father was dead, her mother old and fragile. Things had been changing imperceptibly over the years, and now, for the first time, there seemed none of the life she remembered. She took her mother to a seaside resort where they spent the weeks sitting in what sun there was. They would have seemed to passers-by just a pair of old women, for Edith was now forty-eight and grey-haired, thin, withdrawn.

And a few weeks later, the war to end war broke out. Germany marched against France. With no hesitation, Edith Cavell made her plans to get back to Brussels. She belonged there with her nurses, they needed her, there could be no question of deserting them. It was very difficult to get there, passages to Ostend were hard to come by, for all shipping was in chaos, with Germans rushing home one way, English the other, and half the world caught up in a whirlpool of movement, getting into position as best they could, before the blow fell.

She got to Brussels on Sunday, 3 August, to find the city in a state of wild, unreasoning excitement. Small bands of soldiers, half-armed with obsolete weapons, marched to unspecified destinations while crowds cheered, bands played. Her first, sad, duty was to escort a party of German girls, who had been working at the Clinic, to the railway station. They made extravagant promises to contact each other the moment the war was over, and she was suddenly struck with the futility of a conflict which would make these hard-working, devoted young girls into refugees.

On 12 August she wrote to England, to *The Times*, offering the hospital for wounded British soldiers—though there was never any question in her mind that it should be for the exclusive use of either side, friend or foe. At the same time she begged subscriptions from the British public to make the hospital larger, more able to cope with the work which would come.

A week later, the situation had changed completely. The German army was at the gates of Brussels, flags were hastily pulled down, shutters drawn; the mayor declared the town a defenceless, open city. Two days later it had been occupied by the invader, and Edith Cavell, divided between pity and hatred for these men so far from home, yet bringing ruin to another country, had room in her heart for a kind word: "I saw several of the men pick up little children and give them chocolate and seat them on their horses, and some had tears in their eyes——"

The nurses were offered safe conduct to Holland : Edith Cavell and almost all her staff refused. The war went on, westward, and soon Brussels was a rear area, with most of the hospital's work the treating of wounded Germans sent back from the front which was nearing Paris.

But suddenly the German advance came to a halt, the army withdrew a few miles and settled down to a winter of bloody stalemate. The stationary, dug-in war of trenches that was beginning was to be far more destructive of human life than the lightning advance of the first few months. Casualties mounted at a shocking rate, cemeteries all over Belgium and France began to fill with bodies and to display little crosses— German ones, English ones, French.

The Germans, angered by the thwarting of their advance, turned to atrocity. The beautiful university town of Louvain, twenty miles east of Brussels, was burnt, its civilians massacred.

This outburst of Teuton savagery shocked and distressed the world, and in particular Edith Cavell. "I have seen suffering, poverty and human wretchedness in the slums of London, but nothing I saw there," she wrote, "hurts me the way it does to see these proud, gay, happy, people, humiliated and deprived of their men, their homes invaded by enemy soldiers that are quartered in them, their business ruined. I can only ask myself why, oh why, should these innocent people be made to suffer like this?"

Soon there were no longer any wounded to look after : the Germans were being sent to Germany, the allies no longer came; the patients of the Clinic were almost entirely Belgian civilians as they had been two years previously. But now they came with different troubles, the illnesses of malnutrition, dirt and unaccustomed squalor. The German military governor promulgated a rule that all male patients over eighteen years of age would report on discharge from the hospital to the military police. This would mean, for young Belgians, internment or forced labour, and Edith Cavell made up her mind to thwart the order. She hit upon the idea of ordering each discharged patient to "go to the military police, if you can find them, or to the house of Madame X". She could thus, in her weekly reports to the authorities, say truthfully—and that was the important thing, she would have spoken the truth—that she had ordered them to the military police H.Q. Whether they got there or not was another matter: after all, Brussels was a large and complex city, was it not?

Meanwhile, on the French border, a Belgian princess was busy converting her chateau to a hospital. She would accept any who needed her help, but she was working on a plan to smuggle any Allied soldiers who came to her, right across the country into Holland, whence they could make their way to England. It was dangerous work—far more dangerous for the organizers than for those escaping—and Princess de Croy soon found the parties of escaping prisoners, under a leader she provided for them, would need a staging point, where they could rest, gather strength for the second half of their journey. She decided to approach Nurse Cavell. If she, in Brussels, could help by harbouring the men for a few days, they could be led from Brussels in parties of three or four to the Dutch border and freedom.

Without hesitation, Nurse Cavell agreed.

The scheme at first worked well. The men spent a few days, sometimes weeks, in the hospital, before being led away, often by Nurse Cavell herself, to one of several rendezvous in the town, where other guides were waiting to lead them on to the Dutch border, usually Turnhout. But it was nerve-racking work, and by May of 1915 Edith Cavell had convinced herself the Germans knew Allied soldiers were being sheltered in her hospital. She had given her word, though: she would stick to her promise. Any Allied soldier who came to her would be hidden, fed and looked after, until he and his guide were ready for the last half of the perilous journey to freedom.

In fact the Germans in Brussels had often wondered whether something clandestine was taking place at 149 Rue de la Culture, where the hospital stood, but they had no evidence and few clues which might lead them to investigate further. They had set up a bustling Secret Police H.Q. in the town, had let it be known that they had some six thousand paid spies—presumably Belgians—who had infiltrated every office, every factory, every hospital. This served the twin purpose of making Belgians ashamed of their own country and at the same time frightening

Emmeline Pankhurst fought to win a fair deal for women. She is seen being arrested (*above, left*) after a demonstration outside Buckingham Palace. *Above, right:* Edith Cavell, the English nursing sister who helped British troops to escape German captivity, was executed by a German firing squad in 1915.

Marie Curie, seen here in her laboratory, discovered the element radium with her husband, Pierre. Then she risked her life—and lost it—through a determination to isolate enough of the magic, glowing substance to treat all sufferers.

Above: Scott at the South Pole—the last picture of Robert Falcon Scott, which was found with his body after he and his companions had perished on their way back from the Pole. Captain Oates, Captain Scott, and Petty Officer Evans are standing at the back: Lieutenant "Birdie" Bowers (who released the shutter by pulling a long string) and Doctor Wilson are in front. *Right:* Mahatma Gandhi devoted his tireless energy not only to persuading the British to leave his country, but to working for better conditions for the "Untouchables" and unity between the Hindus and Muslims. Here he leaves at the end of a reconciliation meeting. A few weeks after this picture was taken, he was shot by a Hindu fanatic.

them away from any venture such as the one the Clinic engaged in.

A foolish—almost unbelievably foolish—English soldier wrote a letter of thanks to Nurse Cavell for helping him escape. During a police search (the police, having at last grown suspicious, entered on the pretext of buying some old furniture which was up for sale) the letter was found in her room.

She was immediately arrested, with her English assistant, Sister Wilkins, and carted off to police H.Q. Here the two women were put in separate cells, interrogated.

Sister Wilkins was soon released. She had denied all knowledge of any young men at 149 Rue de la Culture, she had no idea what the police thought they were up to, she was extremely angry at being taken from her work. She was allowed to go back to it. But for Edith Cavell things were different. She seemed to make no effort at all to deny her guilt: what was worse, far worse, was that she provided, by her absolute refusal to tell a falsehood, a list of names of men and women all over Belgium who had helped her by passing along the prisoners, getting them out of the country. She seems to have believed that all the others would automatically confess their parts in the affair— perhaps in order to mitigate whatever sentence they might be given—and so she made a complete and abject admission of her part in the affair—and of other people's. It ended, "My statements which have just been read over to me, translated into French, conform to the truth at every point. They are perfectly intelligible to me in every detail, and I will repeat them before the tribunal——"

Not much room here for a defence. It was a proud confession, there was no trace of despair in it, but it pulled the ground from under the Belgian lawyer who had been detailed to defend her. He might as well not have attended the court martial at all.

The list of prisoners for trial came to thirty-five, including the Princess de Croy and a young Belgian architect, Philippe Baucq, accused, not only of the general "helping Allied soldiers to escape", but of "circulating seditious pamphlets". A list, on the whole, of unimportant little people: coal-miners, clerks, chemists, women from the market.

Edith Cavell, even to those who admired her most, was singularly unimpressive at her trial, which began on 7 October, 1915. She wore, we are told, a dark blue dress and coat with a large, high hat, topped by two ridiculous feathers, "sticking up at a grotesque angle". She looked tired, and listened without interest as her long, detailed and abject confession was read out by the German prosecutor, Dr. Stöber.

The next day, Friday, 8 October, was the climax of the trial. The guilt had been proved of twenty-seven of the thirty-five, and as they stood and listened to what the prosecutor was demanding in the way of sentences, there were gasps, a succession of gasps, around the courtroom. For although some of the sentences demanded were comparatively lenient, a year or two of imprisonment, most were not. And no one had believed the Germans would be severe, even though in the words of the prosecutor—but after all, Dr. Stöber was being paid to do this, he could hardly believe in what he was saying—"all this activity is akin to high treason, and the law punishes it with the death sentence".

He was a fine-looking man, we are told, tall with a reddish face, very black hair and a waxed moustache, and as he made his speech, emphasizing a point here and there with a gesture of the hand, he smiled, so that if one understood neither the German in which he made it nor the French into which it was immediately interpreted, one would have thought he was making an after-dinner speech. When he finished, the defence lawyers, lacking both his presence and his vigour, made tame little speeches—for no one wished to offend or antagonize the judges.

Most of the defendants were in a state of great distress—which is hardly surprising—but Edith Cavell, who calmly, unsmilingly, had admitted all the charges, seemed a woman in a dream. Her answers had a strange dignity about them, as if she were so proud of being English that she could not possibly deny having helped Allied soldiers. Of course she had helped them—and equally obviously and naturally, so had Monsieur X, and so on. Why, she seemed to be thinking, why not?

One of the judges spoke to her. "You are foolish to aid English soldiers. The English are ungrateful."

"*No.* They are not ungrateful."

The prosecutor, Stöber, interrupted. "And how do you know that?"

"Because I have received letters of gratitude—many of them—thanking me."

"Oh. And where do these letters come from?"

"From England."

This—though she could hardly embroil herself more than she had already done—was a bad mistake. If the letters had come from Holland, a neutral country, the crime would have been less serious: by proving she had assisted them to get all the way home, to fight again, another day, it put the blackest of all complexions on the matter.

Then, just when everyone was waiting for the judge to pass sentence, they dissolved the court. With what seems now to have been a calculated cruelty, they refused to promulgate sentence till after the weekend.

One of the defendants (ironically enough, he was among those to be acquitted) hanged himself in his cell. To prevent others from following his example, the prison authorities kept the lights on all night, so that sleep became impossible.

Saturday, Sunday, dragged past. On the afternoon of Monday, 11 October, the accused were once again taken from prison to courtroom and there, briefly, courteously, sentenced. Eight of the thirty-five were acquitted, twenty-two were sentenced to hard labour or imprisonment of between two and fifteen years, and five were sentenced to death. (Three of these were fortunate enough, in the uproar that broke out after Edith Cavell's execution, to have their sentences commuted to imprisonment.)

Despite pleas from the American Minister in Brussels (who yet brought down much American and English wrath on his own head for the oddly unenthusiastic and dilatory way he went about it) the sentence on Cavell and Baucq was carried out in the early morning of the following day, Tuesday, 12 October. Even now no one could believe—least of all the nurses at 149 Rue de la Culture—that the Germans would shoot a woman —a nurse, and one not even accused of spying, only of helping soldiers to get home.

But at five o'clock of that morning, two grey cars came out of the gate of St. Gilles Prison. By this time a small group of nurses had made their way in the drizzle to stand outside, for the unbelievable information that their beloved Directrice was to be shot that morning had reached them. They gasped with horror as the long cars swept by in the darkness and one of the girls thought she saw Nurse Cavell's blue uniform in the front car. A moment later, they were out of sight.

A few minutes later the cars stopped, at the edge of the Place des Carabiniers, in front of the big Brussels rifle range, the Tir National. Everyone got out in a compact group; no barking of orders, clicking of heels, rather like tired revellers coming back, sick and silent, from a late night. Then they entered the building.

There was a delay, and Edith Cavell, standing in the corridor, just inside the door, made one final entry in the margin of her prayer-book: "Died at 7 a.m. on 12 October, 1915. With love to my mother. E. Cavell." Then she requested three large pins from the Commandant. There was more delay while they were sent her, and then without a word the little nurse, who would be as modest in her death as she had been throughout life, pinned her long skirt tight about her ankles.

She was led out on the range, tied to a post some fifteen feet from the one against which Philippe Baucq was standing, blindfolded.

A few moments later, she was dead. The time, as she had accurately noted, was exactly 7 a.m.

The arguments about Edith Cavell's behaviour at her trial, a woman who showed not a flicker of concern at her death sentence, nor at its execution, have raged, simmered, and raged again, ever since.

Perhaps, by her confession, she cost the life of one other person, Philippe Baucq—though he might, with the double charge against him, have been executed in any case. Within three years all the others imprisoned had been released by the advancing Allies. But her execution had at least one important result. As the American author Owen Wister put it, referring to the possibility that America might never have entered the war, it "was killed for ever when Edith Cavell died for England".

And all over the world, indignation, rage and horror mounted. Americans demanded to be allowed to go over and fight. ("I want to arm and equip a regiment of Florida boys ——") In one day in England, after the news was out, ten thousand men enlisted in the army. Girls led recruiting rallies, their younger sisters tore up black dresses, dyed sheets, to hang mourning crape in every window. America, though it would be over a year before the decision was finally taken, prepared to fight.

So—however puzzled we may be by her performance in the dock, she is a hero, a heroine, of a very special sort: a brave woman whose martyrdom shook a weary and—here and there —complacent world. She made victory no longer probable, but a cold-blooded certainty.

Chapter 3

Marie Curie

More than twenty years after Hiroshima, men and women were dying. Dying, years after, as a result of the "pikadon", the "lightning-thunder" which, exactly at a quarter past eight in the morning of 6 August, 1945, had changed the course of history. Thousands died in an instant. They were the lucky ones.

In 1964 alone—nineteen years after—305 victims of "radiation sickness" were admitted to Hiroshima's Atomic Bomb Hospital: 53 died.

But the first victim of radiation sickness, the illness of "radio-activity", was a woman, eleven years before, who had devoted her life to harnessing this strange power, making it serve mankind.

The disease from which Marie Curie died, in July, 1934, was diagnosed variously as cancer, bronchitis, anaemia, tuberculosis —and she had courted it, knowingly, half her life. They called it in the autopsy, "pernicious anaemia, caused by the destruction of bone marrow after a long accumulation of radiations".

An interesting family, these Sklodovski of Warsaw, whose daughter Manya became Marie Curie. They were minor Polish nobility, originally landowners—but as generations wore on, younger sons turned away from the land, experimented with the army, with business, with teaching. One of these was Vladislav Sklodovski, who went as far afield as Petersburg University, did well and came back to Warsaw to teach and to marry. His young wife conveniently started up a small school for the daughters of the aristocracy, and they, and the five children as they came along, were able to live there.

It was a comfortable house, in Freta Street, and when Vladislav got promotion and had to move—a professor now— to new work, the family followed him with heavy heart. Madame Sklodovska gave up the school, prepared to devote herself, from now on, to looking after her family. It was as well, perhaps—for she was ill.

Manya was the youngest. When she was born, Madame Sklodovska was already dying, but had managed somehow to conceal the fact from her family. Apart from bursts of terrible coughing which came at lessening intervals, there was little to suggest to the children that their mother would some day be gone. The eldest sister had already died, of typhus, the family had survived that dreadful sorrow; now, suddenly, the mainspring of life snapped, too.

And, soon after, life changed still more. The professor, ardent Polish patriot that he was, like his children, had been found encouraging pupils to read and study their own language, not restrict themselves, as the edict ran, to the Russian of the Tsars who ruled them. Professor Slodovski was lucky to get away with his life, with only a cut in salary.

But a fifty per cent cut in salary makes a difference. The children, brilliant at their studies, anxious to complete them, were faced with the cruel fact: they would, every single one of them, have to go out and work. The professor earned enough for the rent of the house and a few of their wants—but there were clothes and food to buy. Vladislav felt his shame, his humiliation, deeply. "Soon," he would say wringing his hands, "soon I shall be on your hands myself. *Then* what becomes of you, my darlings?"

And, stoutly, the four children would say : "It doesn't matter. We are strong. We will succeed."

We are strong. We will succeed. The two short sentences burnt their way into the thinking of all four, and as much as any into that of little Manya. They would succeed, the family, because they were strong. But in the meantime, they needed money—and therefore work. They discussed the problem, decided to advertise their qualifications, and were all, within weeks, snapped up as teachers and tutors. Before her seventeenth birthday Manya Sklodovska was making a modest income from tutoring the offspring of the rich. Often, they forgot to pay her at the end of the month. Sometimes they resented the fees, modest though they were. "A person," Manya wrote to a friend, "a person who knew of us through friends came to inquire about lessons. Bronya told her half a rouble an hour and the visitor ran away as if the house had caught fire."

But aside from drumming writing and arithmetic into the heads of the rich, there were real, if clandestine, opportunities for study, and the children seized them. In this Russian Poland, where the rulers restricted learning in an attempt to damp down, stamp out, any incipient rebellion, it was hard to get anything but the bare essentials of an education—but there *was* the "Underground University". Here, attending secret lectures in private houses, sharing out precious pamphlets and books, a young man or woman prepared to take the risk could study the forbidden subjects: sociology, anatomy, history, economics. There were anything up to ten pupils at a time, listening, taking notes. A pupil in one subject might be a teacher in another. And all the while with one ear they listened for footsteps.

If you were fortunate enough to attend such a system of clandestine lectures, you were morally bound to share the knowledge with others—however much this pressed into your scant allotment of time. Manya began to read aloud to the girls who worked in a dressmaker's, to assemble by stealth a shelf full of books in Polish for them to read.

But soon, all this would go. Tutoring in Warsaw was not profitable enough to make ends meet; she would have to teach, full time. It would be best if she could get such a post to become governess in a household. There she would be fed.

Sadly, she advertised her modest attainments a second time and in due course was offered and accepted a post as governess to a family in Warsaw. It would be nice to stay in Warsaw; perhaps she might, occasionally, be able to attend lectures.

But she found she hated her adopted family, their vulgarity, their quarrelling, their arguments over money. If she insisted on staying in Warsaw, she reasoned glumly, this was the best she could hope for. So big as the wrench would be, she must leave the city, get away to simpler, kinder—better-bred—people in the country. For Manya, like all aristocrats fallen on hard times, kept up self-respect with the memory of the age-old nobility from which she had sprung. She was fortunate this time and was offered a position with people she liked immediately, and with whom, for several years, she was very happy. They lived at the unpronounceable "Szczuki, near Przasnysz" and they were, Manya wrote solemnly, "excellent people". Her little pupil, Andzia, aged ten—"though a little spoiled"—was an obedient child and M. and Mme Z were kindness itself. "In this part of the country," she wrote, "nobody works, people think only of amusing themselves". She found it hard to adopt this attitude herself and became, very briefly, an object of pity and amusement by refusing to go to a ball. "But I was not sorry, for M. and Mme Z came back from the ball at one o'clock the next afternoon."

And her new friend, the Z's older daughter, Bronka, her pupil for three hours a day, as against Andzia's four, was "a rare pearl, both in her good sense and in her understanding of life". Soon Bronka, fired by Manya's zeal for teaching, was helping her, two hours a day, with a little class of peasant children.

But throughout this teaching, to Andzia, to Bronka, to the little peasants, Manya was regretting—sometimes in tears in her upstairs room—the education she wanted so desperately for herself. While she grew pink-cheeked and plump as the peasants she taught, there were young men and women in Berlin, in London, and above all in Paris, learning things Manya would never know.

But one had to live—and one could console oneself that it was helping the cause of education; for Manya sent money each month, not only to Warsaw for her father, but to Paris for her sister Bronya. Bronya had managed to get to France for study, was working hard, day and night, it seemed, to achieve a medical degree, lest family poverty drag her back, unqualified, to a menial job in Poland.

Then—for Manya—heartbreak. The Z's son Casimir came home to Szczuki for holidays and was bowled over by the blonde, serious-looking, little governess who looked after his two sisters. He proposed, was accepted—all, it seemed, in a matter of moments—and then turned confidently to his parents, and asked their blessing.

This, to his amazement, and to Manya's shame and distress, was refused. As Manya's daughter, Eve, put it years later in her biography of Marie Curie: "The fact that the girl was of good family, that she was cultivated, brilliant, and of irreproachable reputation, the fact that her father was honourably known in Warsaw—none of this counted against six implacable little words: one does not marry a governess."

The tragedy—incredible to a young girl in love—was that Casimir, stormed at, frightened by, his parents, changed his mind.

But though for a while misery and heartbreak seemed sure to kill her, this rebuff was best for Manya. And best, incomparably best, for the world. Had Manya become young Mme Z, chatelaine of a thousand hectares of sugar beet, there would never have been a Marie Curie.

Fate stepped in. Bronya in Paris married a young Polish exile, medical student like herself. He qualified, got a practice and was able to set up in comfort in a large and rambling house. There was no longer need of Manya's monthly offering and in fact the newly-weds were now able to make contribution to the upkeep of old Vladislav in Poland. If Manya no longer wanted to work as a governess, she no longer had to. She could even, if she wished, come to Paris, remembering, though, to bring, if she came, bedclothes, towels, mattress, stout shoes and both her hats.

Manya, overjoyed, agreed. It was almost too good to be true: not only would she escape from the household where she had been humiliated; she would be able, at last, to study—and in Paris, at the Sorbonne!

Bronya and her husband (another Casimir, this, Casimir Dluski) fussed over the young girl like a pair of benevolent chickens, introducing her to friends, to shops, to the sights and sounds of Paris—and enrolling her at the Sorbonne. Life in their household was almost unbelievably gay; it echoed to music all night: to music and to laughter which would suddenly stop as Dluski heard the door bell and leapt from the piano to let in a late patient. Dr. Dluski was open for consultation, advice—or just music—any time of day or night.

On one occasion the bell rang, Dluski opened the door and another young man came in. They were obviously friends, there was a shout of greeting, then laughter, and they made their way together along the passage. Silence for a moment and then suddenly, drifting up the stairs, beautiful music. It was so appealing that Manya put down the textbook she was reading, made her way on tiptoe down the stairs and into the little room.

The playing stopped and they turned to her. "Oh no!" she said. "Please go on. Please, please, go on——"

"This," said Dluski with a smile, "is my little sister-in-law, Manya. And this——" pointing to the young man rising from the piano stool, "is Ignace Paderewski."

They exchanged greetings and then the pale young man who would one day be world-famous as a musician, and prime minister, at the same time, of a new free Poland, went on playing.

Life at the Sorbonne, studying science, was hard work—for Manya. The French on which she had so prided herself as a governess in the Polish countryside seemed totally inadequate to the task of understanding scientific lectures. She found herself misunderstanding, or failing to comprehend, whole sentences, and she was forced to devote precious time, time which should have been spent in the lab or with textbooks, studying what had become a new and strangely foreign language.

And so, reluctantly, she decided to leave the song-filled Dluski household. The social life, the music echoing about the corridors, the ringing of the doorbell, the conviviality of friends, and patients, and itinerant musicians: she loved it all. But a

few months of it and she risked being asked to leave the
Sorbonne as a failure. And, apart from anything else—this
settled it—one never, never, with the Dluskis, heard a word of
French.

The Dluskis were upset, offended. All work and no play,
surely—even for physicists—was a mistake? But when they
saw her mind made up, they swallowed their disappointment
and helped her find lodgings.

She went to the lodgings, mattress, both hats and all—and
the move was suddenly the biggest step of her life, greater, far
greater, than a mere trip from Warsaw to Paris. For the first
time in life, Manya Sklodovska was alone, entirely alone, without family or friend, or benevolent employer, to catch her if
she fell. She would be free, of course, without human involve-
ment, able to devote her life to study. Could she stick it out?

Would she, in a few years time, creep back to Warsaw, as a
—rather grander, older—governess?

We are strong. We will succeed. The words came back and
she flung open the top of her trunk, dived both hands inside
and started unpacking.

To succeed, she would change her name to its French
equivalent, "Marie". She was as ardent a nationalist as ever but
what mattered *now* was success at the Sorbonne. Anything
holding one back, like being regarded indulgently as foreign,
must be ruthlessly eliminated.

Even one's name.

She planned to get Masters' degrees in physics and mathe-
matics, and now, able to devote each waking moment to the
problem, she made progress. She trained herself to think in
French, to catch every nuance of meaning, every shade of
emphasis in a lecturer's style, and she read and experimented
and read again, far into each night. Almost sooner than
planned, she had got both degrees—and suddenly life was
empty and uncertain. She would have to go back to Poland;
there was nothing left for her in Paris.

Fate intervened. Manya Sklodovska won a scholarship, got
the chance of staying another year in France, doing research.
Delighted, she paid a visit to her father in Warsaw and came
back to start work. She had been invited to do a report on the

magnetic properties of steel. This was wonderful and exciting: it was work which interested her, which she knew she would do well—and it was well paid. To do work one loved, in a laboratory, and be paid for it—Heaven had opened.

The only thorn in her Eden, and it was big, was the equipment required to do the job properly. All of it was cumbersome, some of it expensive: and, taken together, it was far too bulky to fit into her own modest lab. But things seemed to be slipping into position, one by one, like the pieces of a puzzle. She was told of a young French scientist, Pierre Curie, with a laboratory larger than he needed. Perhaps Curie might, for a short time, make room for her in it.

But Marie Sklodovska, bookworm for so many months, was not up to the business of contacting strange young men and asking favours. A friend then conveniently invited them both to tea, and after some thought she accepted.

Pierre Curie was eight years her senior, already famous for his electrical discoveries, and it was, if not love-at-first-sight, love-very-soon, in the lab. He agreed eagerly to let her move in with him, helped her install the equipment—and asked her to marry him. Marie would have none of it: marry a Frenchman? Marry—if one married at all—anyone but a Pole? It was unthinkable.

And so they got married: it was 1895. Two years later Marie had a first daughter, Irene. She, like both her parents, was destined to win a Nobel Prize.

In 1895, uranium was news. Henri Becquerel had played for years with the strange, magic metal which made clear impressions on a photographic plate, even through sheets of thick black paper. He noted its behaviour carefully, decided it was giving off a kind of "radiation", an invisible light which penetrated where the visible variety could not.

The Curies, Pierre and Marie, found the theory fascinating—and Marie, having completed, for the time being, her work on magnetism, decided to write a thesis on uranium for her Doctor's degree. Uranium and its behaviour seemed a far cry from either the magnetic properties of steel or the measurement of electric current, but they wound up the work they were doing and settled down, together, to investigate, for Marie's thesis, "radiation". Pierre's brother, Jacques, helped them. So—surprisingly, perhaps—did Becquerel himself and together they devised equipment to measure the extent of the radiation.

Very soon Marie, spurred on by thought of her Doctor's degree, had left the others behind. Genuinely surprised at her skill, her powers of accurate deduction from the flimsiest tissue of evidence—and perhaps chivalrously disposed to a young woman—they gave her their blessing, promised any help she might need, and went back to their work.

Within a few weeks she had found the peculiar character of uranium in another element altogether, thorium. The property they shared she christened "radio-activity".

She had discovered the disease that would kill her.

Pierre presented her with a sackful of mineral samples from the School of Physics. Perhaps, if she went through all these with her usual thoroughness, she might find the property in other substances.

But it seemed uranium and thorium were, after all, the only two "radio-active" elements. Time and again she found traces of the phenomenon in a rock, and each time compounds of either thorium or uranium proved to be the source. But one sample, a sample of pitch-blende ore, produced—and at first she refused to credit the evidence—a radio-activity far, far greater than either uranium or thorium. What third element, then, had the strange property?

There was none. She had tested every known element for radio-activity—only thorium and uranium possessed it. There could be but one answer, and she caught her breath: she had found a new, brand-new element altogether, an element never previously listed.

Pierre helped her check, cross-check, the evidence. It was right; there could only be some unknown substance producing this high degree of radio-activity. He stopped his electrical work, joined her in the search.

It was 1898 when they began the collaboration, a collaboration broken only by death. And half those eight years, the first four, back-breaking, eye-straining, years were devoted, almost without stop, to the search for the missing element. But they began the work with enthusiasm and excitement. The first thing

46

to do was get sufficient pitch-blende to sift and purify. The missing element, they calculated, would be in the proportion of one part to a hundred parts of pitch-blende ore. The ore was expensive, but as a few pounds of it should yield a measurable quantity of the element, the problem was not insuperable.

They sifted, analysed, compounded the ore—and were left, weeks later, with a tiny spoonful of a highly radio-active substance. But ninety per cent of that spoonful was ordinary, non-radio-active metal: the elusive element must be hiding, somewhere within it—and it must be fantastically powerful.

Had they known, at this stage, that the proportion would be one part in a million, that it would take four years to isolate: would they have carried on? Had Marie Curie known the work would cripple and finally kill her—would she have gone on with it?

We will never know—but a fair guess is: yes, she would have gone on with it. The new element must have a use, and it was Marie's duty, having come so far, to find it.

The problem was to get sufficient pitch-blende. It came mainly from Austria, a dull brown ore used mainly in the manufacture of glass, and it was impossibly expensive, at least in the large quantity they would need. Then it occurred to them that its radio-activity would probably remain intact through the process of manufacture. Taking a chance, they wrote and asked the Austrian Government for a shipment of the residue after glass manufacture. They would cheerfully, they wrote, pay the carriage.

They heard nothing—and then, weeks later, a horse-drawn waggon drew up, and started to unload. They rushed out—and it was the pitch-blende, a whole ton of it, in sacks. Laughing, they helped take it to the back of the house, into the small shed in the garden.

A few weeks and they had isolated a new, radio-active, element. A thrilling discovery—but not the one they wanted: the element was not powerful enough. In honour of Marie's country they christened it "Polonium"—and went on with the search.

At the end of the year they were able to announce the existence of a second new chemical element in pitch-blende. This,

Marie knew, must be the one they wanted. It was one, she wrote in her report on the discovery, "to which we propose to give the name of RADIUM. The new radio-active substance certainly contains a very strong proportion of barium; in spite of that, its radio-activity is considerable. The radio-activity of radium, therefore, must be enormous."

But dedicated as she was to the pursuit, Marie was more than a scientist; she was a human being. Ten days after her momentous announcement of radium, she was able to write, with the explanation mark she had modestly refused to the earlier communication, "Irene has fifteen teeth!"

They went on, reducing the little pile of radio-active substance, largely barium, to its constituents, and each week their original guess of one part in a hundred became more ridiculous. "Pierre," she asked one evening, after they had worked in the shed for the whole of a winter's day, "what do you think it will look like? When we find it——"

He smiled. "I don't know. But I'd like it to have—to have a really beautiful colour."

Pierre was growing sick of the whole business. He had more profitable work to do and his little family had to eat. He was ashamed to leave Marie at this stage of the research—so he tried to persuade her to give up. She had proved that radium existed: was it necessary, then, to go on, till the end of time, trying to isolate it, to see what it looked like, how it behaved, by itself? And what use could this radium possibly have?

Nothing would shake her determination. Reluctantly, he went on with the experiments, stealing moments from them to conduct others in electrical measurement, the measurement of sound, the reproduction of sound, for which industrial firms were prepared to pay. Irene had fifteen teeth. Indeed she had —and like her father and mother, she had to eat.

But the father and mother were not eating, or eating very little; and poverty was not the sole reason. Somehow, their appetites, their strength, seemed to be failing. Perhaps they were getting old. Perhaps they were just overworking.

In 1902, forty-five months after the day she and Pierre had begun research into pitch-blende, Marie achieved what she had set out to do. She prepared a tenth of a gramme of what could only be pure radium, made measurement of its atomic weight: 225. It was even more beautiful than Pierre had hoped, this radium: it shone by itself, like a glow-worm. It glowed with a healing—deathly—light, and they sat hand in hand for an hour in the garden shed, watching.

Radium officially existed. "Without an atomic weight," the chemists had said, "there is no radium". Now there was.

But with the radium came, perversely enough, a grinding poverty. They had devoted four years, largely unpaid, to doing pure research. Now, in the moment of triumph, they were at the end of their resources.

An offer came, out of the blue, to go as a team to the University of Geneva. The salary offered would have solved practically all their problems.

All problems but one: they would be dealing with radium, telling the story of radium—but they would not be progressing in research. And already, at the back of Marie's mind, was the idea that somehow this blue and shimmering element, this ever-burning flame, would be of use to man. Surely those four years in a garden shed would produce something of more use to mankind than a pale blue will-o'-the-wisp? They refused the Geneva post.

Then came the discovery—so wonderful, yet so tragic—that radium would kill human cells. And to Marie Curie this meant one thing: it would kill diseased ones. She pressed on, far into each night, experimenting with ways of making the substance more quickly, more cheaply. If four years non-stop labour would always be needed to sift a tenth of a gramme of it from a ton of pitch-blende, the world would wait a long time for usable supplies. Somehow she had to speed the process.

The application of radium which most thrilled her was its ability to kill diseased cells, but its characteristics, its possible applications, seemed endless. For a start: it gave off radiation two million times stronger than that of uranium. The rays would penetrate everything but the thickest sheet of lead. It made impressions on photographic plates, through black paper; turned the atmosphere about it into a conductor of electricity; reduced, little by little, any container holding it to powder and ashes. It was luminous, one could read by it.

And it gave luminosity—and radio-activity—to other substances in varying degree. Diamonds, for example, were easily made phosphorescent by it. Imitations in paste hardly glowed at all.

Other facts, as Marie experimented, became clearer. The atoms of radium were emitting other atoms—atoms of helium—and changing in themselves. Radium was thus a "descendant" of uranium, after other atoms had left. Polonium, their first discovery, was a descendent of radium. Each of these radio-active elements was destroying itself, and nothing man did could alter the rate at which it did so. The elements lost half their substance in a period of time which, for each particular element, never altered. She proved that radium would diminish itself by half in sixteen-hundred years, uranium in several thousand-million. The descendants of radium took less, down to a few seconds.

But as the news that radium would destroy tumours spread —so excitement mounted. The Academy of Science awarded the Curies 20,000 francs for the extraction of radio-active matter, and they set to work to purify another five tons of pitchblende ore. A French industrialist, catching the prevailing mood, offered to set up a factory for the manufacture of radium, with a laboratory attached for their own research, and they accepted gladly. But now journalists descended on them, discovered or invented details of their private life, hazarded wild guesses about the new element and its uses, succeeded in arousing impatience and anger among the public. Why was the new panacea, the Miracle Medicine, not available now, and to all? What were the Curies doing? Were they waiting for the price to rise so they could make their fortunes? Fortunes from the suffering of others.

And wasn't Madame Curie a foreigner?

Life for these two dedicated, sensitive, people grew grim— and then was brightened by the birth of a second daughter, Eve. This was exciting and unexpected, for Marie was now an ageing, tiring, thirty-seven. And they were still poor. She had refused to patent her process of extraction, even though patenting would have made no difference to the world's supply of radium and would have brought thousands of francs into the little house in the Boulevard Kellermann.

Small quantities of radium, minute quantities packed into lead boxes, for they burnt whatever else they touched, began to leave first one factory, then another. Remarkable cures were reported from allowing the powerful, cell-killing, radiation to pierce tumours and growths. There was still anger and jealousy, but honours, too, began to pour in.

Then suddenly the prop, the main support of Marie's life, was withdrawn. Pierre was killed in a Paris street, killed by a horse-drawn waggon exactly like the one which had delivered Austrian pitch-blende, eight years before. Marie was grief-stricken, but went quietly on with her work. Pierre had been made, just before his death, director of the Physics Laboratory at the Sorbonne, a post with a good salary, and when Marie was offered it she accepted—to become the first woman so appointed. There was more trouble, over this: not only a *woman* in a man's job; a *foreign* woman. A woman who should be doing nothing of the sort, who should be hard at work making sure that there were supplies of radium for the world and all its sufferers. Anonymous letters came in, the Press took up the mad chase of a hunted, sickly woman, accusing her of doing exactly what she was *not* doing. For throughout life, from the moment the pale blue phosphorescence appeared in the garden shed, Marie Curie had devoted herself to finding ways of getting radium. Her ambition was to take radium to every person in the world who needed what radium, and only radium, could do.

She and Pierre had received the 1903 Nobel Prize for Physics, sharing it with their friend Henri Becquerel. A few years after Pierre's death she got the Prize again, for Chemistry. The original glowing substance had turned out, in her later experiments, to be a *salt* of radium, and she succeeded, by an operation of fantastic difficulty, in isolating the metal itself for a short period. As it was completely unstable, altered constantly by atmospheric agents, and lethally dangerous to handle, this was a considerable feat.

War came, she debated what she must do, and took her decision. Radium had much in common with X-rays, and as the world's leading authority on the former she was an expert and more on the latter. She would make it her job to see that the Röntgen X-ray machines, invented twenty years before and still in short supply, got to every major hospital. Correctly used—and she would see to that—they would show the exact position of the shrapnel or the bullet in a wound, would save untold suffering, untold lives.

But for the wounded nearer the front, portable X-ray would have to be developed. Within hours Marie Curie, the woman who was rumoured to think only of radium, to understand nothing else after years of doing nothing else, had drawn an exact blueprint of her "radiological car". It was an ordinary motor car, with Röntgen apparatus, *there*; an examination table, *there*; and a power supply from that large dynamo, *there*, which ran, via this chain, from the car's engine.

The car was built, and it travelled endlessly, with Marie Curie usually inside, lending her store of radiological knowledge, her skill, to the problems of badly wounded men. The Germans approached, her two daughters implored her to leave Paris, move to safety in Brittany, she refused.

Radiation sickness, as we know from Hiroshima, can take a long, long time to do its work. All these years, Marie Curie was dying. Her health failed gradually, she fought back, seemed well for a while, grew worse. She died, in the sanatorium at Sancellemoz, on 4 July, 1934. Two days later, in the cemetery at Sceaux, her coffin was lowered gently on top of Pierre's. A quarter of a century after him, she had joined him, was free at last of the pain, the weakness, which had dogged her. Had Pierre not been run over by that waggon in 1906, he would almost certainly have died of radiation sickness himself. Perhaps he was lucky.

So died Marie Curie-Sklodovska, to give her the name on the tombstone at Sceaux, first victim of a new and dreadful disease, a disease she had courted deliberately, for more than half of her life. She believed that by grappling with the power that caused *this* disease she would find a way to cure others. To a very great extent she was successful, and her courage showed the way to others.

A great scientist; probably the greatest woman scientist the world has ever known.

And, perhaps, the bravest.

Chapter 4

Robert Falcon Scott

One of the joys of the Thames is *Discovery*, moored prosaically between the Embankment and Waterloo Station and a long-ish stone's throw from the Law Courts. The Tower is history, half London is history, but it is on board *Discovery* one gets this almost overwhelming sensation of being in the midst of it. Each tiny cabin is preserved as it was in 1902, with the owner's name above the door: Dr. Wilson, Mr. Shackleton, Commander Scott—and it is easy, particularly on a day when there are few visitors, to close one's eyes and feel their presence.

And above all, the presence of Scott. There is his knife; near to it a plug of tobacco; any minute now he will come in and fetch them before going out on deck. One will straighten up, stop studying the map on the wall, as he strides in and strides out again, a nuggety, round-faced figure with a kindly, frosty, smile.

For with Scott there would be little intimacy: Scott was in charge, absolutely in charge, right up to the end, and it is difficult to visualize a time in his life when he was not. Throughout, he seems to have been the man men look to, take orders from, unquestioningly. That to me is the amazing part of the Scott story; others have perished as hideously; others, like little Edgar Christian, have kept cheerful to the end and literally frozen to death; but Scott, even in the moment of death, could make men do what he wanted, just by the force of his personality. He could make men die—wondering to the end just how they stood in their leader's estimation, hoping with their dying breath that they had shaped well in his eyes, not let themselves down in his estimation.

And yet, there was a soft and gentle, almost effeminate, side to Scott. When his sister, after a difficult confinement, gave birth to a child and he was told, he dropped down in a dead faint. It's interesting to conjecture, in these days of psychiatry, just how a Robert Falcon Scott would fare, today, with a Naval Selection Board. Quite possibly, on the result of a three-page questionnaire, half an hour with an ingenious little wire puzzle and an investigation of his responses to various stimuli, he would be refused a Commission: Psychologically Unsuited to Command.

But no—the true potential, the greatness, of Robert Scott, would have penetrated even the thickest psychiatric skull. It was that which singled him out, still a boy, as the commander-to-be of the British Antarctic Expedition.

And yet there *was* something about Scott which, whether psychiatry revealed it or no, was largely responsible for the tragedy of his second expedition. As much as anything else— and there was a lot else—it cost him his life, as well as those of his four companions. For this great man had one attribute which, in a commander, easily cancels out the rest.

That was Compassion.

A little pity, in fact, goes a long way. But to old Sir Clements Markham in 1887, thirteen years before the *Discovery* Expedition, there was no doubt of Scott's potential. Markham was staying on board ship with his cousin, Commodore of the Squadron, and had been invited to watch a cutter race in the harbour. The race was won by a round-faced eighteen-year-old, Midshipman Scott; and Sir Clements was struck, forcibly, with the obvious guts and powers of leadership of the boy. He invited him to dine, and during dinner made up his mind—without confiding in the young guest—that when his ambition, his dream, of a British Antarctic Expedition came true, this naval officer would command it.

Six years later Sir Clements was elected President of the Royal Geographical Society and was able, at last, to do something about his dream. He had kept a sharp eye on his protégé, often from a great distance, and when he had succeeded in getting official blessing for his scheme he was able to suggest Scott apply to be its commander. Scott did so and in June of 1900 the appointment was announced.

There was much to be done: he had first of all to select a team, then decide on its exact task, the equipment needed for it, the ways of getting it. Most important of all, he had to learn something about polar exploration. A pity, in a way, that Sir Clements never confided, all those years before, that some day he would be leading such an expedition: on his appointment Scott had never donned skis or climbed a mountain, had no experience of working in snow and ice, knew nothing of the history of polar exploration, had read none of its literature.

Robert Falcon Scott had been born near Devonport in 1868. His father, the sickly one of an active family, had stayed at home while his brothers joined the Army and the Navy, to work in the family brewery at Plymouth. Robert, his elder son, entered the Royal Navy via the training ship *Britannia*. He was conscientious, hard-working, admired by his fellows. It was all this which struck Sir Clements Markham.

In the year at his disposal from the date of appointment, Scott dealt with everything; by the time *Discovery* sailed in 1901 he had made himself an expert on his subject and the obvious choice for command. After a final re-loading of stores and personnel, a last revictualling, the expedition left New Zealand on Christmas Eve, 1901, headed south.

They got to the Ross Sea on 7 January, hacked and bashed their way through pack ice in the thick-skinned *Discovery*, anchored in McMurdo Sound. They were promptly frozen in, but the ship conveniently remained their base, a part of dry land, throughout that southern winter.

There was much to learn and as Scott wrote later in his journal of the trip, "Food, clothing, everything was wrong, the whole system was bad". But with trial and error and courage (tents collapsed, clothes refused to fasten, cookers fell to bits) they surmounted their difficulties. In the summers that followed—that is to say, from November to February—twice they had high success. In the first operation, Scott, accompanied by Doctor Wilson and Ernest Shackleton, made a way south as far as Latitude 82 degrees 17 minutes, against every conceivable hardship. The dogs they had taken to draw sledges all died or had to be put down (and this, leading Scott to distrust dogs in polar regions, had its unfortunate effect on the next expedition); the four men had to drag the sledges themselves, pulling as heavy a load as they could, then struggling back for the rest. Shackleton—in these days before Vitamin C, indeed before any vitamins—nearly died of scurvy and they got him back, Scott and Wilson dragging him on the sledge, just in time to save his life. They had been nearer to the bottom of the earth than any men before, nearer to a Pole, north or south, than man had ever penetrated. They had negotiated a hellish round trip of just under a thousand miles in ninety-four days.

The first winter was spent collating results, analysing minerals they had collected (including coal, to their joy, which proved the antarctic continent to have been thick, aeons before, with jungle). As soon as the southern spring returned, Scott went out in a different, westerly, direction, with two different companions, and made an even more remarkable trip, profiting from the errors of the first.

The facts revealed by this appropriately named *Discovery* Expedition were enough in themselves to win Scott undying fame. His party had sounded the Ross Sea, discovered the Great Ice Plateau, mapped miles of new coastline, brought back hundreds of specimens. The Expedition, according to *The Times*, had been "one of the most successful that ever entered the polar regions, north or south". Scott was fêted, given sackfuls of decorations, invited to give lectures, write a book.

Then, as Naval officers do, he went back to the ordinary duties of his calling. He divided his time in the next few years between commanding battleships and doing desk work at the Admiralty. Ernest Shackleton, profiting by his experience under Scott, went back to the Antarctic in 1907 with the intention, this time, of reaching the Magnetic and Geographical Poles— the South Magnetic Pole being that shifting spot near the end of the earth where the south end of our compass needle always points, whether we be in Timbuctoo or Hyde Park. His expedition reached the South Magnetic Pole, brought back quantities of geological, glaciological information. It failed to reach the Geographic Pole. The challenge remained, for Robert Scott.

By 1910, Scott was able to do something about it. He organized a public subscription to finance a scientific expedition: it was not an official one, and though the Royal Geographical Society, the Admiralty and the British public were all behind him, and the British, South African, Australian and New Zealand governments made small grants, Scott had to raise a great deal of money himself. Eventually he scraped together sufficient to buy the 744-ton *Terra Nova*, a Dundee whaler, and have her refitted for his purpose. The avowed main objective of the trip would be the conduct of research in the Antarctic continent, more advanced research than had been contemplated before. There would be biologists, geologists, physicists. Dr. Wilson, old friend from the earlier trip, would be in charge of his scientific staff.

But there was more to it. The team set themselves out to reach, for the first time in history, the South Geographical Pole. Scott knew this was what the public wanted, that this, rather than reports about minerals and magnetism, was what they had subscribed their shillings for. "One cannot afford to be blind to the situation: the scientific public, as well as the general public, will gauge the result of the scientific work of the Expedition largely in accordance with the success or failure of [The Polar Expedition]. With success, all roads will be made easy, all work will receive its proper consideration. With failure, even the most brilliant work may be neglected and forgotten, at least for a time."

The *Terra Nova* sailed from England in June, 1910, got to Melbourne 12 October.

There, to Scott's dismay, was a telegram. "Madeira. Am going South. Amundsen."

This was it, then: the great Norwegian was pitting his team against Scott's. Roald Amundsen had visited the Antarctic way back in 1897, before Scott's first expedition: he was determined to maintain his priority. Norway would reach the Pole first but—always the gentleman—Amundsen would warn his rival.

The British party were downcast for a day—but Amundsen, they reflected, was just another challenge, an encouragement to give of their best. They forgot about him, moved on to New Zealand and sailed south from Dunedin on 29 November, 1910. Scott had only been married a little over two years, his son Peter (one day to be a naturalist) had just been born, and it was a sad, proud farewell when he and his young sculptress bride parted on the dockside in Dunedin.

Two days out from New Zealand the *Terra Nova* was almost sunk in a storm, but survived to enter pack-ice on 9 December, and batter for three weeks getting through it. They reached land, chose a site named earlier as "Cape Evans" and began to unload. Eighteen miles south of them on the coast, but a place which they were unable to reach this time from the sea, was "Hut Point", Scott's earlier H.Q.

Unloading took a week. Then a fortnight for a new hut. Then, after these three weeks of activity they set out—a party of twelve under Scott—to leave a ton of stores in a depot as far south as possible. They took the stores a hundred and thirty-two miles beyond "Hut Point", left a cache there of 2,181 lb.

Meanwhile the *Terra Nova* had done a short voyage eastwards along the coast and found Amundsen's ship at anchor in the Bay of Wales. The news was duly passed back to Cape Evans, and the *Terra Nova* set sail for New Zealand.

The winter, March to October, 1911, was spent in scientific work at Cape Evans. Meteorological instruments, magnetic instruments, were built into huts or sunk in caves of ice, observations were taken, calculations made, A terrible trip in utter darkness (for there is no sun in winter) was taken by Dr. Wilson and two others to Cape Crozier to collect embryos of Emperor penguins, in a temperature of minus 79 degrees

Fahrenheit. When Wilson's party staggered back on 1 August, preparations were in hand for the great trip to the Pole.

The distance from base at Cape Evans, to the objective, was 922 miles. Scott had two new and untried motor sledges, in addition to ten surviving ponies (there had been nineteen when they left England) and two teams of dogs. His plan was that the motor sledges would drive south across the endless, raised plateau, the "Ice Barrier" from Cape Evans, for as far as they could get before being abandoned. Stores from these motor sledges would then be transferred to ponies and dog sledges. Farther on, at the foot of the immense Beardmore Glacier, nearer the Pole, the ponies would be slaughtered, their flesh cached away in depots for the returning parties. The dogs would be sent back. Then three man-hauled sledges—four men to each—would press on south. One of these would make the final assault. Eight depots would be laid along the route (in addition to the earlier "One Ton Depot" laid down the previous year); these would serve to ration returning parties—and the calculation of the quantity to be left in each, the amount to be removed by each party as it returned, was extremely complicated.

By now all were restive, anxious to start—but Scott knew nothing could be done till the end of October: it would be too cold, the precious remaining ponies would die. He had done everything: he was in command: they waited. As he wrote, "The future is in the lap of the Gods; I can think of nothing left undone to deserve success."

He was right. Everything humanly possible had been done—though not every member of his expedition was happy about the ponies, Amundsen had preferred dogs, had made no secret of his preference.

But this was a matter of choice. Scott's mistake was still to come.

The motor party, untried, tentative, unreliable, left first, in clouds of smoke: two roaring monsters with clattering wooden tracks, in the charge of Lieutenant Evans (not Petty-Officer Edgar Evans, of whom more later). They left base on 24 October, 1911.

Not exactly an impressive start. The machines had difficulty getting grip on the ice, and in the first three and a half hours they achieved three and a half miles. It was three whole days before they reached a point eighteen miles from the start, had attained Scott's old "Hut Point" of nine years previous. They spent a night, angry, exhausted by their charges, in the remains of the hut, before pushing on to the edge of the Ice Barrier.

But to the delight of all, the amazement of some, the motor sledges now bit and fought their way up the icy slope of the Barrier, reached the top, roared on south. Scott, who had come this far to see how they fared, waved and went back.

Three days later, both motor sledges had been abandoned: a connecting rod broke in the first, a big end in the other. Lt. Evans and his team, fed up with the problems of starting the monsters in sub-zero weather and keeping them going, left them without regret and marched on, dragging sledges with as much of the motors' load as they could. No one had expected the motors to last anyway; they had been brought by Scott for research into their behaviour. They had taken their loads fifty-one miles before giving up. No one complained.

The pony party was led by Scott himself, and this left a week after the motors, on 31 October. There had been nineteen of the animals; now there were ten, and half seemed unfit for work. The man in charge of these pitiful nags was, ironically enough, a steeplechase rider and cavalry officer, "Titus" Oates, and though Titus did everything in his power to keep the little beasts alive and working, he had no faith in them. They were, he wrote, "the most unsuitable scrap-heap crowd of unfit creatures" yet he devoted himself to them. Scott on more than one occasion in his diary praises his perseverance. From the outset, the ponies were a worry; Scott—unwisely—had put great faith in them. They were intended to be the chief means of transporting a base as far as the point where the three-man hauled sledges went on alone. Yet the dogs, tough little creatures, far happier in the climate than ponies, could only draw a limited amount on their two sledges. A lot—far too much—depended on Titus and his scrap-heap.

The dogs started after the ponies, caught them up on 7 November. A week later they reached One Ton Depot, and here Scott summoned Oates and Bowers into his tent to thrash out the next stage. They agreed to press on at a slightly greater rate, fifteen miles a day, and get to the Beardmore Glacier with the strongest of the ponies. The rest—and these were already in a bad way—would have been slaughtered for food.

This meeting between the three men, all so soon to die together, is interesting. One might have thought that in such a small group, sharing danger so far from home, in sight of such a clear-cut, passionately wanted, objective, the problem might have been discussed over a mug of tea: questions might have been asked and frankly answered, man to man. But no—the other two are brought into Scott's tent and told that he proposes to take the ponies to the foot of the glacier. From this, they *gather* he does not propose taking ponies up the glacier itself, and they are, in their diaries, profoundly relieved: leading a pony—particularly one of these—up a crevassed slope is as risky a job as any they will face on their journey. Neither Oates nor Bowers knows whether Scott has in fact ever considered doing this, but *neither wants to ask*. They leave their leader's tent grateful for this crumb of reassurance.

On 21 November they reach the motorless motor party. Already they are having trouble with the ponies, and—surprisingly early—there is hint in Scott's diary of doubt. "It's touch and go whether we scrape up to the glacier; meanwhile we get along somehow."

They are, at this point, twenty-two dogs, ten ponies, sixteen men. They have five tents to eat and sleep in, thirteen sledges to carry their stores.

And four hundred miles ahead, pushing in from their left as fast as he can go, is Roald Amundsen. His base camp has been reported, everyone knows his intention, yet no one appears to consider it. Someone remarks, "Haven't seen anything of Amundsen," and they all laugh.

They were having to build walls of snow around the ponies at each halt, lest the beasts die of exposure in the wind, and this took up precious time—more time than they had bargained for—used up precious stores of strength when they were beginning to realize they must conserve what they had. Morale was high, but things had not gone well: the long delay in starting, waiting for it to be warm enough for the ponies (dogs would not have minded); the death of nine even before kick-off; the unusually heavy surface: the unusual wind. "It is still rather touch and go. If one or more ponies were to go rapidly downhill, we might be in queer street."

And so they trudged on. Nearing the Beardmore Glacier, still with a few ponies being cossetted by the devoted Oates, they ran into a hellish blizzard which lasted without break for four days, kept them immobile, cursing in their tents, eating up rations. The snow stopped, temperature rose suddenly above freezing, dissolving the surface into two feet of slush, soaking them to the skin. Titus (his real name was Lawrence) was working harder than all of them, trying to keep the last few animals alive. As he was bringing snow or slush in each time he entered the tent, he had stopped coming in, except at night: he spent his day crouching against the snow walls he had built for his ponies.

Four days of this and they were able to move. They were up at five-thirty, but already they were weakening: the simplest jobs had become complicated, the lightest chore a burden. It took two and a half hours to get started. The surface was un-believably bad, but they waded on, dogs often swimming, ponies up to their bellies in slush. Scott dared not stop for a mid-day meal: no one, man or beast, would have been able to get up afterwards.

Fifteen hours' continuous struggle and they camped for the night near the glacier. Oates, by a miracle of devotion to his "scrap-heap", had got five ponies this far, but now these had to be taken away, one by one, and slaughtered.

The meat was cut up for food, entrails scattered about and fought over, in the slush, by the dog-teams. They named it, and with reason, "Shambles Camp".

Men and dogs alone—and a few days later the dogs were sent back. They had been kept a hundred and sixty miles farther than planned, because of the disappointing performance of the ponies. With their two team leaders, Meares and the Russian Dimitri, they had thus consumed far more food than Scott's plan had allowed for. Now everyone went on short rations, Meares and Dimitri sacrificing a meal a day each on their long trek back to base.

Men alone, now, against the cold. They pressed on, over the glacier, three sledges dragged by three four-man teams under Scott, Lt. Evans, and "Birdie" Bowers (and the little man with the heart of a lion, the strength of an elephant, *did* look like a bird), and slowly the going improved. The snow grew firmer and they were able to put on skis which would have sunk without trace earlier. They were laying the all-important depots of food, gradually emptying the sledges, but the ever-decreasing weight seemed to make no difference to their burden.

The first of the two support sledges left to go back on midsummer's day, 21 December. Not until the night before had Scott made a decision as to who should return with it. "I have just told off the people to return tomorrow night: Atkinson, Wright, Cherry-Garrard and Keohane. All are disappointed—poor Wright rather bitterly, I fear. I dreaded the necessity of choosing—nothing could be more heart-rending."

They had been climbing a little each day, and on 3 January they were at 10,180 feet, the temperature minus 18.

Magnetic variation was 180 degrees, so that in order to continue south they were now marching north by the compass, for they had passed the South Magnetic Pole, were between it and the Geographical one. That morning, Scott made the agonizing —and fatal—decision.

He was, as we have seen, the kindest, most sensitive of men. What he now announced, and recorded so flatly in his diary, had given him agony for days. "Bowers," he wrote, "is to come into our tent and we proceed as a five man unit tomorrow. We have five and a half units of food—practically over a month's allowance for five people—and it ought to see us through."

He ordered Lt. Evans, Lashly and Green to return. "Birdie" Bowers should have gone back, as the fourth member of that team, but Bowers had been such a tower of strength and so clearly—in Scott's eyes—deserved to come on, that he invited him to do so.

But Scott had already made up his mind that Wilson, Oates and Petty-Officer Evans were to join him in the final assault.

So, despite the fact that all organization for the assault had been based on a four-man team, Scott now elected to advance with five. His rations had been carefully made up, four men for a week per package; the tent held four comfortably; there were four plates, four spoons, four mugs in the haversack with the cooker. And, because they had jettisoned all but these on the glacier, where they had not been necessary, there were only four pairs of skis.

It was foolish—to say the least. But Scott was *unable*—physically unable—to leave any one of these men behind.

On the flyleaf of his diary is the scribble: "Ages: self 43, Wilson 39, Evans (P.O.) 37, Oates 32, Bowers 28. Average 36".

(Being wise after the event, we may also query Scott's choice of Edgar Evans: a huge man and unlikely to do well on half rations. And of Oates, whose back-breaking work with the ponies had already half killed him. But either of these, like Bowers, would have been disappointed at being left behind. Were they brought because they would be *more* disappointed than the others?)

The support sledge went back and the five men went on, dragging their own.

Two days later Scott writes thirty words in his diary, and then never again refers to the matter: "Cooking for five takes a seriously longer time than cooking for four; perhaps half an hour on the whole day. It is an idea I had not considered when reorganizing."

He had made, and he knew it, a dreadful mistake.

But after this, going is good, spirits again are high. Scott has high praise for his four companions. Wilson, he has decided, is a superb doctor, "ever on the look-out to alleviate the small pains and troubles incidental to the work". Evans is "a giant worker with a really remarkable headpiece". Little "Birdie" Bowers has been organizing them, taking charge of the stores, taking photographs and meteorological readings, often working out sums after everyone else has gone to sleep. He "remains a marvel".

How is Oates? Scott tells us Titus "had his invaluable period with the ponies; now he is a foot slogger and goes hard the whole time, does his share of camp work and stands the hardship as well as any of us".

There is—perhaps—a little of the kindly-report-on-a-well-meaning employee about these words. One wonders.

The three men most involved in the opening of a "Second Front", an Allied invasion of Europe in 1944, and who worked together in planning it, were Winston Churchill and, under him, General Eisenhower and Field Marshal Montgomery. *Above:* Seven years later the old warrior, supported by his two comrades, arrives at the Royal Albert Hall in London for a reunion.

Dr. Albert Schweitzer beside the Ogowe River, a few miles from the Equator. Here, starting with little help and primitive equipment in 1913, he built his hospital for the sick of Equatorial Africa, in particular for those suffering from leprosy. It was more than a hospital: it was a community, with patients bringing their entire families with them to camp in and around the hospital buildings, to cheer them and to cook the food they needed. Others scoffed at this "primitive medicine", but Albert Schweitzer knew this was the way to win the confidence of his patients. By the time he died his hospital was performing three major operations a day and delivering 400 babies a year.

Pope John, though he claimed to be in awe of radio and television, was a good performer. *Above:* He records his Easter message for broadcast to the world. *Right:* Franklin D. Roosevelt, as a young Assistant Secretary, had been "the man who taught the U.S. Navy how to swim". He remained a powerful swimmer even with legs crippled by poliomyelitis—and always happiest when, as here, swimming at his beloved Warm Springs. *Below:* In more sombre mood, he warns the American people, in 1940, of the dangers of isolationism.

There is also, on this page of the diary, an ominous note: "Evans has a nasty cut on his hand."

On they went. Excitement, as they trudged, grew with each day that passed—grew as their strength shrank. Strength was ebbing; no one noticed. Scott observed they were feeling the cold and blamed it on the dampness of the air.

On 15 January, they camped only thirty miles from their goal. "It is wonderful to think that two long marches would land us at the Pole.—The only appalling possibility, the sight of the Norwegian flag forestalling ours."

And the next day Bowers saw it. Not a Norwegian flag, to be sure, but a black one, one of Amundsen's markers. A little farther on: ski tracks, dog prints, sledge marks. Beyond that, Amundsen's tent and above it, flapping and cracking in the wind, the Norwegian flag. Inside the tent, a list of the five names, including Amundsen's, which had reached the Pole. They had been there a whole month earlier, on 16 December, 1911.

Scott's party slept, miserably, at the Pole, near Amundsen's tent, on the night of 17 January. The next morning they took, with Bowers pulling the string, a picture of themselves. Oates, Scott and Evans are standing; Bowers and Wilson are sitting in front, with a Union Jack in the snow behind. The sun is shining brightly in their faces, shining horizontally across the snow. They look terribly, terribly, cold.

They set off on the return journey, carrying a letter from Amundsen to his King, Haakon VII. Amundsen had wished them well in a letter to Scott, urged them, "if you can use any of the articles left in the tent please do not hesitate to do so. The sledge outside may be of use to you——"

And immediately, the tragic, hopeless, nightmare of their return begins to unfold. Edgar Evans's hand has been growing worse, they each begin to have symptoms of frostbite, they struggle, a bit more feebly each day, against distance and the coming winter. A month after their disappointment at the Pole, Edgar Evans dies. He has been staggering, feet nearly useless with frostbite, hand gangrenous, overdue for amputation, bravely trying to pull his share of the sledge. He is the biggest man in the party, unable to keep going on the meagre rations to which they have been reduced by their various delays. He stumbles and falls, gets up, then drops behind. They go on ahead, telling him not to worry, they will pull the sledge themselves, and when they get to the halt-point, put the kettle on, have a hot cup of tea waiting for him.

They have their tea, their meal of one biscuit. Edgar Evans does not appear.

The three trudge back, find him crawling, clothes in disarray, hands bare, a wild unseeing look on his face. Oates stays with him while the other two go for the sledge, bring it back, load him on it. They get him, unconscious, to their tent. He dies during the night.

They bury Evans the next day, grief tempered by the practical consideration that he has held them back: had he remained with them, half-walking, half-crawling, their hope of getting to base would have been zero. As it is, Scott, Bowers and Wilson have an outside chance.

What about Oates? Frostbitten, worn out, indomitable—what about him?

There is nothing to be done about Oates. Only Oates himself can do that, and when, nearing his last gasp, feet gangrenous, almost useless, he asks Wilson, kind-hearted Doc Wilson, what he can do, he is told only, "Slog on, just slog on". "Poor Soldier," Scott writes that night, "has become a terrible hindrance."

But of course no one can tell him.

On 11 March, Scott, still absolutely in command, ordered Wilson to issue the opium tablets with which any one of them could, if he wished, take his life. They were sixty-three miles from One Ton Depot and food, with seven days reduced—very much reduced—ration in hand. But no man in their condition could do sixty-three miles in seven days. If all went well, they might do it in nine, and starve for two of them.

And each day, in black, descending winter, it grew colder. On 14 March, temperature had dropped to minus 43, there was a wild wind blowing. They were pitifully weak now and the boots they had to remove each night to preserve what was left of their feet took literally hours to put on again. Their days, in every way, were getting shorter. Rations which though short might have been sufficient were largely useless because the fuel oil, in the depots, without which food is a frozen, uneatable brick, had leaked away. There was only enough left to thaw—not to cook—a small part of what they had left.

15 March: Oates demanded they go on and leave him. They had to refuse.

The end was near. What had gone wrong? Bad luck, mis-calculation, had beset them from the beginning. They had lost half their ponies even before setting out. Atrocious weather had dogged them, forced them to lie up, time and time again, wasting time, consuming rations. There had been the cruel blow of Amundsen's victory to the Pole, the rapidly worsening weather, the collapse of Evans. And now, of Oates.

That night Oates went to sleep with the other three in the tent. Early the next morning he awoke; there was a blizzard sweeping over the canvas, screeching so a man's words were drowned if he tried to, bothered to, speak. They had all woken in the din, and they heard Oates say something about going out: "I may be some time."

He went out.

"We knew that poor Oates was walking to his death, but though we tried to dissuade him, we knew it was the act of a brave man and an English gentleman. We all hope to meet the end with a similar spirit and assuredly the end is not far."

It was less than a fortnight off. Scott knew they couldn't make it, and he calmly recorded that, "diaries, etc., and geological specimens . . . will be found with us . . . my right foot has gone, nearly all the toes; two days ago, I was proud possessor of best feet——"

And on Thursday, 29 March: "Since the 21st, we have had a continuous gale from W.S.W. and S.W. We had fuel to make two cups of tea apiece and bare food for two days on the 20th. Every day we have been ready to start for our depot, 13 miles away, but outside the door of the tent it remains a scene of whirling drift. I do not think we can hope for any better things now. We shall stick it out to the end, but we are getting weaker, of course, and the end cannot be far.

"It seems a pity, but I do not think I can write more. R. Scott.

"Last entry: For God's sake look after our people."

And so, only 13 miles from One Ton Depot, trapped in a

blizzard, crippled by frostbite and starvation, the last three died. While he waited for the end, Robert Scott wrote twelve letters to those nearest to him and to his companions. They are beautiful letters, for he seems at no stage to have dwelt on his own predicament: his thoughts were entirely for his companions, their loved ones at home.

"Had we lived," he wrote in a final, dying, "Letter to the Public" setting out the reasons for what he regarded as the failure of his charge, the Expedition on which they, the Public, had sent him, "had we lived, I should have had a tale to tell of the hardihood, endurance and courage of my companions which would have stirred the heart of every Englishman. These rough notes and our dead bodies must tell the tale, but surely, surely, a great, rich, country like ours will see that those who are dependent on us are properly provided for?"

The rescue party found him, eight months later, arm over his dearest friend, Wilson, the body of Bowers beside. The remarkable diary, one of the most moving documents ever written, was there, complete, as were the geological specimens with which they had encumbered themselves, slowing still further their agonizing, hopeless journey. Scott knew that if these things were jettisoned, they would never be found: and he had been instructed to get them.

Scott's last Expedition brought back priceless information, down to the minerals he was carrying when he died. He had not been first at the Pole—but perhaps this, after all, means very little.

The significance of Scott's ill-fated, heroic, journey lies outside all that. It was a victory, over suffering and fear, which stands alone.

It was the victory of a leader—for Scott was that above all—who led the whole way.

Chapter 5

Mahatma Gandhi

My great-great-grandfather was, like me and others between, a regular soldier, and although he attained only the modest rank of lieutenant, he had a more noteworthy career than many of us. He served with the East India Company, getting his commission in the Madras Army in 1778 and two years later, during the war with Hyder Ali, he foolishly got himself captured and stuffed into a cage. Just that—a largeish cage, with room for two. He stayed a year in it, cheek by jowl with one Lieutenant David Baird, and for a year the two were a travelling exhibit, studied and gaped at and fed through the bars. No doubt Harry and David ("Lord help the man who's locked up with our Davey" was his mother's comment) were the only British a large part of India ever saw. It makes one wonder.

And indeed I have often wondered, of great-great-grandad Harry who survived his year, was released and went back to Scotland where he lived another half century, even siring his only child, my great-grandmother, at the age of seventy. He appears to have had nothing but respect, even affection, for the people who made him into fifty per cent of a travelling circus. Obviously they treated their exhibits well.

So the intention was always there to visit the great sub-continent, see for myself. And one of the several reasons was the fascination which India's strange mystic, saint and trouble-maker held for me.

One gets, I feel, a clearer picture of him from the early pictures, which show him in western clothes. The later ones, after he had forsworn such nonsense and vowed to wear nothing but *khaddar*, show us very little. He has lost most of his teeth, so one sees a sunken brown face with large ears and very little hair. The eyes, behind steel-rimmed glasses, are almost always downcast; one gets no idea of what is passing behind.

Below this, a home-spun shawl, revealing nothing of the shape beneath. Below that, a pair of match-stick lower legs, in sandals.

But those early pictures, outside the office in Johannesburg of "M. K. Gandhi, Attorney," or in uniform with his Red Cross unit, or as a young man about London, give us a better insight into the man. Mustachioed, arms folded, he looks, at the centre of his ferocious Red Cross group, the virile leader he was. If a man like that gave an order, it was obeyed. Arms folded again—a pose to which he was partial—and leaning against the edge of a table, dressed smartly in grey suit and high stiff collar, he is the barrister whose pleading will command respect anywhere—as indeed it did.

And then there are the pictures, not so carefully posed, trousers a bit baggy, sleeves a little short, which show the shy young man, terrified of public speaking, hands clasped nervously in front of him, a look of absolute defiance on his young face. Here is a man who, though speechless on a public platform, will fight for his ideals till the end.

And in all these pictures, taken in the first decade of our century and the few years before, there are the amazing eyes. Gentle yet piercing; fierce, gleaming like polished anthracite, and absolutely bottomless in depth.

70

Mohandas Gandhi was born, 2 October, 1869, in the tiny Indian princely state of Porbandar, now part of Bombay State. His grandfather had been Chief Minister of Porbandar, as was his father later; but to put this in perspective, we must remember that Porbandar and another two hundred and twenty-one princely states were amalgamated in 1948 into the new state of Saurashtra. And more recently, Saurashtra itself became a part of Bombay State.

So the Gandhi family were big fishes in a very little pool. They were of the Vaisya caste, the third of the four great Hindu orders, a caste concerned mainly, by tradition, with trade and agriculture. Unlike Jawaharlal Nehru, who was from the top caste, a Brahmin, and whose name tells us the family once had a large house by the canal in Delhi, the Gandhis have a name meaning simply that they were originally grocers. Not being of the warrior or Kshatriya caste, they had never been concerned with fighting, and all violence was, congenitally, repugnant to them. Coupled with this caste-ordained attitude was the particular brand of Hinduism practised in that part of western, coastal India. The Vaishnava Hindus, influenced by the Jains, who fear to breathe in violently lest they swallow and thereby destroy an insect, believe all life, down to the humble egg, to be sacred. Gandhi's parents were devout; prayer, diet and fasting, all were parts of life, and this life must be ruled, disciplined, by the taking of religious vows.

And yet Gandhi had his moments of doubt. He questioned, for example, the wisdom of a vegetable diet, when the large, red-faced Englishmen who controlled his country lived on meat. If Indians began, like Englishmen, to eat huge quantities of meat, would *they* not become strong? Secretly, he began eating meat.

But the thought that he was lying—he was only a schoolboy at the time—cured him. He confessed to his father, and his father's complete forgiveness had a profound effect on the boy. From that time on, the doctrine of forgiveness of sin, hence of non-violence, became a part of him.

He was married at this time, aged thirteen, to a girl called Kasturbai, who was to be an important influence on him for the next sixty-two years, when she would die in prison. This was a real marriage, not merely a child bethrothal, and Mohandas found that the duties as well as the pleasures interfered considerably with his studies.

Nevertheless, he managed to matriculate, and now, with his father dead, a family friend advised his mother to send him to England. Here the boy could get a legal training and be better fitted to step into his father's shoes as administrator of some princely state.

And so, after having sworn a solemn oath not to touch wine, women or meat, and having made arrangements to leave Kasturbai and the children behind, Mohandas Gandhi sailed for England. He was eighteen, a married man of five years standing, and of highly sensual disposition.

At first he was utterly miserable—which is hardly surprising. Although he would, without a vow, have remained faithful to Kasturbai, deep carnal desires were to distress him greatly, throughout his stay in England.

Without a sex-life, a man can live. Without meat, in this meat-eater's paradise, Gandhi seemed destined to starve. Did anyone in London eat other than beef or mutton? It seemed not. He found rooms with another young Indian and together they explored the cuisine of the metropolis. What they found was tasteless, insipid, ill-cooked: vegetables whose only excuse was that they had been stewed up with slabs of mutton, were dumped in hideous solitude on their plates, swimming in brown water.

At last they found a vegetarian restaurant—and Gandhi suddenly found himself a vegetable eater by conviction. "I had all along abstained from meat in the interests of truth and of the vow, before my mother, which I had taken; but had wished at the same time that every Indian should be a meat eater, and had looked forward to being one myself, freely and openly some day, and to enlist others in the cause. The choice was now made in favour of vegetarianism, the spread of which henceforward became my mission." In fact, the earliest published writings of Mohandas Gandhi can be found in a London periodical, *The Vegetarian*. Already, he was a man with a mission.

He helped design the badge of the new "London Vegetarian

Society". The rest of its committee was anxious that this young man, whose age-old religion had turned him toward their simple philosophy, should address them. But Gandhi found—to the considerable dismay of one planning to earn a living as a barrister—that he was incapable of saying anything in public. His nerves prevented his even reading a short written speech.

And he was shy, too, in less public surroundings. He resolved to do something about this and bought himself handsome Savile Row clothes, which included a gleaming top hat. He began, at the same time, taking lessons in elocution. Not content with this, he took lessons in French, and dancing. The dancing he soon gave up, but in order to persevere with western music he bought himself a violin.

Suddenly, he realized the futility of it all. "If my character made a gentleman of me, so much the better; otherwise I should forgo the ambition."

He was called to the Bar on 10 June, 1891, and sailed home two days later. As he strode up the gangway he was suddenly struck with the most frightful feeling of inadequacy. He had passed the English legal exams—but what did he know of *Indian* laws? For that matter, though he knew many, many, laws, could he apply a single one?

But home was home, with a wife and small children, as well as his brother's children. Throughout his life Gandhi loved children. One of the great sorrows of that life was the death, at birth, of a child, which he forever afterwards blamed on his lustful nature, which had driven him to intercourse with his wife a few days before the child was due to be born.

And now, while studying at the High Court in Bombay in an attempt to master the laws of his own country, he went to pay an official call on an English political agent. The intention was to put in a word for his older brother, temporarily in disgrace for "having tendered wrong advice" when he succeeded their father as adviser to the State of Porbandar. Mohandas had only recently returned from a cold but courteous England where he had made many friends, and he was shocked and distressed at being treated by this topied fool of an Englishman as an inferior. Indeed, through a misunderstanding of Gandhi's intention, he was literally chucked out by the Englishman's servants.

Throbbing with righteous indignation, he prepared to take proceedings. Then an Indian friend took him aside: "Mohandas, it may be different in England. Here, if you want a professional future, you swallow insults from the English."

And it was at this moment that the offer came, in April, 1893, to go to South Africa and represent an Indian firm in a case out there. He accepted.

Once again he left family behind and there were the myriad temptations of various ports of call, but he made the trip safely and arrived in Durban. South Africa, at first, was like home; there were Indians everywhere he went: labourers speaking Tamil and Telegu, from South India; Hindi speakers from Bihar, and those—mostly merchants—from the Bombay area, who spoke his own, Gujerati, language.

He took train to Pretoria—and here had his first experience of colour prejudice. The Englishman had insulted him because in English eyes he was a dishonest foreigner: the South African did it because of his colour. He was forcibly ejected from his First Class seat and, because he refused to accept this and creep quietly down to a Third Class carriage, he sat shivering defiantly on the station platform as the train moved out.

Eventually he got on another, was able to use his First Class ticket, and got to Pretoria. He was still planning to conduct his legal case with vigour, but now it took second place, in his mind, to another matter. At the first opportunity, he called a meeting of the Indian community. Surprising, perhaps, that when an unknown lawyer gets off a train, a meeting he calls should have much response, but the entire Indian community turned out. He had written himself a speech, and so great was his fervour that he was halfway through it, alone on the platform, when he realized he felt no nervousness at all. Here he was, addressing a very large audience indeed and holding them —there was no doubt about it as he blinked down from the platform—absolutely spellbound.

But Gandhi was not a rabble-rouser. He urged them to get together, present a united front to the Boers, for without that they would continue despised and downtrodden. But at the same time he urged his audience to consider, very seriously, whether their status was a direct result of their colour or not.

Were their business dealings always and absolutely above re-
proach? Were their houses at least as clean and well-cared-for
as those of white people? Before they had a case to fight, the
Indians must make sure of these points. Then, fight they must:
not with sticks and stones and broken bottles, but with dignity
and with argument. Without violence.

He intended, of course, returning to India. His legal case was
concluded (out of court, and to the complete satisfaction of
both parties: this became Gandhi's legal technique), and he
had done what he could to wake up his fellow Indians to the
facts of life in South Africa. He wanted, very badly, to get back
to Bombay and Kasturbai and the children.

But it was at the farewell party thrown for him by the
Indian community in Durban that he looked around him, saw
the innocent, trusting—helpless—faces and decided on the
spur of the moment to stay longer. Without his help, these
simple, good people would never achieve the dignity they
deserved. He would stay—just for a few weeks.

The Indian community was overjoyed. Eagerly, childishly,
they volunteered to help him in his law practice, look after
him, do everything to give him the time to devote to their
problem.

He wrote a pamphlet—his first—on "The Indian Franchise:
an Appeal to Every Briton in South Africa". He helped found
the Natal Indian Congress and become its first secretary. Then
he went back to India to collect Kasturbai and the children. He
intended while there to draw the attention of both India and
Britain to the state of affairs in South Africa. At this time and
for many years he was absolutely loyal to Britain: when he
arrived in India he even joined the committee appointed to
organize Queen Victoria's Diamond Jubilee. He began travelling all over the subcontinent, trying to interest people, British
and Indian, in what he regarded as the terrible plight of his
people in South Africa, people who had been trodden under
foot for so long they no longer had the will or the courage to
fight for themselves. He was persuaded to write a series of
newspaper articles.

On the 18 December, 1896, he was back—almost—in South
Africa, with his family. Two ships from Bombay which had

arrived together, bringing between them eight hundred Indians, were held offshore: the pretext was that plague had broken out in Bombay. In fact, the real reason was report of Gandhi's articles and interviews in India, which had been telegraphed ahead of him, and had roused the white population to a fever of indignation. Furthermore, the eight hundred who accompanied Gandhi (though he knew none and was in no way responsible for their coming) must be part of a dastardly Gandhian plot to submerge all Europeans in a rising tide of "Asiatic blood".

He was already a man of importance, so the Prime Minister of Natal took it upon himself to send a private warning that he and his family should land after dark. Gandhi rejected the advice, landed in broad daylight and was almost killed. He was rescued by the wife of the Police Superintendent who bravely held off a shrieking mob of her fellow-whites with an umbrella, until her husband arrived and escorted the little Indian to safety.

The trouble subsided, it was proved that Gandhi's articles had been in fact most temperate; the eight hundred Indians, including his family, were allowed to disembark.

The South African war came, and now Gandhi insisted that his community, having shouted for its rights, should shoulder its burdens as British subjects. He formed an Indian Ambulance Corps, and it is here that we make the acquaintance of the ferocious-looking leader of men, with the black moustache, the broad-brimmed Gurkha hat and the khaki uniform. He led his Corps with devotion and not a little gallantry.

But, though he had inspired a grudging respect in South Africa for his people, things were still not going well for them. The whites believed—or professed to believe—that he was at the back of a conspiracy to smuggle in countless Indian immigrants, and a law was hastily drafted making it compulsory for "Asiatics" to register their finger prints. Gandhi made plans to thwart the legislation.

It was at this time that he took perhaps the biggest decision of his life. In order to purify himself, devote his entire thought, life and energy to working for his people, he would become celibate. For someone of Mohandas Gandhi's temperament,

this was a sacrifice of appalling magnitude, but he explained it
to his wife, she agreed, and he took a solemn vow of continence,
or *brahmacharya*. That vow was never broken.

In order to fight the legislation, Gandhi worked out a campaign of civil disobedience. This, as its name implies, was the
policy of refusing, but without physical violence of any sort, to
do what one was told to do. In this case, register as "Asiatics"
on penalty of imprisonment, or deportation, or both.

The Act was amended more than once before becoming law
on the first of July, 1907, and Indians were given the rest of
that month in which to register. As the weeks wore on, tension
rose day by day, for hardly a man or woman had appeared at
the registration offices. While time passed, Gandhi considered
the effectiveness and also the real meaning of his strategy.
"Civil disobedience", "passive disobedience", seemed weapons
of the weak and spiteful: he now thought up a new name, and
a new approach. It would be known as "*satyagraha*", or "soul-
force". "To whatever extent there is room for the use of arms
or physical force or brute force, there and to that extent is
there so much less possibility for soul-force. In *satyagraha*
there is not the remotest idea of injuring the opponent—
satyagraha postulates the conquest of the adversary by suffering in one's own person."

At the end of the stipulated month, the Indians—almost all
of them having refused to register—were imprisoned in their
tens of thousands. One of these, of course, was Mohandas
Gandhi, who thus began the series of imprisonments which, in
South Africa and in India, would occupy a sizeable part of his
life. During these two months in the Johannesburg gaol he
wore the white cap of a coloured prisoner, and this, years later
in India, became the badge of Indian independence, the
"Gandhi cap". Soon the fantastic overcrowding of gaols forced
a meeting between Gandhi and General Smuts, after which,
as a result of promises made by both sides, most Indians were
released. But the battle was not over: Smuts had told Gandhi
that if Indians *voluntarily* registered, the hated Asiatic Act
would be repealed; and Gandhi for his part agreed not to hold
inflammatory meetings. Smuts then failed to honour the spirit
of his undertaking: after much legal juggling, the situation

of Indians in the Union remained precisely as it had been before.

So *satyagraha* continued, with a few lapses into violence which Gandhi sternly rebuked. South African legislation, which for a time grew progressively more punitive—prohibiting Indians from entering the Transvaal, invalidating all but Christian marriages, levying a tax on Indians—suddenly did an about-face in 1914, with the Indians Relief Act. This was a tremendous change of direction for the new Union, and all credit for it must go to Gandhi.

His work done, he sailed with his family to England, arriving there the day before the first world war broke out. Already he was a world figure. Such a man, who commanded the respect, the obedience, of thousands of men (soon to be millions) could not be ignored by the British Government. They made haste to hold discussions.

Friendly—and fruitless—discussion over, he left England, arrived Bombay on 9 January, 1915. He stepped ashore wearing Gujerati costume, not the European clothes affected by the Indian leaders of the day, to be greeted—to his surprise—as "a new spiritual force". The great Bengali poet Rabindranath Tagore conferred upon him the title *"Mahatma"*, "Great Soul". The Government of India, not to be outdone, presented him with the Kaisar-i-Hind gold medal, not realizing, perhaps, that they would soon get it back and be flinging its owner into gaol.

Although in many ways he admired his country's British rulers, Gandhi had no doubt now of his ultimate aim: to rid India of them. Self-rule, or *swaraj*, must come. But first of all, having been out of his country for twenty years, he must get to know it. He was shocked by its poverty, shocked too by the working of a caste system which reduced millions of men, women and children, the "Untouchables", to the level of animals. They were worse than animals, for even the shadow of some, should it chance to fall across a caste Hindu, was contaminating. Having educated his countrymen in Africa not only in civil rights, but in civic responsibility, honesty and hygiene, he found he had to do the same in India.

At the same time he began investigating other injustices. There were plenty of these, both Indian- and English-imposed.

But first it was necessary to study his people and their problems, and to set an example. *Satyagraha,* if it were needed, would come later. He had by now given up all legal work and he set himself to building, for a start, a small community which would be an example to India. He selected Gujerat, where he could speak to the peasants in their own language, and in 1916 he settled on the bank of the River Sabarmati, close to Ahmedabad, the great textile centre. Here cotton grew abundantly; but Ahmedabad and its mills had been deliberately restricted so that there would be a thriving export business of cloth to India from the mills of England, notably Lancashire. Gandhi set out to persuade Indians to spin and weave their own cloth. Using the primitive wheel, the *charka,* and the hand-held spindle, the *takli,* the peasants of India were unlikely ever to supplant Lancashire—but it was a step in the right direction and above all it was a gesture of self-reliance and self-respect. Each family, he urged, should spin so many yards a year of cotton yarn and make from that the home-spun *khaddar* cloth—and wear it. And Mohandas Gandhi, barrister-at-law, late of the Middle Temple, sat down and showed them how. From this period till the end of his life he wore nothing but the home-spun shawl, *dhoti,* and sandals. (Years later when he attended, in 1931, the abortive Round Table Conference in London, and was asked if he felt undressed before King George V, he made the immortal remark, "The King wore enough for both of us.")

He worked hard for his Untouchables and coined for them the name *Harijans,* Children of God. He urged them into his community as equals. At first, everyone was shocked, even the Untouchables. That an Untouchable should handle the food, pour the drinking water—and drink it—of higher castes, was unthinkable. To us this may sound ridiculous: to Indians it most certainly was not. (An English observer of a meal in Gandhi's community, all castes sitting down together, watched in wonder and noted that, "they risked Hell at every sip.")

Only Gandhi could have achieved it. Only he could have made men and women, castes and out-castes together, sit down and share food. But this was only the beginning: it must happen all over India, not just in one community, and he vowed to himself that it would. Gradually, this began, here and there, to

79

happen. Then Gandhi, though he never for an instant forgot his Harijans, turned attention to other abuses, and first to the plight of indigo workers on the plantations of Bihar. This was a case—one of very few—of the white man extorting wealth from the labour of peasants, and it seemed to combine all that was the worst in British industrialism, with its long hours, child labour, appalling conditions and pitiful wages, with the Indian feudal system. The tenants of the British "planters" in the district were forced to grow indigo on a large proportion of the land they rented and sell this, at starvation rates, to the landlord. In addition, they paid taxes on marriages, houses, everything they possessed or did. The final injustice had just struck: world prices of indigo were falling against competition from aniline dyes, and now the landlords graciously permitted their tenants *not* to grow the crop—in exchange for a stiff cash payment.

The very arrival of Gandhi in the district caused trouble. The planters ordered him out, then demanded his arrest as a breach of the peace. The Lieutenant Governor of the State over-ruled them, permitted him to begin his enquiry. As he had stoutly refused to leave the State when ordered, and was as stoutly awaiting arrest, The Indigo Affair must be noted as his first act of civil disobedience on Indian soil. This first tussle with the British was clearly won by Gandhi. An Act was passed, on the results of his enquiry, which righted the abuses. Within a year the indigo estates had ceased to exist and peasants were growing their own choice of crops, for their own benefit.

For a while now, Gandhi's history becomes one of battle against British rule. He urges *satyagraha* on the people of the Punjab, a defiance against Acts which give unnecessary police powers to the Government, but he is horrified when the people refuse to consider non-violence. There is rioting and many lives are lost, notably at an appalling massacre in Amritsar.

But other attempts to make the British realize they must, sooner rather than later, give the Indian people self-government, were more successful. The people themselves, as those in South Africa had done earlier, began to realize the tremendous moral weapon that *satyagraha* gave them. In fairness to Britain it must be said that, by now, London knew just as well as did the Indian National Congress that independence must come.

The problem was: How? India was a land of many communities, chief among them the Hindus and Muslims, constantly in a state of undeclared war. Within these communities themselves were the conflicting interests of caste and language. Real unity was hard to visualize—to whom did one give independence, who would hold the reins?

Gandhi was painfully aware of this, and where he stood head and shoulders above the other men who fought for *swaraj* is in his appreciation of the fact. He worked hardest of all for agreement with the Muslim community and at one stage nearly succeeded. Had he done so, the history of South-east Asia since 1947, perhaps of the world, would have been different, happier. He had come "reluctantly to the conclusion that the British connection had made India more helpless than she ever was before, politically and economically".

The acid test in so much of *satyagraha* was the refusal to pay taxes. It had been assumed—and rightly—that if millions of Indians ceased paying taxes, the Government would go bankrupt. Had Gandhi persevered in this—and the people were entirely behind him and would have suffered, if not gladly at least bravely, all the sanctions against them, the confiscation of their cattle and goods—the Government might have had to sue for peace at any price. But each time that *satyagraha* seemed on the verge of succeeding, there was an outbreak of terrible violence, so abhorrent to Gandhi that he called off the campaign.

In fact there were two, quite dissimilar, Gandhis. One was a lawyer and tactician, with ear to the ground and sharp analytical mind, aware that in many cases the end justifies the means. The other was a saint. It was the saint who so often infuriated his associates, like Jawaharlal Nehru.

Saint or no saint, he was gaoled in 1922. He had already returned his Kaisar-i-Hind gold medal and urged others to do likewise with British honours, had staged more than one fast to bring his opponents—not always the Government—to their knees. He would stage many more: for Hindu-Muslim unity, for Government concessions, for an end to rioting; and each one, while dragging his wiry, courageous little frame to the brink of death, would achieve something.

He was released from prison well before the end of his six-year sentence (awarded so apologetically by the British judge: the whole court had risen to its feet when Gandhi came in under escort), but though he resumed his work for *swaraj* with as much vigour as before, he was thinking more of other problems. The *Harijans* were, next to Hindu-Muslim unity, his greatest worry, and he worked unceasingly on their behalf. One of the hurdles to getting a plan for an independent India, acceptable to all its people, was the question of votes for Untouchables, and he demanded they be put on the electoral roll, treated like everyone else—against opposition which wanted them deprived of all voting rights or put on a separate roll.

He started a newspaper which he edited until his death, *"Harijan"*. As it dealt with every topic under the sun and was the mouthpiece of Mahatma Gandhi, it was eagerly purchased and read by everyone who had an opportunity, and the proud name, as well as the proceeds of the paper's sale, did their bit to raise the status of the "Children of God". A few months after starting it he went on a ten months' tour of the subcontinent to put the Untouchables' case and to collect money for their relief. He collected about £60,000, mostly in coppers and small trinkets of jewellery, but he knew as much as any man that more was needed than charity and legislation. What was needed was a whole new way of thought. In the meantime, he would teach them, himself, to tan the leather of the skins they took from the animals they slaughtered (without payment: scraps of meat sticking to the skin were their only reward), to make tools and ornaments from the bones. At the same time, by his example, much as Our Lord's of washing feet, he led parties of men to clean latrines, carry *Harijan* corpses at their pitiful funerals. One by one, others followed. Temples, schools, wells, began—terribly slowly—to be thrown open for the use of *Harijans*.

He seemed now to be opting out of the struggle for *swaraj*, if only because there were others to carry on where he had left off, to organize *satyagraha*, and there was so much which only he was able to do. In April, 1935, he settled into a small community, more or less exactly at the centre of the Indian peninsula, called Segaon. It was primitive, isolated, and he took up residence there, in one small room which he shared with two Untouchables. Here by his example—which was noted and studied all over India—he began, again, to build up his ideal community.

When war broke out in 1939, Gandhi felt himself, for the first time, unable to side with the British. The Viceroy, while urging the Indian people to fight against the German Oppressor, refused to hold out hope for freedom after the struggle. This, for Gandhi, was just not good enough. He refused to help recruitment as he had done in both the South African and 1914 wars, and his attitude, though constantly being modified in the light of circumstances, was throughout hostile to the war effort. In 1942 he was imprisoned yet again after a "Britain Must Quit India" movement which degenerated, to his distress, into bloody violence, a violence which redoubled when he was arrested. The imprisonment lasted just under two years, but his wife Kasturbai, who had shared his fortunes without complaint for sixty-two years, died there. Shortly after this, Gandhi himself was released. He was now 74, but he devoted himself with the energy of a young man to reasoning with the Viceroy, Lord Wavell, the case for postwar freedom, and with the Muslim, Jinnah, the case for unity.

War ended, independence drew near. It had been granted in principle for many months and now, with a change of British Government, plans were made to implement it as soon as possible. There were many who felt it was coming too soon. There were others, like Mountbatten who succeeded Wavell, convinced it must come immediately. He signalled the Government in London that plans must be drastically speeded up, or there would be bloodshed.

There was. It began even before independence had become a fact. Rumours spread of a Hindu-dominated nation, then of a Muslim one, rumours of partition. As each took hold, there was rioting and wholesale murder. No one could have done more than Gandhi to stop it, and in many places he was successful. In fact, every place he reached, in a tireless, desperate journeying, stopped its quarrel when he got there. After one pre-independence riot between Hindus and Muslims, which stopped as soon as his presence in the district was made known, he told the bruised and bleeding survivors that although Mountbatten's promise of independence was "deliberate, unconditional and unequivocal" these people before him might well "tempt him to eat his words".

Mountbatten did not, could not, eat his words. Independence came on 15 August, 1947. Two Dominions were set up, India and Pakistan, predominantly Hindu and Muslim respectively. Bengal and the Punjab, because of their close balance of communities, were split, and the Indian Army, that superb, largely British-officered force, without which the Japanese and perhaps the German wars might have been lost, was divided.

There was universal rejoicing. At first. But the man more responsible than any other for achieving independence was nearly heartbroken. To have these two, rival, states, was not only lunacy: it was a sin against God.

In Bengal, a riot began that bid fair to be worse than anything so far. Gandhi, with heavy heart, went there and his presence—he stayed in Calcutta with a Muslim household—stopped the riots. But they began again; the arson, the bloodshed, grew. He announced his fast unto death.

The riots stopped. As the London *Times* put it, this one old man had achieved more than could have been effected by divisions of troops.

There was one more fast to come—and though it has been suggested, more than once, that these fasts were a stunt, no one who knew Gandhi, or even followed, as I did from a comparative distance, the working of his mind, the unfolding of his strategy, could doubt that he would literally and cheerfully have starved to death, if that had been necessary. Fasting to him was a purification; as the body wasted, so the mind grew clearer. He rose from each fast a little weaker and a little wiser, and if it were necessary to fast unto death, that was God's will.

On 2 October, 1947, there were congratulations from all over the world on his seventy-eighth birthday, but there was agony in his heart. Wholesale migrations of Hindus, Sikhs and Muslims were taking place in both directions over the new borders, innocent travellers were being butchered on their way. He prepared for yet another fast.

84

This, the world felt and feared, may be the last.

It was—but for a different reason.

The fast occupied five days in the middle of January. Then Gandhi learnt that a pact had been hurriedly drafted and signed. He stopped his fast and the world rejoiced.

Twelve days later, on 30 January, he sent for his personal attendant. "Bring my letters," he said. "I must answer them— for tomorrow I may never be."

At five o'clock that evening, as he climbed the steps to the platform for his prayer meeting, leaning, for he was not only old now, but tired, on the shoulder of a grandniece, he was shot three times at point-blank range. Blood spurted from his chest, dyeing the undyed *khaddar*, and he fell back, saying, *"Ram! Ram!"* "O God! O God!" As they picked him up, his hands clasped themselves in prayer.

Thirty minutes later, the saviour of India was dead, butchered by a fanatic—a Hindu. The world had lost, in one moment of that mad, unthinking violence against which the Mahatma had fought all his life, the wisdom of perhaps its greatest son.

Mahatma Gandhi—Gandhiji—was unique. There are no more like him.

Chapter 6

Winston S. Churchill

"The car weighed some 2,400 pounds. With my evening coat on I could not have weighed much less than 200 pounds. Taking the rate of the car at thirty-five miles an hour—I think a moderate estimate—I had actually to absorb in my body 6,000 foot-pounds. It was the equivalent of falling thirty feet on to a pavement. The energy absorbed, though not, of course, the application of destructive force, was the equivalent of stopping ten pounds of buckshot dropped 600 feet or two charges of buckshot at point-blank range.

"I do not understand why I was not broken like an egg-shell, or squashed like a gooseberry. I have seen that the poor policeman who was killed on the Oxford Road was hit by a vehicle travelling at very much the same speed and was completely shattered. I certainly must be very tough or very lucky, or both."

Tough, yes: lucky, perhaps. But above all, of an insatiable, restless curiosity. If you or I had been run down in the street, had suffered internal haemorrhage and the fracture of fifteen bones—would either of us go to the trouble of working this out?

When I came to England and to boarding-school between the wars, as a gangling youth of fifteen, I regarded myself as British. This despite an appearance, a manner and an accent which made me, to everyone else, laughably, hilariously, *not* British. Even the masters, when in doubt, hailed me in the High Street or on the playing fields as "I say there, American boy . . ." My first weeks at Harrow were not particularly pleasant and I spent much time bemoaning an incomprehension of rugger, fives, Harrow footer, cricket and Latin and wishing I were thousands of miles away.

The dining-room of the Headmaster's House where one seemed to spend so much time having one's name called out, praying, eating, singing and doing prep, was a sober, dark-brown box with windows set high in its walls so one saw nothing but sky and roof-tops through them. Around these cocoa walls were panels—in fact the walls, from head-height up, were panels of carved names, two inches high, inlaid in gold. During these first weeks, as gradually life became bearable, workmen came in, took down an uncompleted panel, carted it away. A few days later they brought it back with my name and those of others who had just entered the House, gleaming in gold upon it. I began to take an interest in these panels, which went right round the room, and to sympathize with the boys, presumably long dead, whose panel had been removed to make way for ours. For the progression was clockwise, the dog ran round in a circle, eating its tail, and every few years, as a new panel was completed, the oldest one, next door to it, was taken away to make room for a virgin new one.

There were few names I knew, though I could fritter away the odd minute of prayers or prep in wondering whether that Redman on the farthest panel was father to the one sitting opposite me, whether the two Bethels on the same panel were brothers.

One of the names I recognized was: Winston S. Churchill. I can't remember the year against which he was shown, for though I know now that he went to Harrow in 1888, he spent a few terms in one of the "Small Houses" farther down the Street before entering the H.M. Perhaps it was 1889. At any rate, it was an old and faded panel, a poor thing against the gleaming near-virginity of my own. I knew very little about Winston Churchill, except that he was a dynamic fellow, a restless thorn-in-the-flesh English politician who was, for the moment, out of favour. He was also, and this interested me, half an American. I wondered how he'd liked the place.

And so, when he burst over my limited horizon four years later, in the blackest moment of the war, he was familiar, but an unknown quantity. A name, in faded gold, almost ready to take down.

A few months later he was the greatest man on earth, the man without whom, Vera Lynn notwithstanding, there would not have Been An England by the end of 1940.

It is an impertinence to sit down and write a biography, however short, of someone who has won the Nobel Prize for Literature and already written it. For Churchill the man is in his writings. Every bit of him is there—and written incomparably better than I can.

But if one sets out to write of Heroes, one cannot leave out the greatest of them all. Nobel Prize or no.

He was the grandson of a Duke, and not a particularly notable Duke. Five of them had walked on from the wings, carrying spears, between the time John Churchill won his Dukedom with the dazzling victories of Blenheim, Ramillies, Oudenarde and Malplaquet and the time Winston's grandfather inherited it. Perversely enough, John Churchill chose for himself the Dukedom of Marlborough and elected to build his 208-room palace in Oxfordshire. Appropriately enough, he styled it Blenheim.

The seventh Duke had three sons and of these Lord Randolph Churchill distinguished himself—briefly, brightly, like a passing comet. He had the good luck to meet a remarkable American girl, Jennie Jerome, during Cowes week in 1873, when he was twenty-four and Jennie five years younger. Jennie's father had had a lively career in law and newspaper publishing and at this time was proprietor and editor of the *New York Times*. She was startlingly beautiful, Randolph was good-looking, and they were both of an energetic, forceful disposition. The day after they met, each admitted to a friend that their fate had been decided: the next day, Randolph proposed and was accepted. Almost every obstacle available was flung in their path, but eventually they succeeded in getting married, and after rather less than the customary interval, for Winston was a premature baby, *The Times* announced, in December, 1874, "On the 30 November, at Blenheim Palace, the Lady Randolph Churchill, prematurely of a son".

Lord Randolph—and far the best about him has been written by his son—flashed briefly on the political scene when Winston was a small boy. He became Chancellor of the Exchequer; then after three times threatening to resign over a matter about which he felt deeply, he was allowed to do so. He vanished from politics at the age of thirty-seven, and was dead by the time Winston, who loved him deeply, reached the age of twenty-one.

But before that, Winston had been sent, not to Eton like other members of the family, but to the school on the Hill, where refreshing breezes, it was hoped, would help his "weak chest". There is no record that they did, but we do know that he disliked much of his four years there: they were "a sombre grey patch upon the chart of my journey". On the other hand, he apparently changed his mind—perhaps he wondered whether the fault had been his own—and was, to the year he died, an ardent supporter of Harrow, regularly attending its annual "Songs" in Speechroom, encouraging the school in every way he could.

At school, though, he managed to combine sensitivity with naughtiness and a firm distaste for learning. (A dancing teacher of a few years before, remarked, "I used to think he was the naughtiest small boy in the world.")

He despised, was bad at, Latin. (And if ever there was a case for reducing emphasis on this deadest of tongues, surely Winston Churchill has argued and proved it.) But he thrived on English. Harrow has always been a good school for English and I look back on my own days with gratitude to the masters who taught it me with imagination and gusto. When, as Churchill put it, his fellows who had been so good at Latin "had to come down again to common English, I did not feel myself at any disadvantage."

It was during a school holiday from Harrow that his father paid a visit to his room and admired the boy's collection of tin soldiers—no less than 1,500 of them, all of which you may see displayed today at Blenheim Palace. There was, sadly enough, little contact between pre-occupied father and sensitive son, and when Lord Randolph abruptly asked the boy if he would like to go into the army, Winston, almost without thinking, said, "yes".

In just this way are many of life's biggest choices made. "For years I thought my father, with his experience and his flair, had discerned in me the qualities of military genius. But I was told later that he had only come to the conclusion that I was not clever enough to go on to the Bar."

The boy who might have become an advocate became a soldier—but a soldier with a restless, searching mind. He had been taken to the House of Commons when Gladstone paid tribute to the father-and-son team of Joseph and Austen Chamberlain, and even with Sandhurst and an army career looming ahead, he had considered a career, some day, beside his father in public life. A commission in the army need not, after all, be a life sentence.

Two months before he got that commission, Lord Randolph died.

He was gazetted to the Fourth Hussars. But now suddenly the whole *raison d'être* of soldiering seemed to vanish. How could an officer, and a young one, expect to command men without an experience of fighting, of action?

In those closing years of the Victorian era, war seemed to have become extinct, at least for England.

He wasted no time. There was a little war in Cuba, nothing to do with England: he arranged to spend his 1895 leave there, as an observer. Like his father before him, who had done newspaper articles on a tour of South Africa, he arranged to do a series for the *Daily Graphic*, at £5 each. He was not a rich man—he became one later, entirely through his own efforts—and he needed the money not only to live on, but to pay his fare.

He arrived in Cuba, was attached to the Spanish commander

and came under fire for the first time. It was his twenty-first birthday. A horse was wounded, mortally, and as the young subaltern-journalist watched it die, he "began to take a more thoughtful view of our enterprise than I had hitherto done".

The enterprise, for Churchill, was a success. He had been blooded, had found his self-respect as a soldier, and his Editor liked his work. He returned to England and prepared to sail for India with his regiment.

And it was with his Hussars, in Bangalore, that the young subaltern became aware of the gaps in his education. Many of us have done just that—and nothing more. Winston went into top gear, ordered quantities of books from England, cursing himself for not having seen the light before he left, for not bringing a library with him. The books arrived, months later, and now, while brother-officers slept in the heat of the afternoon, he hacked a pathway through Macaulay's *History of England*, carried it on through Gibbon's *Decline and Fall* and thence through crate after crate of literature, in a non-stop intellectual do-it-yourself which was to continue throughout his life.

But still, for the Fourth Hussars, no fighting; and a soldier could not spend his career swotting in a tent. Churchill demanded to join a field force on the North-West Frontier and—military custom being rather different then—was allowed to join it, if a newspaper would commission him. There was no trouble about this; his fame had spread from Cuba, and Lieut. W. L. S. Churchill, special correspondent of both the Allahabad *Pioneer* and the London *Daily Telegraph*, presented himself to the H.Q. of the Malakand Field Force.

There is no space to describe it; you must read *The Malakand Field Force* yourself (the author, unperturbed by hand-to-hand combat, for "after all, I had won the Public Schools Fencing Medal——"), which is a thrilling account of action. It was also—and this did him no good at all—highly critical of government and of generals. It was a best-seller, in 1898—and it was described, angrily in Whitehall, as "A Subaltern's Guide to Generals".

So it was hardly surprising, when he tried next to join Lord Kitchener's force in the Sudan, that he got a sharp rebuff. But through a masterpiece of intrigue, in which his glamorous mother, the Adjutant-General, and the Prime Minister were all involved, he managed to join the force. It was stipulated that if he was unfortunate enough to get wounded or killed he would not become a charge on Army funds. To keep the record straight, he could have a commission—unpaid, of course—in the 21st Lancers.

He arrived outside Omdurman to take part in history's last classic cavalry charge. His description of it must be unique in military history, for authors are not usually privileged to take part.

Once again he came back to offer advice to his superiors. But now he decided that, as he was earning more as a journalist than as a soldier, and seeing just as much action, he would resign from the army. But he would not become a full-time journalist: he would become, like his father, a politician.

He resigned and was invited to stand for the Conservative Party—his father's party—in a by-election at Oldham. Oldham, though, was strongly Liberal and he was soundly beaten. Now, like his father, he proceeded to disagree with his party on an important tax bill. Like his father—but more so—he fell into disgrace.

Fame and fortune came at this convenient moment with the publication of his book, *The River War*. It was followed immediately by war in South Africa, to which he made haste, again as war correspondent and this time as a civilian.

His capture—by no less a person than General Botha—and his subsequent remarkable escape were front-page news, and when he returned, in 1900, it was to find a markedly different climate in which to air his politicial opinions. He was offered Oldham again and now, as a hero, he won it. (He had wisely taken the opportunity of praising the efforts of Mr. Dewsnap, of Oldham, who had helped him in his escape by hiding him at the bottom of a mine. The crowd shrieked with delight and he won by a majority of 230 votes—a good showing in a strongly Liberal constituency.)

He was now, in 1901, the year of Queen Victoria's death, a Member of Parliament. But without a sizeable private income a young M.P. could be even poorer than a young Hussar. He immediately took steps to right this and made a lightning five-month tour, lecturing on the South African War, over England and America. It netted him £10,000 which he gave to a friend to invest for him: he was able to enjoy himself on the proceeds for years.

At about this time the London *Daily Mail* was running a series on prominent young men, and it is interesting to see what they said about "Winston Churchill, the Youngest Man in Europe". He was, they felt, a boy in years and in temperament, but "in intention, in deliberate plan, in relating means to end, already a man. . . . He derives the hereditary aptitude for affairs, the grand style of entering upon them, which are not the less hereditary in British noble families because they skip nine generations out of ten." And from his American mother the young man had inherited "a keenness, a shrewdness, a half-cynical personal ambition, a natural aptitude for advertisement and, happily, a sense of humour". He had, the *Mail* concluded, "qualities which might make him, almost at will, a great popular leader, a great journalist, or the founder of a great advertising business".

Six months after being elected Member for Oldham he began to attack his party's defence policy. That party—his country's Government—listened aghast as he went on to castigate everything in both Conservative and Liberal policy which offended him. But, in fact, he was being drawn more and more towards the policies of the Liberal Party, which stood for free trade, social reform and financial retrenchment. At a public meeting on free trade he suddenly roared out, "Thank *God* we have a Liberal Party!" then announced that he was, on this matter, "an opponent of this present Government". This present Government could hardly believe their ears, and it was well that he followed up his remarks by resigning from the Conservative Party. It was 1904.

In a short time—as doubtless he had expected—he was offered the chance of standing as a Liberal, for a Manchester seat. He won it and returned, utterly ostracized by the Conservatives, to sit opposite them in the House of Commons.

After the General Election of 1906, in which the Liberal Party came to power, he was made Under-Secretary of State for the Colonies. He was thirty-one years old. Three years later he was President of the Board of Trade, with Cabinet rank.

And now—a nasty set-back. Under Parliamentary procedure, since changed, a new member of the Cabinet had to offer himself anew to his constituents. The Conservatives, still smarting, mobilized to defeat him, and he was exceedingly unlucky in that the Suffragettes chose to teach the Liberal Government a lesson in his constituency. In a close-fought contest they turned the tide against him by interrupting each and every one of his meetings with anything from screams to the clang of a muffin-man's bell.

He was to spend, years later, much time in the political wilderness, but the time was yet to come: he was immediately translated by his party to a safe Liberal seat in Dundee, won it despite renewed effort on the part of Suffragettes who had followed him north, and returned to the House of Commons. But it had been in more ways than one a smiling fortune which sent him north of the border; in Dundee he met Clementine Hozier, twenty-three years old, a girl of beauty and intelligence. Not only that, she had decided to earn a living by giving French lessons, thereby displaying a strength of character which fascinated the new President of the Board of Trade. And she was an ardent Liberal.

It was the wedding of the year on 12 September, 1908; "I married," Winston wrote, "and lived happily ever afterwards."

And now, for a while, he moved up steadily. By 1910 he was Home Secretary, still counselling caution in financial matters.

Twelve months later he had changed his tune. Germany, he decided, with the intuition born of knowledge which he displayed not only in 1911 but again twenty years later, was a menace to world peace. Money must be poured out in military preparedness, particularly on the Navy. And he began, with the same intensity he had shown in Bangalore, a course of study: this time into the military preparedness and strategic position of every nation in Europe.

Nineteen hundred and ten—First Lord of the Admiralty. And three years later—war.

He was a fine First Lord, but he was forced to resign in 1915 after the failure of the Gallipoli campaign. He was given a sinecure post, but this was not at all to his liking and he resigned it and joined the army again. Soon he was in France commanding a battalion of the Royal Scots Fusiliers. For a while it must have seemed to him as if none of those years in politics had happened. He was happy back in uniform—and his men, though occasionally baffled by their C.O., loved and respected him. You could never tell, they wrote home to their families, just what Colonel Churchill would do next. If the battalion had to go off and get deloused, he was quite likely to give you, first of all, a two-hour lecture on the rôle of the louse in history. And he wore such funny hats.

But Parliament wanted him back—after all, it was pointed out, he was still an M.P. If the Prime Minister refused to let him into the councils of government, then he must snipe at that Government, keep it on its toes.

He came back. Soon he was appointed Minister of Munitions. His first long exile from political power was over and he tore into the new job. Lloyd George maintained later that in five months he increased the number of tanks by 27 per cent, of machine guns by 41 per cent.

Came peace, and now Churchill became Minister of War with the problem of demobilization. There was fighting still going on in corners of the world and had he had his way there would have been little demob—the army would have gone out to Russia to defeat the new and "foul baboonery of Bolshevism". He managed to send about £20 million in supplies and weapons to the White Russians fighting that "baboonery", but the British Government refused to consider direct intervention.

He went on stating his views on Russian Communism, a voice crying in the wilderness. Small wonder that his relations, twenty years on, with Stalin were at times a bit strained.

But was he right? He had been right in 1911, he would be right again in the 1930s, and again in 1946, at Fulton, Missouri. Was he right in 1918? We can only guess.

A spell as Secretary of State for the Colonies, and then, in 1922, Lloyd George's Government fell. Once again he had to contest Dundee. This time he lost.

But for Churchill there was always something better to do. He took himself to the South of France and wrote *The World*

Crisis, which earned him a great deal of money. With this he bought himself a country house, Chartwell, in Kent.

In 1924, disenchanted with the Liberals, who had now aligned themselves with the Labour Party, he changed sides again. Now all was forgiven, and the Tories welcomed him back with open arms, let him contest the safe Conservative seat of Epping. He won it easily and soon, like his father, he was Conservative Chancellor of the Exchequer.

Not, though, the happiest of appointments. On the mistaken advice of the Bank of England he returned the pound to its pre-war gold standard and indirectly—by ruining the export coal industry and depressing miners' wages—precipitated the 1926 General Strike. This, with its scent of real emergency, appealed greatly to him, and he enjoyed himself insulting trade unions in the Government broadsheet *British Gazette.* Accused of angling the news, not being impartial, he replied cheerfully, "I cannot undertake to be impartial as between the Fire Brigade and the fire".

And soon he was out of a job once more—but this spell in the wilderness was to last a long time. Now it was a life of his illustrious ancestor, Marlborough, the First Duke, which occupied him—with a little painting, which he had recently taken up, and bricklaying at Chartwell, which relaxed him. Had Winston Churchill not spent those several spells out of office, English literature would be the poorer. At the same time he kept a wary eye on Germany, and he tried, again and again, with less success than in 1911, to draw his Government's attention to German preparation for war. "All those bands of sturdy Teutonic youths, marching through the streets and roads of Germany, with the light of desire in their eyes to suffer for the Fatherland, are not looking for status. They are looking for weapons——"

But the British Government, in the disastrous hands of MacDonald, Baldwin and then Chamberlain, was in no mood to listen.

And, as he had forecast, war came. He was brought back on the afternoon of the day Britain declared war against Germany and made, once again, First Lord of the Admiralty —the post he had held twenty-five years before at the start of an earlier war. "Winston is back!" was the delighted message from Sea Lords to Fleet.

By May of the following year the years of neglect and moral cowardice against which he had fought for so long, and in vain, were being paid for and in full. He became Prime Minister at last.

The rest is too recent history to need a gloss from me. By exhortation, inspiration, sweat and genius, he pulled Britain and the world through the greatest war in history.

And then—in what must be one of history's strangest backhanders—his people threw him out of office. The blow stabbed to the heart but, as he remarked wryly, "In a war you can only be killed once, but in politics many times."

He was far from out of sight. A few months later President Truman, in a scribbled note at the bottom of an official letter, asked him to speak, during his forthcoming American trip, to "a very fine old college in my state". It was at Fulton, in Missouri.

He did so. I was in New York at the time on a fleeting, end-of-war visit to relatives, and the howl of rage that went up from Manhattan Island, to say nothing of the Middle West itself, where the solecism was made, was frightening. He had described a Russian-built "Iron Curtain" as descending over the continent of Europe. "Last time I saw it all coming and cried aloud to my fellow countrymen and to the world, but no one paid any attention——"

But the Russians were our gallant allies. This was an outrageous slander, and the world, particularly the United States, was shocked.

A year later Churchill pointed out, a little sadly, that, had he made his Fulton speech then, in 1947, it would have been totally ignored: too trite, too obvious—*everybody* knew there was an Iron Curtain.

Once again he used each moment out of office; now he wrote six massive volumes of *The History of the Second World War*. It was reprinted, paper-backed, serialized, translated. In its original form it sold just under nine million copies.

He was awarded the 1953 Nobel Prize for Literature.

Another General Election—he was 76 now—and he was

again his country's Prime Minister. Two years later he at last accepted a Knighthood from his Queen. "Sir Winston" now, there were millions of people who would always remember him as "Mr. Churchill".

But at last age began to catch up. A glittering banquet at 10 Downing Street with Her Majesty as guest, and the next afternoon, though the world was not to know it for another day, he handed in his resignation as Prime Minister and leader of his party. It was 5 April, 1955.

He continued a further nine years as the Member for Woodford. On 27 July, 1964, he attended his last session of Parliament. Perhaps the best and truest of the many tributes he received that day came from a man, considerably his junior, who had recently handed over his own office as Prime Minister to another, younger man. "The life," said Harold Macmillan, "of the man whom we are honouring today is unique. The oldest among us can recall nothing to compare with it, and the younger ones among you, however long you live, will never see the like again."

Seven months more and that life was over. And while most of a saddened world mourned, history's greatest Englishman, rejected more than once by the people he had served and saved, was honoured as no commoner had been before.

Then, the old warrior who had served under five sovereigns, and fought death as valiantly as he had fought tyranny, was taken away and laid to rest in an English village churchyard.

Chapter 7

Albert Schweitzer

Great men have enemies. Every person in this book—as, in most cases, you will see—has his own devoted team of haters, shooters-down-in-flames. And probably Albert Schweitzer, theologian, organist, medical man and near-saint from Alsace, had more than most. People who had never seen an African outside the London School of Economics accused him of having no understanding of African needs, African feelings; people with neat minds deplored the simplicity of his treatments, his equipment, the general living conditions of his patients and staff at Lambarené.

Only the young die good. So they say—but old Albert Schweitzer, I suspect, was as near a saint as makes no difference.

In 1965 he achieved his ninetieth birthday. Ninety years on earth; rather more than half of that with his hospital at Lambarené. For it was in 1913 that the newly-married Schweitzers arrived in this inhospitable and forbidding part of Africa, determined to do what they could for its inhabitants.

They did—against appalling odds—a very great deal, and now the hospital, ten minutes by motorboat up the Ogowe River from Lambaréné, performs on average three major operations a day, delivers between three and four hundred babies a year.

Albert Schweitzer was born, on 14 January, 1875, in the village of Gunsbach in Alsace. There, where the shifting tides of empire had left a population speaking both French and German, his father was the Pastor. Albert went to the village school and it was there that he discovered, to his distress, that his family, the Pastor's family, was more fortunate than most others in Gunsbach. They had plenty to eat, their clothes were warm—but the village children were often cold, often hungry.

This was awful: he had had no idea it could be so. And as one could not possibly be different from one's fellows, the friends one loved, there was nothing for it but to discard one's overcoat, well-fitting boots, warm hat.

Try as they would to make an exasperating small boy see reason, Pastor Schweitzer and his wife were unable to make him wear—ever again—his expensive clothes. He wore wooden clogs like the rest of them, ill-shaped mittens, and a large, ridiculous, woollen cap. He was happy.

A trivial anecdote—but it gives a pointer to the man who would some day win a Nobel Prize for Peace. Schweitzer could not bear to think there was anyone, anywhere, deprived of something he, Albert Schweitzer, had.

One thing he had, was unable to share, was a talent for music. His father gave him a first lesson on the piano when he was five and was surprised at the boy's talent. Within a few months he was reading music faster than he read his schoolbooks, and when he asked to be allowed to learn on the church organ, the Pastor agreed. By the time he was nine he was playing it for services.

At the age of fifteen opportunity arose for him to study the organ regularly, at Mulhausen, where he had gone on to school. The church organist there was a particularly gifted man, Eugene Munch, who taught well, inspired his pupils with love for the instrument, so that by the time Albert was eighteen he had decided to make the organ his life, become a professional performer.

100

He went to Paris on a visit and was given the opportunity, by an aunt, of playing for the great composer and organist, Charles-Marie Widor.

"But this," said Widor after he had listened for a few minutes, "this is genius. A little work and you would be the finest organist in the world. I want to give you lessons."

That settled it: stunned by the praise, Schweitzer stammered out that he would be only too happy to have lessons, even though he went seldom to Paris. He would try to come more often.

Widor agreed and for many months Schweitzer paid regular visits to Paris and studied with him.

And then, to Widor's disappointment, he decided quite suddenly that he would be a Pastor, after all, like his father. He went to Strasbourg University to study theology.

As if music and his church were not enough for him, he decided to write a book, a controversial, rather shocking, book. He called it *The Quest of the Historical Jesus* and in it he considered carefully, analytically, the various attempts which had been made over the centuries to write the life of Christ. Among other heresies, the book denied Christ's divinity and thereby horrified many readers. "But a faith which refuses to face the facts," Schweitzer pointed out, "is not faith at all." He was a mature, thoughtful man now, sure of himself and his ideas.

Not content with setting the religious world on its ear, he proceeded, urged on by Widor, to write a two-volume life of Bach, one of the most penetrating studies ever made of the composer.

He left his church of St. Nicholas to become, at the age of twenty-eight, Principal of the Theological Faculty at Strasbourg. He was world-famous as author, musician, hard-hitting theologian, in demand all over Europe to give organ recitals, lecture on music, preach. And he had, in addition, a full-time, exciting job helping pupils iron out their beliefs and their doubts in the College.

Surely, could such a man ask for—or want—more?

He did. Schweitzer had read, shortly after going to Theological College, a report by the Paris Missionary Society on the needs of Africans in the Congo, and had been deeply shocked. It was, for those first few moments of shocked disbelief, like going back in time to the village of Gunsbach, a bewildered six-year-old, finding that his little playmates envied him three square meals a day and his warm, well-fitting clothes.

The idea of Africa continued to nag at the back of his mind: was it Christian to allow black people to starve and die of foul disease—without lifting a finger?

Of course, one could always collect money for them, send medicines, food, clothing. That would be practical and wise. And not too difficult.

But Albert Schweitzer, to the distress of his Faculty, resigned his august position and went down the road to study at the Medical School. He would there get the qualifications, learn the skills the people of the Congo so desperately needed of him.

Schweitzer was so long at Lambaréné that one tends to think of him as born to mission life. In fact the decision he now took was the equivalent of Maria Callas taking the veil and going out to nurse in Central Africa.

The medical course took six long years. And then, when he was at last able to place the title of Doctor before his name and know he was a practical healer, not just a man who wrote theses on theology, he found the Paris Missionary Society had long memories. Schweitzer, eh? Wasn't that the man who'd written that outrageous book about Our Lord? They refused to send him to Africa—or anywhere else. Better the natives should die of leprosy than be infected with the heresies of a renegade Lutheran.

Schweitzer was not author and preacher for nothing. He marshalled his arguments, explained precisely why he *was* going to Africa. They gave way.

He had married during his medical studies a girl called Helen Bresslau. She was ready to go with him wherever the Paris people chose to send him—and this turned out to be French Equatorial Africa, one of the most disease-ridden spots in the world. The Society had a mission station on the Ogowe River, a fly-blown settlement about a hundred miles in from the West Coast, and less than a degree south of the Equator. The new recruit's job would be to make a hospital there. To help him, they would order material for a proper building, send it out from France. That, however, would take months. In the meantime he would have to make do.

Helped by Helen, he made do. There was a filthy chicken house, the only place large enough, and he cleaned it out, set up shop inside, arranging bottles, jars and instruments on a table near the door. Then he waited.

Within a day, news had got round. At dawn there was a cluster of puzzled, trusting black faces outside his door, a sudden gleaming crop of dark flowers. He set to work immediately. Some of the Africans' ailments, despite the final months he had spent in France on tropical medicine, were a mystery, but they learned to trust him: the firm, gentle touch, the raised bushy eyebrow when shocked or laughing, the walrus moustache which made him, still in his thirties, into an ancient, pale-faced deity. Many of the cases needed surgery and Schweitzer embarked on this without previous experience, trusting in God and a knowledge of anatomy. He had primitive anaesthetics with him and these in particular fascinated both patient and onlooker. "First," one of them explained later, "the white man kills the sick man. Then he cures him. And then, he wakes him up." One wonders if this new technique was ever tried out by witch doctors in the dark-green world behind Lambaréné.

In his first nine months, Albert Schweitzer treated two thousand African patients, men, women, children. There was scarce time to read or write—but there were always a few minutes at the close of day for sitting down at the piano, the one he had been given, as a parting present, by the Paris Bach Society, and playing music. Then, with darkness falling, with Africans clustered outside, the jungle seemed to quiver and shake to the music of Bach.

This peaceful, hard-working life was shattered within eighteen months of his arrival by a world war. The Schweitzers were German citizens, and even though they were trusted members of a French mission they were now ordered into house arrest. Except under escort, they must stay inside their hut, right until the end of war. They could not enter their own new hospital.

The ridiculous edict was gradually relaxed and soon Schweitzer was back at work. The tide of suffering humanity, leprous, blind, crippled and deformed, seemed never to recede. He went on, helped by Helen, dealing with diseases of which he had read—but which he found hard to believe.

Just when it seemed he was effecting cures faster than new cases came in, another blow fell. There was a change of attitude in the colonial government: the Schweitzers were still enemy nationals, time could not alter that, and they could still not be trusted. A year before the end of the war, doctor and wife were bundled on to a ship, sent back to France for internment.

A sad disappointment: so much to be done, and a lifetime would not have been sufficient to do it in. But Schweitzer shrugged his shoulders, sat down to write another book. This time—a world away from the heat and smell and death of Lambarené—he wrote of the history of European ethics. He entitled the monster work *The Philosophy of Civilization*. His idea had begun to take shape in Africa, and now he worked far into each night on it. The book, in several volumes which succeeded each other in the bookshops and libraries of Europe, came out between 1923 and 1925. He became so involved with the work that, even though the war was long over, he felt himself unable to go back to Lambarené. He loved his hospital, he loved the African people—but his heart and mind were bursting—he had to put a little of his thoughts into words, before it was too late.

Lambarené won. In 1925, when he was fifty years old, he and his wife returned. But before they could actually set sail, there was something to be done. The hospital, in order to catch up with modern development, needed money and lots of it: Schweitzer would get it.

There can be few doctors of medicine able to finance their work by touring Europe and giving recitals of organ music. But for a man who was, as well as missionary, surgeon and controversial author, one of the world's greatest musicians, it was easy. He toured vigorously, made a lot of money, sailed for Lambarené.

Medicine had progressed, was progressing fast, pushed onward by the horror and the speed of war, and now Schweitzer set to work modernizing his settlement. Old shacks came down, new and permanent buildings replaced them, new instruments and drugs came into the surgery. But the routine stayed much the same. Healing, kindness—and a little firmness. Music and, on Sundays, prayer.

By now his fame had spread over the world and visitors and press began to trickle in. Most were full of praise for the work he was doing, but there were others who protested that this ageing, unkempt man had no business to be running a hospital in the twentieth century. There were half-naked Africans squatting outside the new bungalows, cooking filthy things in a most unhygienic way, feeding them through the doors to the patients. Indeed, some of those squatting in the dust and the flies were actually patients. And why were there goats and chickens everywhere? This was no way to run a hospital; it wouldn't be allowed in Manchester, or Cleveland, or Berlin.

But it *was* the way—the only way—to run one on the Ogowe River, a hundred miles from the sea, a stone's throw from the Equator. The Africans trusted Schweitzer, understood him and, most important of all, he understood them, knew that no patient, not a one, would remain long enough for a cure if incarcerated on the fourth floor of a modern block and fed from a trolley. And without goats and hens there would be little enough to eat: it was rather simpler, buying eggs and milk in Birmingham or Strasbourg.

And as for the unhygienic-looking goats—without those restless, searching jaws the jungle, bursting out all round them, would swallow the tiny settlement within a year.

Slowly, as he assembled a trained staff, he began to have time to write and think again. Volunteers began to come from all over the world, to be doctors, nurses, helpers. Young women from England and America, some trained, some not, doctors from East Europe, from Canada, helpers from every continent. Schweitzer's own thinking was turning now to the philosophies of the East. "Indian thought," he wrote, "presses forward to a stage of knowledge which is quite outside the purview of European thinking. It reaches the point of taking into account the fact that our ethical behaviour must not only concern our human neighbour, but all living things."

All living things. And to many critics, when this great thinker and musician deserted Europe, vanished into the stink and heat of Africa, this was what he would be dealing with. Savages —just Living Things. A man like Schweitzer had no right to bury himself among them; he had a duty to real people, at home.

The climate of opinion had changed—and now Schweitzer, a very old man who liked respect from the young, was accused of being a despot in his little kingdom; Africans even had to stand up when he came in. What sort of democracy was that?

But Albert Schweitzer went on doing, while others talked. One of the controversial points of that first book, all those years ago, was that Jesus had failed. Failed by not rolling up his sleeves and going to work.

We may not agree with the theory. But Schweitzer went right on through a long, very long, life, sleeves rolled up all the time, working.

In 1957 his wife, devoted helper and support for forty-five years, died, and her ashes were buried at Lambaréné. She had lived long enough to have her husband receive, in 1953, the Nobel Peace Prize, and to see every penny of the money it earned sunk into new quarters for lepers. Two years after that he received the Order of Merit, in England.

Albert Schweitzer, musician, mystic, surgeon, physician and author, hacked out a clearing that started with the little one by a slow-moving African river and came to embrace the whole world.

"I am just a simple doctor. All I wanted was to found a small hospital. But patients came and came—and then people gave me land, and people came to help, and now we are a big family—a family with doctors, nurses—and patients. People come here, ask what they can do. They do what they can and when they want to leave, they leave."

But for Albert Schweitzer there could be no leaving. His wife, before she died, asked how long he intended to stay in Africa.

Without a moment's hesitation he replied, "As long as I draw breath."

And he did. Albert Schweitzer died in 1965, working to the end.

Chapter 8

Helen Keller

"Early one morning the fever left me as mysteriously and unexpectedly as it had come and I fell into a quiet sleep. Then my parents knew I would live and they were very happy. They did not know for some time after my recovery that the cruel fever had taken my sight and hearing, taken all the light and music and gladness out of my little life.

"By and by the sad truth dawned upon them, and the thought that their little daughter would never more see the beautiful light or hear the voices she loved filled their hearts with anguish.

"But I was too young to realize what had happened. When I awoke and found that all was dark and still, I suppose I thought it was night, and I must have wondered why day was so long in coming. Gradually, however, I got used to the silence and darkness that surrounded me, and forgot that it had ever been day.

"I forgot everything that had been, except my mother's

tender love. Soon, even my childish voice was stilled, because I had ceased to hear any sound."

Not a bad essay for a twelve-year-old. Any twelve-year-old. But when this appeared in *The Youth's Companion,* in 1892, it was, as the Editor pointed out, "written wholly without help of any sort by a deaf and blind girl, twelve years old, and printed without change".

The story of Helen Keller is almost incredible—and were it not so exactly documented, one would be tempted, as indeed others have been, to disregard the whole thing, dismiss it as an ingenious fraud. But, of course, it is nothing of the sort: it is one of the most startling examples we have of courage and sheer determination against appalling odds—and it is vouched for, checked, cross-checked and proved by more, and more solid, authorities than any other case in history. Half history, written as it is in arrears, may be a fraud—bunk, Henry Ford called it, not without justification. But this bit is different. Helen Keller has been studied, fought over, reported, ever since she was eighteen months old. We can say of her case, with more certainty than we can of the Battle of Waterloo, that we know each detail and that it is genuine, unquestionable.

And at the same time almost totally incredible.

Old Captain Arthur Keller (there must have been a time when he was not old, but with his wispy, Chinese-style beard, his narrowed, pale blue eyes and his scowl, it is hard to believe it) was of Swiss descent. His family had arrived in the deep south, in Alabama, via a generation or so in Maryland. The Captain had fought gallantly in the Confederate Army, he ran a fine plantation in Tuscumbia, and he was Editor of the *North Alabamian.* He was a widower, and Kate, his second wife, was twenty years his junior.

From Arthur and Kate Keller was born, 27 June, 1880, a normal, blue-eyed, lively baby girl. The eyes in particular were remarkable, for they were the same pale blue as her father's, but they sparkled with the flame of life. By the time she was a few months old she was—so her mother told her, years later —"picking up needles and buttons which nobody could find." At six months she was clearly and correctly demanding "tea" and "water".

The future for little Helen Keller looked bright indeed; a lively, intelligent and very pretty girl with prosperous, popular parents living in a lovely old house surrounded by friends. What more could a girl, or her parents, want?

Then, with a crash, life folded.

But not all at once. At the beginning of 1882, when the weather, even in Alabama, was treacherous, cold and damp, the child went down with a fever: she was not quite nineteen months old. The fever mounted, day by day, and the doctor, diagnosing it as "a congestion", warned Captain and Mrs. Keller that their child was unlikely to live.

Then—deliverance. Or so it seemed. The temperature dropped. The parents gave thanks to Almighty God who had spared their child. Neighbours called with congratulations, good wishes; brought little coloured toys for the child, snatched from death, to look at, play with.

And as Mrs. Keller bathed her child one evening soon after the emergency was over, she noticed that the blue eyes, when she put hand and sponge over them, didn't close.

Mrs. Keller did it again. Then she screamed.

The child heard nothing, smiled happily, sightlessly, at the ceiling. Helen Keller was totally blind, totally deaf. And soon, as she wrote later, even her voice was stilled, "because I had ceased to hear any sound".

Only a miracle could help her. And none came.

To say no miracle came is to be strictly accurate—but Annie Sullivan, nearly blind herself, was the nearest thing. This chapter is as much about Annie as it is about Helen, and you may take your choice as to which is the greater heroine.

Helen was six before her mother decided to chance a visit to a Baltimore doctor. The man held out no hope of a cure, but he urged the Kellers to take their child to Alexander Graham Bell. Bell, whom we know as the inventor of the telephone, was far more than that: a great man, to whom deafness was a challenge. Both his mother and his wife were deaf, his wife since the age of four. The telephone was only invented as a by-product of a system to help Dr. Bell's deaf pupils.

Alexander Graham Bell was the first of the world's great

men to know and write of Helen Keller. We know of her childhood, her youth, from many sources, but none, surely, as unimpeachable as this. Bell examined the child, suggested Mrs. Keller get in touch with the Perkins Institute in Boston. Mrs. Keller had heard of the Perkins, she was delighted so wise a man should recommend it. Years earlier, Charles Dickens, in his *American Notes*, had described the place, the miraculous way Dr. Samuel Gridley Howe had taught a deaf and blind child, Laura Bridgman, to communicate with the world, become a part of it. Mrs. Keller remembered reading this. Now she sat down and wrote the present head of the Institute, Howe's son-in-law, Michael Anagnos.

Anagnos recommended the Institute send a teacher to Tuscumbia, to live with the Kellers and try to help the child. He suggested a recent graduate, twenty-one-year-old Annie Sullivan. No one could forecast success, but Annie might be able to teach the child something, even if the goal of speech, total understanding, were too remote to contemplate. The Kellers accepted, and Annie Sullivan, suddenly very frightened, rushed through the records of Howe's training of Laura Bridgman and set off. "I realized," she wrote later, "that I didn't know a single subject thoroughly. I could not possibly teach, and I had no urge to teach. I knew better than I had six years ago how abysmal my ignorance was."

But, urged by Anagnos, she went. The day she arrived in Tuscumbia, 3 March, 1887, was forever after, to Helen Keller, "my soul's birthday".

But at the time there was no indication at all that she felt this way. Annie put down her suitcase on the porch, asked, "Where is Helen?" and was shown, at the far end of it, a little girl, not yet seven, with uncombed brown hair, a dirty dress and black shoes done up with white string. Annie went up, tried to kiss her, and the child ran away.

A minute later Annie, locked in her room by the child, was leaving it, with some annoyance, through the window, down a ladder.

Just who *was* Annie?

She was the child of poor Irish immigrants. Her mother had died when she was eight, her father had deserted the three children. The other two had been taken to State Institutions, but Annie, born nearly blind, had been sent to the Massachusetts State Infirmary. Here she learned of the Perkins Institute. One day when the Infirmary Board of Governors was paying one of its visits, she tore up to a tall man in the corridor and flung her arms round his waist. She was too blind to know, as she cried, "Mr. Sanborn, oh please, Mr. Sanborn!" that this was not Mr. Sanborn, the Chairman of the Board, at all; but she was allowed to blurt out her request to be transferred to the Perkins Institute, and a few months later it was granted. When she was admitted, almost totally blind, in the autumn of 1880, her future pupil was three months old and in full possession of her faculties. By the time Annie left the Institute she could see fairly well and was top of her class: Helen Keller was blind, deaf and dumb.

Annie's first weeks with Helen were worse, far worse, than she had feared. The child was a savage to whom it seemed impossible to communicate any idea whatsoever. It screamed, wept, kicked and bit. But slowly they made progress, and after only a few weeks Annie could write to Anagnos: "The wild Helen has become gentle, learned to crochet, learned to spell words, but still has no idea that everything has a name."

Everything has a name. This discovery, so obvious to a normal child, is the key to all knowledge. On 5 April, only a month after her arrival, Annie took the child to the backyard pump, let the water run over her hand. As she did, she spelt, over and over again, in the finger alphabet into her palm, the word, "water".

Suddenly, it was clear: the symbols Annie had been tapping in her hand meant something, were no longer just part of a foolish game. The little tattoo of five letters, W A T E R, on one hand meant cold, wet stuff on the other.

Helen pointed to Annie and got the message back, in the palm of her hand, "Teacher".

The key of knowledge had turned. From this day on the child made almost incredible progress. She learnt to read Braille, and to write its little raised dots on thick paper with a Braille Writer, not only in English but in Latin, Greek, French and German. She learnt to converse fast and easily through finger language, the remarkable tactile alphabet brought to France from Spain by Trappist monks sworn to silence. She began to notice what was going on around her, to comment on it, be affected by it. By the time she was ten she had heard of a child in Norway, suffering from the same afflictions as herself, who had been taught to speak. She demanded to be given the opportunity. It was given her. After the eleventh lesson she said, quite suddenly and in a strange, half-human voice, "I am not dumb now."

She had been sent, because Annie was trained to teach the blind, not the deaf, to a special school in Boston. Later, the principal, Miss Fuller, was to write, "I began by familiarizing her with the position and condition of the various mouth parts, and with the trachea. This I did by passing her hand lightly over the lower part of my face and by putting her fingers into my mouth. I then placed my tongue in the position for the sound of 'i' and let her find the point as it lay perfectly still and soft in the bed of the jaw, just beyond the lower front teeth, and discover that the teeth were slightly parted. After she had done this, I placed one of her forefingers upon my teeth and the other upon my throat or trachea, at the lowest point where it may be felt, and repeated the sound 'i' several times. . . ."

From this point on, Teacher took over, forcing practice upon her, sitting for hours with Helen's hand on her throat, carrying on because the improvement went on, excitingly, day by day.

By the time Helen was twelve years old she was, thanks to her uncanny abilities and the notice taken of them by men like Bell and Mark Twain, a bit of a public figure. Very few children, even without her handicaps, would have been able to assimilate the knowledge which was now a part of her: the foreign languages, the history, the understanding of world affairs. And because, in her small way, she was famous, she had made enemies. Enemies she had never seen, would never see, and with whom she had had no contact. And she was twelve years old!

She had the idea of writing a story as a birthday present to Mr. Anagnos, with whom, through Annie's regular reports of their progress, she had corresponded. Anagnos was extremely proud of her, of Annie Sullivan, and of himself for throwing the two together, and he had already published a pamphlet: "Helen Keller, a Second Laura Bridgman".

The story Helen wrote, aged twelve, was entitled, *at her family's suggestion,* "The Frost King". Anagnos, who burst into print at the slightest provocation, had it published.

Then came the uproar. Someone decided it bore similarity to a story by Margaret Canby called "The Frost Fairies". Word spread about, particularly among people who had read neither, and within days a twelve-year-old girl had been branded by press and public as a fraud, a plagiarist. Not only, they said, had she copied her story, almost word for word, from another, published one, but she was—quite obviously— not blind at all.

This, to me, almost unbelievable tale of the jealousy, blind, unreasoning, cut-'em-down-to-size phobia, which afflicts so many people in the presence of greatness, is a pitiful comment on human nature. But it has wounded, nearly destroyed, many others—some of them in this book. And it terrified a little girl out of her wits.

I have seen both stories: the resemblance is slight indeed. Were it not for the title, which was supplied by Helen's family, one would not think twice about it. It is, apart from anything else, the simplest of fairy tales, which might have been thought up by anyone, or passed down, with countless others like it, through the generations. What probably happened was that Helen, years before, had had the Canby story read to her, and it had stayed at the back of her mind.

(Though one must, with Helen Keller, be careful to avoid a "years later" figure of speech: her progress in everything she did was so startling that it was not years, but months, or only weeks, between the time she decided to master a subject and the time she had done so.)

There was wild, intemperate, outburst in which Anagnos, amazingly, shared. The child, terrified, denied having heard a story like her composition—and quite probably she had no recollection of it—but this merciless hounding of a child, already a symbol, a badge of achievement to people like Michael Anagnos, probably had a permanent effect.

113

But in the meantime it was left to Mark Twain, great and kindly philosopher—another of the men who wrote and spoke and knew so much about Helen Keller—to put things into perspective. "As if there was much of anything in any human utterance, oral or written, except plagiarism!—substantially all ideas are secondhand, consciously or unconsciously drawn from a million sources — ignorant damn rubbish about plagiarism. I couldn't sleep for blaspheming."

She loved Mark Twain. He never tailored his conversation to her, spoke his mind all the time. Though occasionally, as they sat talking together, he would take her hand gently away from his lips and say, "Now, Helen, I must curse." Once someone, one of the numberless, sniping, "well-wishers", sniffed and said life for Helen must be "terribly dull". Twain nearly blew her out of the room with his explosive reply: "You're damned wrong there—blindness is an exciting business, I tell you. If you don't believe it, get up some dark night on the wrong side of your bed when the house is on fire, and try to find the door."

To Helen he said, "The world is full of unseeing eyes, vacant, staring, soul-less eyes."

She entered Radcliffe College at the age of twenty. Annie Sullivan, now forever "Teacher", went with her, to share digs in Boston, for there were no Braille books on most of the subjects she was to study. Teacher sat with her in class, spelled lessons into her hand and, incredibly enough, managed to keep pace with the lecturers. But if your hands are busy "listening", you cannot take notes, so Helen had to remember everything she "heard" and write it down later. When this was over, late in the evening, Teacher would read to her, holding the books hard up against her own weak eyes, till Helen, realizing the faithful Annie would go blind herself unless this stopped, refused to listen.

She had a natural talent for expression, and her writings, whether she punched them out on a Braille machine or a typewriter, or wrote them carefully, long-hand, against the corrugated board, like a washboard, she used for getting lines straight, they were all of them little gems of thought and feeling. In 1902, still at Radcliffe, she published her first book, *The Story of My Life*—and at twenty-two she had lived a pretty eventful one—which was soon published all over the world in some fifty languages, and became a minor classic. She was helped in editing the letters and articles which formed part of the book by a young man who was later to become a successful author and critic himself, John Albert Macy. Macy went on to marry Annie Sullivan, on the firm understanding that the two women never be separated. But by now Helen's journalistic offerings were being snapped up by papers all over the country, and soon, much as with "The Frost King", they were dismissed as being simply the mouthpiece for the "radical" views of John Macy. Helen had sincerely and passionately written of the problems of the poor, but all this was now seized upon, worried like a bone, and rejected as the second-hand ideas of a "socialist". Sadly, Helen gave up journalism. She had talent and a great deal to say; but she was a freak, and unless she wrote as a freak no man would trust himself to read it.

Eventually, Annie's marriage broke up, and the two women, on their own again, decided to earn a living giving lectures. They found audiences insatiable: people would flock in their hundreds from miles away, to appear at any hall where Helen and Teacher were booked to appear. Helen's speech, though fluent, was hard to follow, and at the lectures Annie would translate some of the more guttural noises, and demonstrate her methods of teaching.

Then a sad complication arose: Annie's eyesight, always weak, began to fail altogether. They were fortunate in enlisting the services of a Scots girl, Polly Thompson, who had come over to America to visit relatives and now agreed to stay with them, as their companion and their eyes. For Polly was the sort of girl who could book train and steamer tickets, argue with tradesmen over the size of a joint, the change from the milk money, look up telephone numbers—who would keep, literally, an eye on everything they did.

In 1918 a Hollywood company headed by Mary Pickford and Douglas Fairbanks suggested Helen make a film for them about a little blind girl, under the awesome title *Deliverance*. Reluctantly she agreed, and the film, using every dramatic cliché and ludicrous situation (Helen Keller flying to France to demand an end to war, Helen Keller as Joan of Arc) to replace the more commonplace-seeming details of her real life, was what *Variety* would call a box-office clinker, a flop. Frightened by impending poverty, Annie and Helen, foolishly perhaps, rushed into vaudeville, sandwiching their act between acrobats and performing bears. There were enraged howls of "Exhibition for profit", and soon Helen, who had been supporting two other women as well as herself by it, had to give the work up. It seemed that society, which had so applauded her efforts to lead a normal self-supporting life, was determined not to let her. But by now there was hardly any need to work for herself. Gifts poured in, to be poured out again on the needy, and the philanthropist Andrew Carnegie persuaded her to accept a small annual pension. ("But, please, Miss Keller, cut the admission price to your lectures—the world must hear them.") She went on with lectures and vaudeville, but to the outcry against "Exhibitionism" was now added the whispered suggestion, soon to become a shout, that she was a charlatan, a perfectly normal woman making a living out of the credulity of others. Some, accepting that she was blind, deaf and dumb, hinted that she was an idiot as well, Annie's puppet, Trilby to her Svengali.

By now, though, she knew what she had been sent into the world for: to help others as handicapped as herself. She joined the American Foundation for the Blind. She was already a pillar of strength and support to those who had been blinded during the war, and with her multiple affliction she was able to set an example of full and worthwhile living which others might envy and emulate.

By 1936 Annie Sullivan, having worked unceasingly, devotedly, for and with Helen for almost exactly fifty years, was completely blind herself. Before she died in October of that year, someone said, "Teacher, get well. Without you, Helen Keller would be nothing."

"Then," said Annie Sullivan, "—then I have failed."

But, of course, she had not. She died, and her death was a shock and a cruel blow to Helen—but Helen Keller was by now quite capable of looking after herself. And there was always Polly Thompson who, in quite a different, businesslike way, took over the rôle of companion, a woman who could balance a bank account, deal with the press, eject time-wasting callers.

During the Second World War, Helen Keller made almost continuous tours of war theatres, talking to blinded soldiers, sailors and airmen, infusing them with her courage and her gaiety. The pictures—which Helen, sadly, never saw—of the delight on the faces of the young men she is talking to, dancing with—and she could have been any of their grandmothers— are as moving as any I know. When the war was over, she went straight on, straight into another world trip with the faithful Polly Thompson, spreading her own special brand of courage.

By 1959 Polly, too, was gone, and Helen was alone in the world. Now, though, she no longer needed people : people needed her. Her work for the Foundation for the Blind in New York, answering with a message of hope and commonsense hundreds of letters a week, travelling over the country to inspire—and to inquire—was occupying all her considerable energy. For Helen Keller, in her 80th year, had the drive of a woman half her age. She had a message and she knew it, which no one else could impart. And she had to impart it— to as many people, wherever they were, as would listen.

In honour of her 80th birthday, on 27 June, 1960, the United States Senate passed a resolution that "in recognition of the vast contribution made by Miss Keller to the well-being of all humanity, the Senate hereby extends its greetings and best wishes to Miss Keller on the occasion of her 80th birthday".

A pretty thought, and gratefully, gracefully, accepted. But Helen Keller, the girl who had almost been given up for lost seventy-eight years before, had been saved by the devotion of a half-blind Irish pauper and gone on to become one of the finest minds of her generation, had a debt to repay. And perhaps not too much time to pay it. She smiled, said thank you, and went back to her work.

Chapter 9

Pope John

I am not a Catholic and for years I was glad of the fact. I was brought up as a child within the American Episcopal Church, opting out of that for a couple of years at boarding school in New England where we were allowed to choose our places of Sunday morning worship, in the town, to become a devout Unitarian. It was the heyday of the Italian-born Chicago gangster and, in Boston, near my school, that of the Irish Catholic political boss. Prim little Protestants all, we viewed them with distaste, and discussed in voices not yet broken the morality of a Capone or a Luciano, belting down the street to the nearest confessional after each revolting murder; the propriety of countless seedy small-time politicians doing the same after each major electoral swindle. On our screens at the Newsreel Theatre, and in our Sunday papers, we saw regularly huge funeral processions waddling and moaning down the streets of New York or Chicago, with thousands of dollars' of flowers and wreaths, paid for by crime and bearing

118

the scrawls of "Lucky", "Waxy", "Al", "Nino" and the rest, and
followed by hordes of wailing, bogus mourners.

I had other, rather more logical, reasons for being glad not
to be a Catholic, but this is no place for them. Perhaps, though,
my main grievance against that Faith was the galling fact that
its adherents regarded *my* religion—never mind whether I
was passing through an Episcopalian, Unitarian or even Church
of Scotland phase—as wrong. So wrong and so infectiously,
contagiously, wrong that no Catholic was allowed to enter my
church, on pain of something frightful. Or so I believed.

These were my views—or a cross-section of them—in adoles-
cence and I deliver them now because, although I have changed
them, they are still the views subscribed to by many millions
of reasonably intelligent people. Particularly in the United
States. John Kennedy scraped home by a few votes in 1960,
for which we must thank, if not God, at least some cosmic
guidance; yet we know now, from a University of Minnesota
survey, that his majority would have been vastly greater had
he not been a Catholic.

But when the two-hundred-and-sixty-third Pope since St.
Peter died, I wept. And it was not just for the gallant manner
of that death—it was for the loss of a man which the Church
—any church—has not seen in modern times.

He was elected to the supreme office at the age of seventy-
eight: an old has-been, men said, put there to keep the place
warm for a year or two and then die, by which time the jockey-
ing for position in the College of Cardinals would be over and
there would be no argument about his successor.

Instead of which, this short fat man with the elephant ears
and the round, kind face, had, in the four years and seven
months of his sacred office, begun to revolutionize his Church,
a thing men said could never be done, and with it, the world's
acceptance of it.

Angelo Giuseppe Roncalli, born in Sotto il Monte (Under
the Mountain), near Bergamo, on 25 November, 1881, was
one of a family of thirteen children, the progeny of a small
farmer, Giovanni Roncalli. They were poor, there was never
any meat on the family table, or wine, but "in the morning we
had porridge, at noon some vegetable soup and a little cheese

119

or sausage, and the same again in the evening. We were very poor, but we were happy, and we were never aware that we lacked anything. In fact, we lacked nothing at all."

And young Angelo, who wrote those words many years later, and who showed great intelligence at the village school, was pushed by his anxious parents and entered for a small seminary some two hours' walk from his home. He went there, but the four hours' walk each day, the long hours after that, working by candlelight to prepare for the next morning, weakened him and he became ill. He fought against the illness, went back to school, but he was fast dropping behind the others, and the harder work he had to do, to catch them up, brought on more illness. His parents decided the boy must give it all up—they had made a mistake, they were quite prepared to admit it, he just wasn't up to bookwork—and join the rest of the family in working the land. They gave young Angelo a letter to the head-master, explaining all this, and sent him off on what they imagined would be his last walk in that direction.

Halfway along the road, Angelo decided to open and read the letter. He did so and quietly tore it up, letting the hundreds of little pieces flutter away into the hills.

The immediate result of this disobedience is unknown—though the story is true and vouched for—but a little later Angelo was accepted by the Diocesan Seminary in Bergamo. In the fullness of time he was ordained—he was just short of his twenty-third birthday—in the Church of Santa Maria in Rome. He offered his first mass the next day, at St. Peter's, but made haste to his own Sotto il Monte to say the next one there.

And now: one of those rare strokes of luck. The Pope appointed to the See of Bergamo a remarkable priest, Giacomo Radini-Tedeschi, and consecrated him himself, in the Vatican. The new bishop was deeply involved in the fighting going on at the time between Church and State in Italy. Looking around him for a suitably energetic, understanding secretary, he chanced on the young Roncalli.

The future Pope (when he had visited Sotto il Monte to say that second mass the village doctor had said, "Young man, you will be Pope," and they had both laughed) was now secretary to one of the most controversial bishops in the Church. The fight against anti-Christ was joined forthwith, and in no time at all Roncalli and his superior were involved in every sort of industrial dispute, forcing themselves to understand the real problems of working men and help solve them, showing thereby that the Church had the terrestrial as well as spiritual interests of its flock at heart. To the distress of many employers, both Tedeschi and Roncalli were up to their necks in the big workers' strike at Ranica in 1909, ardently supporting the strikers. The young priest went on to organize a chain of Catholic Action Groups, at the same time teaching in the Bergamo Seminary and publishing parish news bulletins—all with the intention of correcting, as far as he could, the reactionary bias, as he felt it, of his Church and its senior officials. In his few leisure moments he began a study of St. Charles Borromeo, taking notes in the Milan library of documents concerning the saint which interested him—and many years later, in 1952, his five-volume history was published. Already he must have felt: if only one had the power, the authority and the influence over the whole of this Church, that my bishop has over Bergamo. Perhaps—for every private has that baton in his knapsack—he may have wondered whether it might come to pass.

The war found him, in 1915, a sergeant in the Medical Corps, as was the custom with priests—though in fact he had earned his rank the hard way a dozen years before when he had done a year's service as an ordinary soldier in Bergamo. He had done it for the experience it would give him, and been promoted to that rank. Now Sergeant Roncalli was sent back to Bergamo, to the military hospital, where he was immediately made chaplain with the rank of lieutenant—and with a huge black moustache which, in the photos of the time, sits imposingly on the familiar round features. He spent the rest of his war going from hospital to hospital, comforting, talking to and, above all, *listening* to the maimed and dying around him. One recurrent theme cropped up—why had they been sent into battle to kill and be killed by men exactly like themselves, fearing, worshipping and loving God—just wearing a different uniform?

In the evenings he would ponder this and work on his life of St. Borromeo.

At the end of 1920, Pope Benedict XV called him to Rome

to help reorganize Catholic missions. Here, with the travel it would entail, the opportunities for spreading the Faith in person, was a job to the liking of Roncalli. He took it with open arms, hugged it to his breast, went to work. The strange, almost childlike, enthusiasm he showed for the work, his wonderful good nature and, above all, the absolute naturalness of the man seem to have strengthened the faith of thousands he met, and to have won over thousands more who had not shared it. By 1925, such was his success with mission work, he had been elevated to the rank of Archbishop and appointed Apostolic Visitor to Bulgaria. There—and in Greece and Turkey where his work took him—he acquired an almost unique understanding of the Eastern Church. Slowly he began to realize the futility of a separation from such a body: a bridge could be, *must be,* built.

But when?

It was December of 1944 and he was in Istanbul, looking out from a window over the Bosphorus, when a servant came in with a telegram from the Vatican. All his life Roncalli had enjoyed doing things for himself, finding out, and now, with his secretary out of the room, he gleefully seized the code book and began to decipher.

It began "284145 stop 416564——" and he knitted his brows as the answer emerged. Then he decoded again—at which point his secretary came in and checked what he had done.

Yes—there was no doubt about it. The message read, "Return immediately. Transferred Nuncio Paris. Tardini."

His first, alarmed, reaction was to ask not to be sent, that the job was too big for him to handle. Good soldier that he was, he prepared to leave his palace in Istanbul, but he took the precaution of sending a mildly querulous message back to the Vatican. By return came his answer: Angelo Roncalli was the best man to handle a difficult task; he was the personal choice of Pope Pius XII, and he would go.

It was, indeed, an uphill task that the sixty-three-year-old Roncalli was facing. The Provisional Government of France, headed by General de Gaulle (not an easy man to deal with, as half the world knows now), had demanded that his predecessor be withdrawn: the man had been accredited to the despised Petain government and must, therefore, de Gaulle maintained, have collaborated with the Germans. The Pope himself was not above suspicion.

It was into this atmosphere that Roncalli came, to be greeted not only with the suspicion verging on hostility which he had expected, but by a terse demand that he remove bishops—droves of them—who were accused of helping the enemy.

Roncalli, presented with the great dossier by the General himself, looked carefully at it, flipped over the pages. Then he looked up—a long way—to the towering figure over him. He stared up into the damp, indignant eyes and then, with a slight smile, placed a pudgy finger on the document.

"May I, then, have the evidence? This—this is a book of newspaper cuttings."

He was right, it was. Not without much muttering and complaint, evidence was assembled. Or rather, orders were given for its assembly; the process took no less than ten months. In the end de Gaulle was forced to agree that he had been wrong over thirty bishops. Out of the thirty-three he had demanded be sacked, only three were removed from their posts.

Many men have argued with Monsieur le General. None with as great success. From the moment he arrived in Paris, Angelo Roncalli showed that beneath the smiling peasant exterior was a will of iron—and a sense of absolute fairness.

The war ended, Roncalli stayed on in France and soon he was fighting, as he had been, all those years before, in Italy, fighting the battle of Church against State; fighting, but with absolute honesty and sincerity, the age-old battle over money for Catholic schools. And yet he was travelling: there was no point in being a Papal Nuncio unless one knew the views not only of the Vatican but of the little men and women at the receiving end, and he travelled all over France. Often he was on foot, because he met more people this way, and with his fluent French and his understanding of men he made friends everywhere he went.

In 1953 he was created a cardinal and the red biretta was, according to custom, placed on his head by the Head of State, President Auriol. But the new Cardinal Roncalli was grieved by his elevation, for it would take him, he thought, out of the sphere of human relationships. When the Archbishop of Paris, puzzled at Roncalli's gloom, mentioned it, the new Cardinal agreed that he had been honoured, but "I should have been content just to be an ordinary pastor. Somewhere near Bergamo."

But the next news from the Vatican cheered him immensely. He was to go to Venice as Patriarch, he would be a shepherd of Christians, after all. He made his farewells in Paris—there was almost universal sorrow at his departure—and headed for Venice.

Once there, he became the bustling "ordinary pastor" he had wanted to be, red hat and all. A breath of fresh air whistled through the Venice palace and soon that building was, for the first time, open at all hours of day and night for any member of his flock to come and visit him. He worked hard to bring the Church to his people, make it, to them, the vital twentieth-century force he knew it was. Anything which brought the Church to the man in the street was all right by Roncalli, and it was he who hit upon the magnificent idea of playing the religious works of Stravinsky in the great Basilica of St. Mark's, where in fact they had their first performance.

Pius XII, the aristocratic Cardinal Pacelli, died on 9 October, 1958. He had held the office of Pope for nearly twenty years and during that time he had been feeling his way slowly towards reforms in his Church: one was the introduction of evening mass. He had already begun to widen contacts between the Vatican and the world outside, giving audiences not only to kings and queens and presidents, but to actors, film stars, artists and just ordinary people. Yet, when he was not at one of his many audiences (never had a holder of the supreme office granted so many) he was an aloof, retiring figure, unwilling to share his problems and his thoughts with others. He had held back from creating new Cardinals and as a result, when he died, the College was small. Only fifty-one Cardinals were there in the Sistine Chapel in October, 1958, to vote for his successor. And that successor must come from among their number.

Voting was close. For the first eleven ballots it was quite indecisive. Then, on the twelfth, Roncalli was elected.

124

He received the fact of his elevation with humility and said that, if this were the case, he would like to be known as Giovanni, or John. Not only was that the name of his father, it was the name of the patron saint of his home village, Sotto il Monte. On 4 November, in the glare of television floodlights, he was crowned Pope, in St. Peter's in Rome.

To the world outside—and perhaps to the Cardinals within —the election in the Sistine Chapel had been to find an aged caretaker for the office, to give the Church time to think out its policies and its future. And no doubt the thought occurred to the new Pope John XXIII that he had been chosen for just that purpose. When someone congratulated him and offered good wishes for the future, he replied, "One who is Pope at seventy-eight does not have a great future."

How wrong he was! Almost immediately there was a wind of change gusting through the Holy City. Pius had long since cancelled the regular audiences of fixed days of the week— the "Tabella"—for the Cardinals and certain prelates; the new Pope reinstated them, then went on to create twenty-three new Cardinals, many of them foreign, raising membership of the Sacred College to a higher figure than it had been since the 16th century. New blood, he had decided, must come in, fast, and with it new ideas. In 1960 he created the first African negro Cardinal.

And, peripatetic as ever, John began visiting outside his Holy City, partly because he loved meeting people—all sorts of people—partly to point out that he was not only Pope but Bishop of Rome. One of his first visits, which deeply shocked some and delighted many more, was to the great Roman prison, the Regina Coeli, where he made a point of talking to all, and longest of all to those locked up for the most serious crimes. He told them—and the appalled press hastily altered the statement—that an uncle of his had once been imprisoned for "lawlessness".

No Pope in history had begun—or, no doubt, even considered —getting so close to his people, but this to Angelo Roncalli was only the beginning. And yet there was so little time. The world was one, he had always known it in his heart and his travels had proved it, and in particular *the Church was one.*

It was vital, urgent, in the few years which might be granted him, to build a bridge over which the first faltering, timid, steps of unity might be trod. He must meet the other Churches, understand them, draw them closer together in the one universal Church. He must find a common basis for all Christians, and he moved fast to do so: the Russian Orthodox Church was invited to send representatives to call on him; the Archbishop of Canterbury accepted an invitation and became the first of his office to come to the Vatican since England's Henry VIII had repudiated all Popes four hundred years before.

And he announced plans for a second Vatican Council.

The first one—and both have been called variously Vatican, Universal, and Ecumenical Councils—had been in 1870. It had resulted in much legislation, including the dogma of Papal infallibility. It had been a huge undertaking, getting bishops and clergy from all over the world, and the projected second one was daunting to many in the Holy City. "I doubt," said one of John's advisers, "I doubt that we will have time to organize such a council for 1963——"

"I see," said the Pope. "But I mean the Council to meet in 1962." Then, with a wide, kind smile—this, surely, disposed of the problem—he turned to other business.

And so the huge "Vatican II" was assembled, with 2,500 bishops and other lesser men coming from all over the world. The purpose, John declared, would be the renewal of the Church—*now*—and ultimately, building on foundations which would be laid—*now*—the unity of all Christians. To this end the vast Council, inspired by the words of their Pope, turned (partially, at least) away from the conservatism and reaction which characterized so much of Church government, and started thinking, thinking hard, about change. Everything which made it difficult for men to understand was to be examined, thought out again. This was not a religious feast, John pointed out. Far from it; it was a parliament, and there would be, must be, hard debate.

One of the reforms instituted was the use of vernacular tongues instead of Latin for certain parts of the Mass. The fact that a large proportion of Catholic worshippers outside

Italy had forgotten, or possibly never known, the exact meaning of their ceremony had been ignored for years. Now, with John pushing hard, this was changed.

This Vatican Council, the first for 92 years, must be regarded as Pope John's monument. The idea had come to him, he said, during the annual week of prayer for Christian Unity, and he decided then and there that the Council must have both a long-term policy and a short-term one. The short-term would be to reform the Catholic Church and make it, quite simply and frankly, more attractive to those outside. (John knew only too well how many men looked on it with fear, distrust, and worse.) The long-term policy, which must follow, would be the unity of the Christian Church: not just a metaphorical unity; a real, factual one. "First—there must be a Council to reform the Church and to revive the spirit of the Gospel. *Then* shall we be able to understand our separated brethren, and they will understand us."

So John's Council was a different one to earlier Councils. The Council of Trent in the sixteenth century was an attempt to consolidate, pull the Church together after the body-blow of the Protestant Reformation. The first Vatican Council in 1870 had been an attempt to shore up the authority, the dignity, of the Church against the attacks of liberalism. But the second Vatican Council, John's Council, was outward-looking: looking at the Church's position in the world, her relations with other Christians *and with non-Christian religions,* at religious liberty and at the Church's mission to the world. It was a monster undertaking, with these two and a half thousand bishops giving up nearly three months of each year for four years in succession. As perhaps he anticipated, John did not live to see the end of his four-year Council, but before he died the ground-work had been laid for many reforms. The Catholic attitude to birth control came under close scrutiny, as well as the doctrine of the Pope's infallibility, the form in which the Holy Sacrament would be taken, and a host of other matters.

But the Vatican Council is not John's only memorial. He produced eight important Encyclicals—Pope's letters. In the two most far-reaching, *Mater et Magistra* of 1961 and *Pacem in Terris* of 1963, he set out the guiding principles of his own life and his instructions to others. In the first he brought up to date the traditions of Catholic social teaching, defending both man's right to private property and at the same time the legitimacy of "socialization" for the common good. The second was the first encyclical ever to be addressed not just to the bishops and the faithful but "to all men of good will". This one had somewhat of a revolutionary effect throughout the world, for in it John told men that "error is not to be confused with the errors of persons" and at the same time pointed out that a false creed, by implication Marxism, should not be identified with or confused with a genuine historical movement like Communism, in which there might well be some good. He appealed for co-operation between all nations and specifically mentioned the Communist countries.

There was angry criticism in the more conservative Italian newspapers that John, by this "ill-considered encyclical", had given moral support to the Communist movement, particularly in Italy, and increased the number of its adherents. The considerable increase in Communist votes in the 1963 Italian Election was quoted as bearing this out—but to the world at large, particularly to the non-Catholic world, it brought an encouraging, cheering, realization that a bridge could be, and was actually being built, between the Catholic Church and the world.

He gave an audience to the daughter of Nikita Krushchev and her husband Adzhubei, editor of the powerful *Izvestia*, and made a start in breaking down the colossal, man-built barrier between the world's second most powerful state and its most powerful religion. "You say," he said to them, "that you are atheists. But surely you will receive the blessing of an old man for your children?" Humbly and gratefully, they did.

Among conservative elements in his Church he was still viewed with some dismay, but slowly, very slowly, he won them towards him. However much they may have quarrelled with his ideas, few men were able to feel anything but love for John as a person. His predecessor, Pius XII, had also been a kind man, though of a different temperament, and he had allowed the almost Byzantine rigidity of much Vatican protocol to submerge him, but John XXIII was a man of the people who liked people above all—better than ideas, even, and certainly better than dignity.

But he knew the sands were running out, and when his doctor warned him that he might have a tumour in the abdomen, he said, after a short pause to consider the implications, "Very well, then; God's will be done. But don't worry about me, doctor. My bags are packed and I'm ready to go."

Gradually the symptoms developed, became unmistakable, irrefutable. The pain worsened. The first general intimation that all was not well came in November of 1962, almost exactly four years after his enthronement. He was forced to cancel a general audience because of a "gastric disorder".

John recovered slowly and only partially from that disorder. By now he knew his illness was incurable, but as soon as he was on his feet he was out again, indomitable if pale, visiting, talking and, as ever, listening. Occasionally his knowledge of what lay in store would slip out. He told a group of visitors in April, less than two months before his death, "That which happens to all men may happen, soon, to the Pope who speaks to you now."

On 21 May, the Vatican announced that the Pope had cancelled all public appearances for nine days. He would pray and rest, before the Feast of Pentecost. In fact, the brave man was forced with continual internal bleeding to spend most of that time in bed, though he rose from it time and time again to pray with the crowds below in St. Peter's Square.

And now began that almost incredibly heroic battle against death itself. The world realized—with a shock, for John had impressed himself on it; was doing so much, had so much unfinished business on hand—realized that John's short, packed reign was drawing to its close. Doctors moved into the Vatican to try and ease his pain. The agony mounted and yet he refused even to admit it. His old friend and physician, Dr. Gasbarrini, of Bologna, who had been with him, announced that the end was near but that his patient had "the constitution of iron to go with his will of iron".

Days after the time when, by all medical prognosis, he should have been dead, he got out of bed, ash-white and in terrible pain, but smiling, to hold a conference on Vatican business. "He has," said a Vatican official, "the heart of a horse." But the periods of coma were increasing, and when his old sister and three brothers from Sotto il Monte were led to the bedside, he failed at first to recognize them.

Then, in a sudden flash of memory, he did so. He sat up in bed and embraced them all.

In his moments of lucidity he would bless those about him and pray for the success of the Vatican Council, and for peace, and each time he sank into unconsciousness all around were certain the end had come. A doctor leant over to see, and the Pope opened his eyes, smiled, and said, "With death, a new life starts". A little later, having made another impossible fight back from the edge of the grave, he remarked, "I have been able to follow my death step by step. Now I am going sweetly towards the end."

And yet the end was still some days off. As with most famous men, from Charles II to Winston Churchill, who take "an unconscionable time a-dying", there are those around who grow restive: one French bishop, asked for his views on a successor after the Pope should be dead, said tartly, "As far as we are concerned, he has been dead for a month".

When one dies it is better to die by the hand of an assassin, like Kennedy, or the wheels of a cart, like Pierre Curie, than to take one's time.

And yet there were millions all over the world who followed the struggle of this great man with respect, admiration and a profound sorrow. Thousands of them were in the square below his room; others, huddled against the great stone pillars of the colonnade, listened to transistor radio sets for bulletins of his passing, watching, as they did, the huge bronze doors of the Apostolic Palace.

Slowly, on the morning of 3 June, they swung shut. The Pope was dead.

Popes have always tended to be a bit of a surprise: the office reveals the man, and often a most unexpected one. In the Renaissance, Cardinal Piccolomini busily fathered illegitimate children, no doubt as a practical demonstration against that celibacy among clergy he fought so angrily against. He then became Pope Pius II, famed for his personal rectitude. Cardinal

Pacelli, John's immediate predecessor, had been a famous and a worldly diplomat—but his reign as Pius XII was hardly notable for this. And his successor, Cardinal Roncalli, Pope John—likeable old fellow, just a peasant, really—would leave the Church to slumber just a few more years and let the real makers of policy consider their next move.

How wrong they were! The peasant from the north made a bigger, far bigger impression, both as man and as Pope, than had any other modern Pope. For, through the trappings, the gold and scarlet and purple of the Supreme Office, one could always discern the man—and this, as much as the work John did for that office, gave the Catholic Church, in the eyes of those outside it, as well as those within, a completely new perspective. In the words of the ad men, a New Image—but this cant phrase is less than accurate, for the fostered image of a toothpaste or a cigarette is the reverse of the absolutely solid, factual, tangible shape the little round Pope projected of himself and his Church.

But he was conscious of the value of twentieth-century "media": of things like television, radio, the press. And startling, mind-jolting innovations like a sudden Papal descent at Lourdes by jet-plane. Only television, though he wanted it, and demanded that it help him spread the word of his Church, worried him. He watched himself, before his first television appearance, on a monitor screen, the round, good-natured face occupying two-thirds and the projecting ears the rest, and was clearly heard to say, "Oh Lord—this man will be a television disaster". He was far from it, much the reverse, but he had his own private doubt to the end of his life.

He made mistakes, but they were utterly trivial set against the good he did. The one, apocryphal, perhaps, which has always appealed to me was his painstaking effort to master a few words of English, of a chatty, hail-fellow-well-met sort, to greet the visiting General Eisenhower. John spoke many languages, but English was not one.

Unfortunately—he was, perhaps, a President too early—he had chosen a priest to instruct him whose rich Irish brogue was almost incomprehensible outside Erin. Delighted to be of service, the man taught his Pope a series of bright observations which John carefully repeated after him and noted down in a little book.

But when Dwight Eisenhower was shown in and the smiling Pope began, the President frowned. Not a word of this extraordinary Italo-Galway could he comprehend and, try as he would to look pleased and understanding, he was forced to shake his head. The Pope's face fell. Then, with a shrug and a broad smile, he beckoned the interpreter and conversation began.

But the message Pope John gave to the world, which stays behind him, needed no interpreter.

Chapter 10

Franklin Delano Roosevelt

Franklin Delano Roosevelt, as I have said elsewhere, is an intensely real hero to me, an intensely personal one, and in order not to inflict too personal, too family, a view of heroism on the reader, his entry in this book will be as short as I can make it. But I would not be honest to myself, or to the memory of someone for whom I had the greatest admiration as well as love, if I left him out.

His mother and my grandmother were sisters. As the family has always been close-knit, this fact in itself would have ensured that I follow his career, whether he had been President of the United States or the man who delivered the milk. It also would have meant that he and I would have corresponded, as grown man and growing boy, over the years, for ours is a letter-writing family. He had children of his own, five of them and all older than me, but his interest in other cousins, old and young, was real and ceaseless. We corresponded regularly throughout the blackest days of the war—and it is only now that I realize just how black those days were for him, and how remarkable that he should have bothered to do so.

For my mother, he felt a particularly deep affection. He was fourteen when his father, aged sixty-eight, decided he was too old to take on the responsibility of being godfather to a young sister-in-law's new daughter. The old man was discussing it with his wife Sara when there came a shout from the next room: "Never mind—*I'll* do it——"

So my mother became, more or less by accident, Franklin's god-daughter. Years later, when she married my father, Franklin gave her away. A few days before, he had, as the strapping, athletic Assistant Secretary of the United States Navy, been a noisy, delightful and hilarious guest at my—British—naval father's bachelor party on H.M.S. *Warrior* in the Potomac River.

The rôle of godfather—perhaps because it had been entered early in life and somewhat unconventionally—always appealed to him. The various books he gave me in childhood, the signed photo I begged from him, all come from an "Affectionate Great-Godfather" Franklin, who might or might not enclose the relationship in inverted commas, as fancy took him.

So it was as a kindly and brave older relative that I knew him. He became Governor of New York State when I was seven and I was not impressed: the office, in my eyes, added not an inch to the stature of the man.

It was 4 March, 1933, before I began to consider that stature.

I had been invited, with my parents and young brother, to attend his first Inauguration as President, in Washington. Suddenly, things were in different perspective. I lay in bed for hours that night, in our hotel room, thinking over the parade, the oath of office I had heard, the thousands of people. As I thought these thoughts, a family party was taking place in the White House, and my parents, in a tiny way, were making history as the only British subjects to have dined in the building on an Inauguration Night. I was twelve, and aware now of what was going on in the United States, aware that today, however glamorous, glittering and noisy it might be in Washington, was a real day of crisis for the country as a whole. Bankruptcy—and that was a word, in 1933, one understood only too well—faced the country. I knew men and women all over the U.S. had been flocking—fighting—their way into banks to withdraw their savings, hide them away, anywhere, under the mattress, in the jam-jar, rather than have them vanish. The Governors of most States had already closed banks to prevent their doing so.

It was—apart from the Civil War—the most severe crisis ever to afflict the United States. People not living there at the time can have little idea how serious, how hopeless, it seemed.

A restrained presentation of how things stood comes from Franklin Roosevelt himself. "Those who lived through the months immediately preceding March, 1933, do not require a description of the desperate conditions into which the American economy had fallen since the crash of 1929. By Inauguration Day, the banks of the United States were all closed, financial transactions had ceased, business and industry had sunk to their lowest levels. The widespread unemployment which accompanied the collapse had created a genuine feeling of utter helplessness. I sought principally to banish, as far as possible, the fear of the present and the future which held the American people and the American spirit in its grasp."

In this he succeeded where probably any other man would have failed. For this was the second monstrous crisis in Franklin Roosevelt's life, and he was able to defeat it as he had defeated the earlier one and would defeat the third when it came. The first had been his sudden, crippling, and permanent paralysis from the waist down, at the age of thirty-nine. Of the three, I suspect this is the only one he had doubts—very secret doubts —of overcoming. The second—the bankruptcy of his country— was dealt with in a whirlwind "Hundred Days" (or so the Press saw it) which no man had believed possible. The third, his country's entry into the Second World War and the defeat of both Germany and Japan, was the third and final of his life.

He was of part-Dutch descent. With the Dutch were traces of German, French, Swedish—and far more than a trace of English. His ancestor, Claes, from Roosenvelt, in Zeeland, arrived in the New World, in New Amsterdam, in 1644, at much the same time that his maternal and my ancestor, Philippe de la Noye, later Delano, arrived in Massachusetts from Leyden. A few years after this, New Amsterdam was captured by the English, became New York.

Claes van Roosenvelt had two grandsons, John and James (or, if you prefer, Johannes and Jacobus), and from these two stout fellows were descended one line, remaining stolidly Dutch and culminating in Theodore Roosevelt, and another, more gregarious, perhaps, which produced his fifth cousin, Franklin.

Franklin Delano Roosevelt was born on 30 January, 1882, at his parents' home in Hyde Park, above the Hudson River in New York State. His father's first wife had died, he had married Sara Delano, much younger, and the boy was strongly attached to them both. The attachment survived his being sent, much against his will, to that most aristocratic of American schools, Groton, with a heart set on joining the navy. It was during early days at Groton that his mother startled both locals and school authority by overcoming, in a typically dramatic gesture, the school's quarantine against scarlet fever. She arrived at Groton, straight from a transatlantic dash by steamer from the Continent where the rest of the family had been holidaying, to find her son recovered—and still locked up. Without ado she produced from somewhere a long ladder, placed it against the wall of the school infirmary. For the next fortnight, at certain times of the day, the young and beautiful Sara Roosevelt could be seen balancing gracefully, precariously, at the top of her ladder, talking with a young man inside in his pyjamas.

From Groton to Harvard—showing no interest at all in politics, until September, 1901, when fate pushed an older cousin into the White House. Theodore had been Vice-President when McKinley was shot and now the fact of having him suddenly the country's Chief Executive aroused an interest in the country's affairs which had been dormant. The two cousins were of opposing parties. Once, all Roosevelts had been Democrats, but many had become Republican with the Civil War, because the south—the enemy, Confederate South—was Democrat to a man. Franklin's branch of the family had clung to their first allegiance. Now—but without any real idea of becoming involved himself, he began to take an interest in the running of his country.

THE WHITE HOUSE
WASHINGTON

August 15, 1940.

Private

Dear Ian:

It was grand to get yours of July
twenty-eighth as quickly as this and to know
that all goes well with you and that you are
in the south of England with, I take it,
several million others who are doing a grand
job.

Slowly, but surely, we are waking up
in this country in spite of the definite campaign
for appeasement -- the same thing that happened
in England a year ago.

I hope that all goes well in this
definite attack which is being made on Great
Britain as I write.

The good old Alcantara seems to have
come through all right but I wish we could hear
from your old man. What an unlucky shot it seems
to have been into his boiler room! I take it,
however, that his repairs have been made good
and that he is off again on the South American
patrol.

Much love to you all. Tell your
mummy that we miss you all very much.

Affectionately yours,

Ian Fellowes-Gordon, Esq.   *Franklin D Roosevelt*

In the darkest hours of the war, Franklin D. Roosevelt found time to
write letters of encouragement to a young relative in Britain. This one to
the author was written at about the same time as Roosevelt's "Fireside
Chat" to the American people (facing page 65).

A year after leaving Harvard and going on to the Columbia Law School, he married his distant cousin—on Theodore's side of the family—the shy, gawky, Eleanor, and the President agreed to come to New York and give her away. He was coming to that city on St. Patrick's Day to inspect the annual parade and he announced that he would now make the visit serve both ends. Apart from the drowning of the parson's words by frenzied singing, in the street outside, of "The Wearing of the Green", the ceremony was satisfactorily concluded. Though, as Franklin's mother wrote later, there was an awkward moment for the newlyweds, when "they were left entirely alone while the crowd hovered around Mr. Roosevelt, shaking him by the hand".

Franklin was still a student and it was two years before he joined a firm of New York lawyers. But soon after that the Democratic Party in New York State found themselves in difficulty and approached him. They needed a candidate for the State Senate: no one would run. Hardly surprising, perhaps, as no Democrat had won the seat since the year Franklin was born. But it was important for the honour of the party that someone—someone sufficiently young and resilient not to mind being overwhelmingly defeated—contest the seat.

He thought about it for twenty-four hours. Then—as a campaign, a wordy, no-holds-barred battle, like this one, might be valuable experience for a young lawyer—he agreed.

Determined not to let the Party down, he put all his energies into the battle—much as he did with every battle he fought—and to his and the Party's amazement he was elected, on 8 November, 1910, to the State Senate in Albany.

No time to examine in any detail his life and work in the State Senate, except to note that he discovered, during these years, that politics was in his blood. By the Presidential election of 1912, so passionately did he feel about it and about his Democratic Party, that he attended the Democratic Convention in Baltimore to support Woodrow Wilson. Here he had one of his first experiences of the rough-and-tumble of American politics, found he could be as tough as the next man. He learnt that the supporters of Wilson's chief opponent, "Champ" Clark, were proposing to storm the Convention with a hundred men wearing Clark buttons, shouting "We Want Clark". They had bribed the doormen to admit anyone wearing a Clark badge.

Roosevelt calmly mustered two hundred opponents of Clark, provided them with Clark buttons and got them past the doormen. Then, as soon as the shouts of "We Want Clark" began, they were drowned by twice the number of stalwarts roaring "We Want Wilson!" Wilson—though probably his young supporter's undergraduate trick had little to do with the result —was given the nomination.

Wilson was elected and to Roosevelt's surprise and delight he was offered by Josephus Daniels, Secretary of the Navy, the job of his Assistant. He had refused other jobs in the new Administration; he disapproved of a system of Spoils For Supporters of the winning team, but this offer was too good to be refused. For someone whose parents had refused to allow him to go to sea, the job of Assistant Secretary of the Navy was a gift, not from Daniels or Wilson, but from God. On 17 March, 1913, the eighth anniversary of his noisy, St. Patrick's Day, wedding, he took the oath of office.

Now, much as his contemporary Winston Churchill was doing across the Atlantic, he flung himself into the business of making a modern fleet from an out-of-date, forgotten, one. He scrapped the antique battleships, built new ones, converted the country's navy yards into major industrial plants, each specializing in certain equipment: radio from Brooklyn, paint from Norfolk, Virginia, and so on. One of the first things he did was teach his Navy to swim: half of it couldn't, numbers were being drowned every year. He tempered stern and uncompromising orders that in future they would swim or get out, with a silver cup, to be awarded annually to the ship with the highest score in his "Roosevelt Test"—an eighteen-foot dive from the deck, followed by a hundred-yard race in the open sea.

The war—and some thanks is due to the United States' Assistant Secretary of the Navy—was entered, successfully concluded. He was at the height of his physical powers, could do his own "Roosevelt Test" faster than anyone else. He was persuaded to give up the job and the sea in order to run for Vice-President, in 1920, but there was a Republican land-slide and he failed. Now, for the first time in ten years, he was entirely out of politics.

There were no regrets: after all, his chosen life's work was that of lawyer; now was a chance to get down to it. Even, at last, to earn, as all self-respecting Americans must, a little Real Money.

Some years before, a quiet little gnome of a man had offered him, with no strings attached, his advice, his much greater experience of politics and his friendship. The offer had been accepted and Louis McHenry Howe had helped in countless different ways since he and Franklin Roosevelt had become friends in the early days of State politics. A newspaperman from Albany and—surprisingly, perhaps, in that most cynical of trades—an idealist, he had decided the young politician, eleven years his junior, deserved to, and would, go far. But he lacked experience, and this little Louis Howe was eager to lend.

In August, 1921, on holiday with Eleanor and the five children on their favourite island off Campobello, off the Maine coast, Franklin went swimming in ice-cold water. The chill he contracted worsened mysteriously into paralysis. After a month of critical illness he was left—an active, some said a brilliant, man, and not yet forty—paralysed from waist down with polio-myelitis.

Louis Howe was already on his way to Campobello to say his farewells, get back to newspaper work, when the illness struck. When he arrived and discovered that the young man in whose future he had so firmly believed had been stricken, he decided, on the spot, to give up journalism, give up the plum job he had just accepted, and devote the rest of his life to Franklin Roosevelt.

But, of course, without the patient's own will to recover—to go on living, doing, achieving—all the care, the encouragement and the support of Louis Howe and Eleanor Roosevelt would have been wasted.

There was no danger of this. He fought himself back to health and mobility, after the specialists had told him this would be out of the question; he taught himself to move swiftly on crutches. Egged on by restless, chain-smoking little Howe, he agreed to be campaign manager when his old friend Al Smith ran for the Democratic Presidential nomination. Al Smith failed, but now—and perhaps this is why Louis Howe forced Franklin into it—he knew his physical handicap could never stand in his own way.

Soon after this he learnt of a small settlement in Georgia, styling itself Warm Springs, whose clear spring water was supposed to be helpful to people with limb injuries. He took a few days off from his law work, went there, and found it a down-at-heel holiday resort with a small hotel and a pool, fed by a warm spring. A few days in the pool, using his powerful arms to drag himself through the water, made his legs noticeably stronger.

This was a tremendous discovery—as much for other sufferers as for himself. Almost on the spur of the moment he endowed with his own money a "Warm Springs Foundation". Then, when he was satisfied the place really *would* help all sufferers, he began to enlist aid from friends and public and raised over $1,000,000 for his Foundation. Thousands of sufferers to this day have cause to be grateful to him.

Soon he had thrown away crutches, could walk, slowly and carefully, with a pair of sticks. He acquired, and partly designed, his own car, with hand-operated controls, like a motorbike. Al Smith, relinquishing the Governorship of New York State in 1928 in order to run for the Presidency (in which he failed), urged him to run for the Governorship. Roosevelt did so, was elected by a huge majority.

Now came an opportunity as exciting as the one presented by Assistant Secretaryship of the Navy, to do something about social injustices which had, throughout life, distressed him. His Governorship covered the 1929 stock-market crash and the immediate aftermath, and he worked hard through those dreadful months for "the forgotten man at the bottom of the economic pyramid"—the man who always, throughout American history, has been ignored, left to fend miserably for himself.

And so—leaping on—we find him, four years later, President of the United States. In his first Hundred Days, as dramatic as any achieved by Napoleon, he lifted his country out of desperate trouble by its boot-straps. He took it off the gold standard; partially repealed the corrupting Eighteenth Amendment to the Constitution which had forbidden the sale of alcohol; set thousands of jobless, starving men to working for the Government, planting trees (urgently-needed trees, in dust bowls and drought areas, but no one had thought of it before), making roads. He set up the Public Works Administration; the vast, imaginative, Tennessee Valley Authority.

In short, Franklin Roosevelt got his country moving—in an incredibly short space of time—as it had never moved before.

The rest is history. He was returned again, with more huge majorities, in 1936, in 1940, in 1944. For the first nine years of those unprecedented terms of office he fought a spirit of isolationism. "If war comes," he declared to an apathetic American audience in 1937, "let no one imagine the United States will escape". When war did break out, in 1939, he recast, against huge and vocal opposition, his country's Neutrality Act so France and Britain could buy arms on a "cash and carry" basis. He bullied his country into giving Britain fifty desperately-needed destroyers after Dunkirk, then pushed through a "Lend-Lease" Act, in 1941, whereby the trickle of food and munitions which had done so much to keep a weary Britain going became a mighty flood.

Japan's strike against Pearl Harbour brought what he had known to be inevitable—the open alliance of the United States with Britain.

He died almost in the moment of victory. He has been accused, not without reason, of grievous errors of judgement towards the end, errors which gave half Europe to the Russians. The evil that men do lives after them: men are prepared to forget—if in fact they ever knew—that without the fight back to health of this brave and obstinate man, a man who knew right from wrong and preferred it to expediency, the war would have ended very differently indeed. An America which had all but collapsed in 1933 had been dragged to her feet and gone on, a decade later, to drag the free world back to its own.

And while it is true to say—as elsewhere I have said—that Britain would have collapsed in misery and defeat without a Winston Churchill urging, inspiring it on—there is more to the truth than that.

Even Churchill, the incomparable Churchill with his example and his exhortation, could have done little more than prolong his country's back-to-the-wall resistance.

From 1940 onward, the ultimate outcome depended on the moody, bigger, not-entirely-friendly, boy behind that wall. That he was persuaded to hop over it, was able then to deliver the knock-out blow, is entirely thanks to the man whose statue now stands in London's Grosvenor Square—to Franklin D. Roosevelt.

Chapter 11

Thomas Edward Lawrence

I would have loved to be there, hiding under desk or behind filing cabinet, on 27 December, 1922. For then I would have heard—more or less—this dialogue between Adjutant and Guard Commander at R.A.F., Farnborough.

"*Yes*—Watkins?"

"Beg pardon, sir—there's a hundred blokes, looks like it, with cameras——"

"*Cameras?*—what the hell d'they want?"

"Aircraftsman Ross, sir."

"Ross?"

"Yes, *you* know, sir. Skinny little bloke. They say he's Lawrence of Arabia, sir. Lawrence of f——ing Arabia. Begging pardon, that is, sir. . . ."

And so on. Probably it was different. But the fact remains that on this cheerless winter morning near the end of 1922 the *Daily Express* had announced to its readers that the fabulous, mythical, eccentric T. E. Lawrence—*Colonel Lawrence*, no less—was hiding from the world, skulking as an aircraftman in the R.A.F. The rest of the Press had come along to see. Aircraftsman Ross, he was calling himself.

So he was. But, thanks to the *Daily Express*, his position became, overnight, quite untenable. His engagement was terminated.

For months he pestered his friends in high places to get him back into the Air Force. There was no question of a commission: he would join, that he made plain and definite, as an aircraftsman, or not at all. He would enlist, and stay, in the lowest rank provided by the British armed forces.

That was Ned Lawrence's plan. But obviously this sort of a man, who has been a senior, much-decorated officer, who knows everyone from the Prime Minister down and is not averse to letting people know it, is a disaster in the non-commissioned ranks of any service. He has but to suggest, by word or innuendo in his barrack-room, that such-and-such an officer isn't what he's cracked up to be, is rogue and poltroon and having an affair with the colonel's wife, and everyone believes him. Any order from a mere flying officer, even from a squadron leader, will look pretty silly against the reasoned advice of a battle-scarred colonel who has rejected the fruits of high office to Be Like Everyone Else.

And, as Lawrence continued to refuse a commission, the R.A.F. refused to let him re-join. Once was enough; never again.

He joined the Army—the Tank Corps. And as, thanks to the Press, the "Ross" pseudonym had become world-famous, he chose another, "T. E. Shaw". This time he changed it legally, by deed poll.

One of his joys had always been fast motor-cycling, and one of the men he knew well was George Brough, who manufactured expensive, custom-built models. It was through Brough that he got, at a greatly reduced price, one of those superb machines. He could easily have afforded a car by now, but to him cars were hideous, stuffy things, to be used, if at all, in the rain.

He was mad on speed, he would tear over the countryside at speeds of over a hundred miles an hour, visiting friends,

testing a new carburettor setting. just travelling. The friends,
and he had a great many, were odd ones for a private in the
Tank Corps; they included men like Thomas Hardy and
Bernard Shaw. And it was during this period that Lawrence—
for, deed poll or no deed poll, we cannot think of him as anyone
else—bought the only bit of real estate he ever owned, a
tumbledown cottage in which to entertain them. It was called
Clouds Hill, only a few minutes' walk, a second or so's sprint
on a motor-bike, from his Bovington Camp in Dorset. He set
himself to "improve" it.

Certainly it needed that attention. It was damp, it leaked,
the windows were broken, and he set to work with a will to
do something about it. In a few weeks he had made it, if not
attractive, at least habitable. It had a bed, some chairs, a
gramophone and bookshelves, and now a stream of friends
began to make their way south-west across England to Clouds
Hill.

For the most part, they were friends indeed—for there was
very little more to be had than friendship in Clouds Hill. Their
host hated the smell of cooking. Many people do—but with
Lawrence, as with so much he did, this was carried to extremes:
he firmly, flatly refused to have any cooking done on the
premises. If you dined with Lawrence, you did so straight from
the tin—everything was tinned at Clouds Hill—and thus
avoided the insanitary nonsense of plates.

(Years later, the wife of the artist Eric Kennington, who did
a fine painting of Lawrence and was to do many more of
heroes in the public eye, the men of the Battle of Britain,
including Richard Hillary, reported that the method of washing
up after tea, when this meal took place, was to set dirty cups
and plates along the stepped garden path, then pour boiling
water on the top step, let it splash on down.)

But though Lawrence had complained of life in the R.A.F.,
its brutality, its squalor, he pined to go back. The Army was
a thousand times worse. He was "queerly homesick whenever
I see a blue uniform in the street".

The R.A.F. was less than keen about his return; application
after application was refused. At one stage he thought he
might achieve it when the Secretary of State for Air asked him

to write an official history of the Air Force: he imposed the condition that he be allowed to re-enlist when the book was finished—and was deeply distressed when the proposal was withdrawn.

Eventually he made it, by the simple device of threatening suicide. This, had he done it, would have been a public scandal, for Lawrence would not have gone to his Maker without leaving behind a few thousand words of explanation. "War Hero, Sacked from Air Force, Heartbroken. I Cannot Live Without the Air Force"—the publicity was too appalling to contemplate. On 16 July, 1925, after frantic juggling behind the scenes between Lawrence's friends, the Secretary of State for Air and the Prime Minister, "Private T. E. Shaw" transferred to the R.A.F.

Even now he was denied the peace, the anonymity he wanted. He was posted to India in December, 1926, at his own request, because he wanted to be out of the country and avoid publicity when his book *Revolt in the Desert* came out. But it was while he was at a station on the North-West Frontier that the Press, once again, undid him. A story was printed that the great Colonel Lawrence was doing secret work in Afghanistan. This was seized upon by the Soviet Union, which insisted that the "secret work"—he was checking airframes, in full view of all who cared to watch—was espionage.

Again he returned to Britain—and, by unfortunate coincidence, a revolt broke out in Afghanistan. The Left Wing Press gloated: Lawrence had done it, all right. His effigy was burnt on Tower Hill.

He managed to convince his persecutors that he had nothing to do with it, and his remaining years in the R.A.F.—almost his last years of life—were peaceful. He did much to organize the Schneider Trophy seaplane races and he also began work on a technique of air-sea rescue, which would have a marked effect in the coming war. His interest in this came by accident when he was involved in a tragedy in Plymouth Sound. He was crossing in an R.A.F. launch when an aircraft above him suddenly got out of control and plunged into the water. He opened full throttle, tore across the water—and failed to get there in time. His boat was just incapable of the speed

147

required. At the same time it lacked any equipment for keeping the aircraft afloat for those vital seconds which would give the crew a chance to escape.

This became an obsession. He spent his last years in the R.A.F. developing and testing fast boats for rescue operations. Countless pilots owe their lives today to his work.

And in a quiet but persistent way he did a lot for the day-to-day life of the R.A.F., making it more pleasant, more humane, somehow persuading the powers above him to alter tiresome regulations, let in a bit of light. The military historian Liddell Hart wrote: "He was a greater spiritual force than the whole Board of Chaplains in raising the standard of decency, fair play and unselfish comradeship."

Not a mean achievement for an aircraftman.

A little later he was dead. He retired to the peace of Clouds Hill, and on 13 May, 1935, coming back from a visit to the post office—as ever, on the motor-bike—he swerved to avoid two children, crashed and was killed outright. He was forty-six.

He was born 16 August, 1888, in Wales, illegitimate son of Sir Thomas Chapman, Seventh Baronet of Westmeath in Ireland. A romantic beginning, but one that affected his whole life and was largely responsible for the neurosis which dogged him throughout it. Chapman had left Ireland at some speed, running away with Sara, the governess of his older children. On arrival in Wales, he cut all links with the past, changed his name to Lawrence. His Sara, sadly prevented by the divorce laws from ever becoming Thomas's wife, was a fine woman who bore him five sons. "Ned", T. E., was the second.

He was ten years old when he made the discovery that he was illegitimate. His father took him aside, explained that marriage had not been, never would be, possible. Lady Chapman still refused him a divorce.

The shock was great: and when he had recovered from it young Ned resolved—so he later explained to a few close friends—to be better at everything he set his hand to than anyone else. He would prove, illegitimate or not, that he was as good a man as the next.

And the frank dislike of young, attractive women which was so typical of him in adult life probably dated from this discovery that he was the product of a moment's passion between two people he had loved and respected.

One of his earliest crazes—and life for Lawrence was made up of many—was toy soldiers. The family left Wales, moved to Scotland, thence to the Isle of Man, to Jersey, and finally to Oxford, where he was sent to the High School, and throughout this time he collected, mobilized and deployed—much as Winston Churchill had done at the same age—armies of tin soldiers. The hobby became an obsession with castles, medieval archaeology. When the time came for him to write a thesis for his B.A. degree at Jesus College, he elected to do it on "Crusader Castles".

For this, he would have to travel through the Middle East. He leapt at the opportunity and headed there during the summer vacation of 1908, when he was just short of his twentieth birthday. By now he was in many ways an odd-looking youth: a magnificent head that should have belonged to a man six and a half feet tall was attached to a short and slender body, the whole reaching only to five feet six inches. The eyes were deep-set, piercing, the mouth wide and firm, chin strong, prognathous.

He was fascinated by the people and set himself to learning Arabic. He worked exceedingly hard at it—and did badly. Right to the end of his desert days, when he was leading an Arab army to blow up Turkish trains, he spoke Arabic with a comic English pronunciation. Paradoxically, this made the Arabs love and respect him: Arabic is not a hard language to learn, and plenty of Englishmen have done so, not all for the best motives. If this was the best the little man could do with their language—well, he could hardly be a spy. They took him to their bosoms.

He passed his finals, was awarded a "Research Demyship" at Magdalen College, a grant which would enable him to travel for the purpose of study. Immediately he headed for the Middle East, to where the famous archaeologist, D. G. Hogarth (who was to become lifelong friend and confidant), was excavating the ancient Hittite city, Carchemish, on the Euphrates.

Work on this "dig" was a continuing, daily, adventure, and Lawrence, having arrived here in the spring of 1911, found himself staying three years. Quite apart from the archaeology, he had found the political problems, the history, of the Arab peoples, absolutely gripping. Within weeks of his arrival, he had begun to identify himself with the Arab dream of shaking off the hold of Turkey: evenings in his tent, he would pore over a map, deciding where he might place the capital of this hypothetical Free Arabia.

And while he did this, war drew near. Another man considering maps was Lord Kitchener, British Resident in Egypt. He was studying, with considerable urgency, the defence of the Suez Canal. To do so effectively would require control over the Sinai Peninsula, now under Turkish control and quite unmapped.

The first thing, Kitchener decided, was to get it mapped. Much thought was lavished on the question and at last an ingenious plan was produced: a British expedition would be mounted and sent, with Turkish permission, to map "The Itinerary of the Israelites During the Forty Years in the Desert".

What the Turks really thought of this idea we will never know, but the expedition duly set out, including Lawrence as one of its members, mapped the whole of the Sinai Peninsula and went back to England to assemble maps and information into an Army manual.

With the job half-finished, war broke out. Lawrence, who had just completed his share of the work, was now posted back, as a junior officer in the Army, to Cairo.

Immediately he took a violent and largely irrational dislike to senior officers, to most of military life. Gone overnight was the love of soldiers, tin, lead or flesh. In its place came a new love, the love of fast, sleek, shining machinery—the high-powered motor-bike. He bought one, tore round Cairo on it, deliberately enraging senior officers, "the fat and lazy ones" he saw sitting at Shepheard's Hotel, drinking, taking tea.

An idea, entertained briefly at G.H.Q., had been the sponsoring, somehow, of an Arab revolt against Turkey. This was so close to what Lawrence himself had been considering as he rootled in the dust of Carchemish that he grabbed hold of the idea, worried it like a bone, demanded to be allowed to help organize it. Eventually he was granted permission to contact the Grand Sherif of Mecca, see what could be done.

The Sherif had five sons, scattered about the Middle East, each descended from the Prophet, and each in control of a sizeable area, with wealth and with influence throughout the Arab world. Lawrence's job was to visit them in turn, sound them out on the possibility of a rising. He did so, deciding that the best man would be the Emir Feisal, to whom he took an instant liking, and rushed back to Cairo.

At G.H.Q. the idea had been entertained with a minimum of enthusiasm and there were senior officers who had hoped and assumed the Lawrence mission would be a failure, that no protagonist would be found. But now G.H.Q. found itself being swept along on the tide of this one young man's enthusiasm, agreeing to support his revolt, supply him with arms.

The deal was clinched by Lawrence's announcement that he would require no British troops. It was an Arab revolt, an Arab war, and the Arabs required nothing but arms from the British.

Arms, and, of course, Lawrence.

The Commander-in-Chief had been reluctant to supply troops and this information was as welcome as it was puzzling. How on earth did the young chap propose to overthrow the might of Turkey with a few thousand Bedouin on camels?

From Lawrence's point of view, it was all exceedingly clear. He felt sincerely that he knew more of what was to be done than any Englishman living—and he would brook no interference, take no advice, from anyone. It was quite clear in his mind : he would adopt Arab dress, the Arab tongue, their way of life, and in this way bind them to him by ties of respect and affection.

There could be no room in this sort of dream for other Englishmen. The tale of Lawrence's dealings with Army officers of his own seniority, throughout the war, is a sadly disappointing one, for so great a man. Without exception he quarrelled with them, and if they happened to possess a knowledge of the people and the area rivalling his own, he was consumed with jealousy. He avoided them whenever possible, but at one stage G.H.Q. insisted on attaching to his

Arab force a regular officer, a young man who had the misfortune to speak far better Arabic than his unwilling host. Lawrence behaved so outrageously to the poor man that he was forced to ask for a posting away—anywhere—to escape.

The Arab revolt took place—and it worked. Under the combined leadership of Feisal and Lawrence, the Arabs rose, captured the Red Sea ports which were under Turkish control, reduced them one by one. In one battle a heavy defeat was inflicted on the Turks with Lawrence himself on horseback, leading the Arabs—but this was one of the last straightforward combats in the campaign. He had discovered that the Arabs, not always reliable in battle, were superb in any manoeuvre requiring stealth or cunning. He took to organizing and leading raids on railway lines, blowing up enemy trains, with huge success. Soon the Turks, having only heard the name from Arab sources, were advertising a reward for the capture, dead or alive, of the fantastic "El Orens, Wrecker of Engines".

The war moved on. Damascus fell in 1918 to Lawrence's force, but during the advance on it he had the misfortune to be captured. Fortunately, the Turks never seemed to realize they had in their hands no less a man than El Orens, and he managed, as he said later, to convince them his light skin was Circassian. Whether they believed this or not is another matter, but they thought sufficiently ill of this prisoner to subject him to brutal torture, throughout which he prided himself on "not groaning in English".

Eventually he was released, thrown out on the sand outside the Turkish camp. Weak from beatings and loss of blood, he managed to steal a camel, ride it back to his own camp.

Controversy has raged ever since over whether the Turks knew they had Lawrence, the hated El Orens, after all. Had they calmly reduced him to within minutes and inches of death, then flung him out, just in order to show the Arab world how pitiful their leader could be? I doubt it: Lawrence, pitiful as he may have looked arriving back on a stolen camel, went on to become a still greater figure in the Arab world. And—from the Turkish point of view, the point of view of the soldiers who captured him, there was too great a reward on Lawrence's head for anyone not to make sure of getting it.

Armistice came in November of that year, and a few months later Lawrence was summoned to the Peace Conference in Versailles. By now he was a world figure and with the flair for personal publicity which dwelt alongside an almost pathological desire to be left alone, he arrived, to the delight of the world's Press, the scepticism of its negotiators, in full Arab dress.

He argued forcefully for the Arab cause: freedom, no alien domination, a united Arabia. Then, when he saw he had failed, he was heart-broken and nearly collapsed. France in particular had shocked and grieved him: the French, promise or no promise (and every sort of promise, in the heat of battle, had been made), had every intention of staying on in the Middle East. England, less vigorously, concurred. Turkey was out of the way, the area was free for exploitation by the first man in.

This, even more than the discovery at the age of ten that he was a bastard, seemed to tear the ground away from under Lawrence's feet. He had given his personal word to Feisal, indeed to the whole Arab world, that a free Arabia would be set up at the end of the war. It had been—though Lawrence would not have dreamed of using the word or even seeing it in this light—the bribe for Arab help in driving out the Turks. He spent a few weeks, vainly, desperately sniping at the entrenched positions of the great powers, and then, sadly, returned to England to write an account of his desert campaign.

Months later, with manuscript almost complete, he left it in a railway carriage. Perhaps, a century from now, it will reappear, be auctioned at Sotheby's, but since that day it has never, so far as as we know, been seen.

Calmly, Lawrence sat down and rewrote the entire thing, a long and immensely powerful book, eventually published as *Seven Pillars of Wisdom*.

As he had foretold at Versailles, things in the Middle East went from bad to worse. Feisal crept into exile—and Lawrence, who had been given a Fellowship to All Souls College and was using it to get on with his writing, raged against the perfidy of his own country, and of France, which had made such a disaster possible. Nobody paid the slightest attention. No one, that is, except for one man, who also figures in this book.

Winston Churchill had been made Colonial Secretary, he had met Lawrence at the Peace Conference, and he trusted and believed in him. He invited Lawrence to join his Department as Political Counsellor. Furthermore—and this was unusual for Churchill—he agreed to listen to that counsel.

The final result was that Feisal became, if not King of All Arabia, as Lawrence had originally planned, a King of Iraq, elected by his own people, under British auspices, with an overwhelming vote. The British Army left Iraq.

Lawrence was overjoyed. Churchill, he knew, was the only man in Britain who would "set honesty before expediency".

Perhaps he was unjustifiably gladdened: after all, this was a long way short of the promise he had made to Feisal. But Lawrence, who hated many with a waspish hate, admired Churchill profoundly. He went on record as saying: "England is out of the Arab affair with clean hands."

Now, it is doubtful whether even Churchill felt this: there had been too much dishonesty and self-interest at Versailles for that. The mere bringing out, from his English exile, of one Arab chief and making him King of a part of the Middle East, leaving the rest under Western control, was hardly concluding the affair "with clean hands".

Perhaps by now El Orens, the man who had driven the Turks from their Middle Eastern empire, had wearied of man's perfidy to man. Perhaps he wanted to escape from the whole affair. He had done the best he could—no man could do more. Now he wanted to be free, utterly free, of the Middle East. If he convinced himself that his country had done the best possible for the Arabs, he would be free.

We may never know whether Lawrence believed this. I suspect not, and this is why the man who, only a few years before, had been one of the world's great commanders (though only Colonel El Orens, he had an influence in the Middle East equalled only, since then, by Gamal Abdel Nasser)—why this man now submitted himself to the indignity of the lowest rank in the R.A.F.

Why the R.A.F.? Because it was new and young in outlook, dealing with engines and with speed. And because he believed it was totally different from the Army.

His first term of service was short—for, as we have seen, a newspaper report broke it up at the end of 1922. But then, after a short and unhappy period in the Tank Corps, he got back again and seems to have been content to mix with the simplest of men, to lose his identity among them.

He never married. The few women he knew were all older than himself, and with several of these he indulged in long, literary flirtations. One of them was the wife of Bernard Shaw. When she died, Shaw, going through her letters, remarked: "She told Lawrence many things she never told me." No doubt she did, for our odd, complex, waspish little hero inspired a love and confidence in some people as violent as the dislike he inspired in others. He was capable of great friendship, even love—though not physical love for women. Driven always by ambition, ambition which had hit him in the face at the age of ten, an ambition not far removed from despair, he fought the world and nearly won.

He was often ridiculous: his sudden, feline jealousies; his posturing, as with his flowing Arab robes in Oxford, or in the Bois de Boulogne. Yet this odd, illegitimate and possibly homosexual little man, with the great, handsome head on the little man's body, was loved and admired by more men—and women —than is the lot of most of us. Only a man like Lawrence, with a generous, slightly twisted, nature, a boundless enthusiasm and a limitless courage, only a Lawrence could have welded the quarrelling tribes of the Arab world into a fighting machine —and with it driven the might of Turkey from the Middle East.

Circumstances alter us all. How much, if any, of this would have happened if Ned Chapman, younger son of the Seventh Baronet, Sir Thomas, had been born and brought up in Ireland, a respectable member of a respected family?

But Ned Lawrence did *not* grow up in Ireland. A less idle conjecture is: How long would the First World War have lasted—indeed, who might have won it—had there been no "El Orens"?

For this—quite apart from his writing, and the legend he has left us—we owe a deep, very deep, debt of gratitude.

Chapter 12

Mao Tse-tung

When I was in North Burma during 1943-45, the little Kachin soldiers we were trying to organize into an anti-Japanese force seemed to spend as much time fighting the Chinese as the Japs. A little-known fact, I suppose: but without knowing it no one can understand Burma. There was scarcely a month when messages were not being sent over the Kachin Hills, by radio or runner, warning that another lot of the hated "Miwa-ni" had crossed the border from Yunnan and announced their intention of taking over that part of the country. As a result, over vast areas of Burma, the Chinese were more hated than the Japanese. No one had a kind word for the Chinese, and with reason: but in the south, as we knew only too well, there were Burmese happily, sincerely, collaborating with the Japs.

The invasions kept up, and soon we began to take them in our stride. The Chinese—those we tangled with—were not only woefully incompetent as soldiers, despite their American, British and Russian arms, they seemed to be cowards to boot.

156

One platoon of Kachin Levies, barefoot and armed largely with vicious long-bladed dahs and, if they were lucky, a Bren gun, could disperse a company of Chinamen as soon as say Chiang Kai-shek.

And yet, somehow, one knew: given a leader and a cause —and these people so obviously had neither—they would be a very different proposition. When—and if—that happened, one wanted to be on their side.

Apart from these more-or-less private invasions from the east, we had, in the west, Fred Karno's army of American-trained Chinese, lagging far behind the spearhead of American troops, the superb (we had nothing, but nothing, in Burma, to compare with them) "Merrill's Marauders". Without these Americans in front I have no doubt that they would still, a generation later, a little grey and toothless, be a dozen miles south of Ledo, quarrelling with, looting, local inhabitants. All over Burma, in fact, the cry was never chuck out the Japs, but God save us from the Chinese. They were cruel, they were cowardly, they were totally undisciplined; and I for one find myself looking back over twenty or so years and feeling that we fought a war against China, not Japan. And won.

But would we win today?

I love the Chinese. For what they have taught the world, and me; the beauty, the thinking, even the point of view they have given us.

My last memory—also unfortunate, but absolutely indelible —of Chinese soldiers, is of a day when I lay uncomfortably, hour by hour, on my face, having foolishly driven my jeep over a land-mine. The jeep had been blown to pieces and one of the larger bits had come down again and pinned an American sergeant under it. He, poor fellow, had been attached to a battalion of American-advised Chinese, which had dug itself in some miles behind us. We had stopped to give him a lift back north to Myitkyina.

Now he was badly wounded under a sizeable piece of our jeep, surrounded by hurt Kachins, one of whom was dying. We lay there, none of us able to lift the jeep off Ed's back, even to move ourselves, cooking quietly in the sun.

Hours later, a group of Chinese soldiers from Ed's battalion appeared, coming down the road from Myitkyina, back to camp with two stolen bullock-carts, piled high with loot. They reached us, were fascinated by the sight and stood chattering and laughing among themselves.

Then they came over and a dozen lifted the chassis off Ed's back and dumped it in the ditch. After this they went methodically through our kit, which was scattered over the road, and distributed it among themselves, down to the individual rounds of our ammunition which they counted out carefully and shared. A precious bottle of rum we were transporting, wrapped in a blanket, was miraculously unharmed and this they fought over, and decanted into their water bottles.

Then they loaded us on one of the carts, not unkindly, transferring the loot to the other. Little Hkaw Zung was now dead, and after removing his Boy Scout belt and a few paper rupees from a breast pocket they dumped him in the ditch with the jeep and headed south with the rest of us.

And so Chinese soldiers, as I knew them then, seemed a cruel, unorganized mob. Yet one knew, because news filtered over the border, that a strange new wind had blown up over their vast country. A new force, a new leadership, was springing up, a spirit that would unite these people, all six hundred million of them, as they then were (and terrifyingly more now), into one proud state.

And then—God help us if we weren't on their side. The days of frightening off a muddled, demoralized Chinese company with a platoon of half-armed tribesmen wouldn't last. If these men found themselves someone to fight under, someone more inspiring, more attuned to their way of thinking than Generalissimo Chiang Kai-shek (though, to give Chiang his due, half his soldiers had never heard of him, had never weighed and found him wanting; they had simply not known of his existence), and also found a cause worth fighting for, they would be the most powerful, dangerous force on earth.

They have and they are.

But in those days of 1944 and 1945 they seemed to be divided into enclaves all over China, some led by self-styled war lords, some owing allegiance to the Generalissimo, some to Mao Tse-tung. This last was only one of a group, or so we learned from our trans-border intelligence, a group which included men with improbable names like Liu Shao-chi, Chuh Teh and Chou En-lai. The Lisu tribesmen who worked with us, more Chinese than the Chinese, knew of them: they lived in caves romantically situated at the top of the map, up against the Great Wall. They called themselves Communists, but the idea of a rural, peasant China going Communist seemed far-fetched: general opinion, not only in our remote Kachin Hills, was that they had adopted the title through a combination of ignorance and respect for the Soviet Union.

But, whatever they were, they were a force to be reckoned with. More and more Chinese, of this we were certain, were joining them.

That part of Burma, between Myitkyina in the north and a little below Bhamo in the south, where a great lump of China sticks westward, almost to the Irrawaddy River, is a good place for information. Without doubt the people up there know details of the latest Chinese bomb tests and the state of play in the undeclared war beneath China and the U.S.S.R.

They also have a fairly good idea who the successor will be to Chairman Mao.

But in the meantime, let us consider the man himself, for at the moment he is China. The new, emerged—not "emergent" —China. For, make no mistake about it, these people have erupted into the mid-twentieth century (700,000,000 now, and a lot more by the time you get to the end of this article) with a vigour, determination—and success—that has outstripped many nations. Like, say, Britain.

He comes from Hunan Province, a little below the middle on the map of China, where he was born in the village of Shao Shan on 26 December, 1893. His parents—for the sake of the myth they had to be poor peasants, and if they were nothing of the sort we will probably never know—worked the land and they do differ from the standard pattern in that the father accumulated a few acres. Hunan is one of the richest granaries of China and the hardy, thrifty, peasant-traders have, not for nothing, been described as the Germans, sometimes the Scots, of China. The old, old saying goes: "China will be conquered when the last man in Hunan is dead."

Mao's youth need not concern us, for he only began to exist, for the purposes of China and this essay, when he was a grown man. The backgrounds of most great heroes—particularly Communist ones—tend to be limned in with all the accuracy of the Old Testament, and his biographers, who have written backwards and stressed the revolutionary traits which were so manifest when he was five, can be taken with a pinch of salt. But we do know, because everyone else in Shao Shan was and many still are, that the family were Buddhists. They also respected the teachings and ceremonies of Confucian China.

It was when he was eighteen years old, a tall, pale, rather effeminately pleasant-looking young man, that Mao led his first revolt, and this, thanks to a biographer, Emi Siao, who was with him at the time, we can believe. He had become inspired by the writings of the remarkable Dr. Sun Yat-sen, the southerner who had grown up in Hawaii, gone on to practise medicine in Hong Kong, then given up medicine to devote himself to saving China from the Manchus. That dynasty had ruled for three hundred years and it was, Sun knew, responsible for his country's low standing in the world, her regular defeats in war, the poverty and misery of her masses. Mao for his part decided to do something dramatic. The symbol of subservience to the Manchus was the ancient pigtail: he seized a pair of shears one morning at school, clipped off his own and rushed wildly about the classroom doing the same for the other pupils.

He seems to have survived this rather odd little demonstration, and a little later a more practical method arose of showing his true feelings. There was a bomb explosion in Hankow and a number of the supporters of Sun Yat-sen, believed to be responsible, were executed out of hand. The army revolted, and within a day or two had driven Manchu governors out of several Chinese cities. Mao promptly joined it, and with the calculating fervour which would mark everything he did, became a superb guerrilla fighter, sworn to throw out, for ever, the hated Manchus. In between his military exercises he became a modest pamphleteer, sticking up wall-newspapers with morals like: "Out with the Manchus!", "Set China Free!", "Freedom for Women!"

By the end of the year Nanking had fallen to the rebellious army. Sun Yat-sen, who was in America, was brought back and made provisional president of the new Chinese Republic. There were still centres of Imperial power, notably Peking, and it was not until February of the following year, 1912, that the Manchu dynasty fell. Mao, now eighteen, resigned from the army, confident that he had played his part, that his revolution was successfully over. From now on, China would change, a little more each day, and always for the better.

China did change, but not along the lines he had expected. He spent the next five years, from 1912 to 1918, in the Changsha Normal School in Hunan, learning to be a teacher. He had been keen, when he left the army, to educate himself, keep up with the brave new, westernized future (in those last days of an old order, soon to vanish in a world war, the sun, for China, rose daily in the west). The realization that he must look much harder at the west came from his nineteenth birthday, when he saw for the first time a map of the world. He was dumbfounded: no wonder China, which had once been so sure it was the centre, the hub, of the world, was not seen in that perspective outside its own borders. China was not even the largest nation.

On the other hand it had, would always have, the largest population. This fact, central to all Mao's thinking, impressed itself deep on his formative mind.

Dr. Sun Yat-sen's supporters—against his advice—formed themselves into a political party, the National People's Party or Kuomintang. The Manchus had gone but there was plenty of fighting to be done, not only against pockets of Manchu supporters but among the revolutionaries themselves. Sun Yat-sen, again against his own judgement, had been forced to make the old Imperial General Yuan first President of the new Chinese Republic, if the General would persuade—as he did— the old dynasty to resign rather than be annihilated. But almost immediately Yuan began to plot for a return to the monarchy, with himself as Emperor. Very soon, Sun Yat-sen's party had been outlawed, Yuan had declared himself Emperor, the Republic was over.

Yuan died eighty-three days later, leaving anarchy behind.

Hundreds of petty war lords were fighting among themselves to take over, if not the whole of the nation, at least as much as they could grab before it was too late. Sun Yat-sen, discouraged, almost heartbroken, escaped to Japan. From there he appealed for western help. This was China's last chance to avoid total anarchy and collapse. Was it not worth while for the rest of the globe to see a strong, friendly China?

It was not. Then, towards the end of the world war, there seemed a little hope: President Wilson's principles would surely prevail, the western powers would give up their extra-territorial rights in Chinese cities, long a bitter point, give the new Republic the economic and military aid it needed to get on its feet. But in May, 1919, came the shattering news that the Versailles Peace Conference had no intention of supporting democracy in China, would retain all extra-territorial rights in the country for westerners. Far worse, it would legalize the encroachment of Japan.

Suddenly, China was electrified—and not least the twenty-five-year-old Mao Tse-tung. On 4 May five thousand students in Peking marched on the legation quarter to force European and American diplomats to intercede with their own countries. They were not allowed into the legation area—this was the unkindest cut of all, there was this sizeable bit of China in so many Chinese towns, forbidden to her citizens—and rioting broke out.

The outbreak—the "May the Fourth Incident"—started other riots in other cities and is now regarded in China as the start-point of the second stage of the Chinese Revolution. Sun Yat-sen had done his best—but developments from now on would be very different. Russia appeared on the scene.

With the western powers holding parts of the country as more or less a colony, shared out among themselves, with Japan encroaching daily into the rest of it, China's taste for west-European democracy faded. The Chinese turned to Russia for help and it came: money, arms, advisers.

So impressed was the young student-teacher by this that he resolved to devote his life to emulating the new Russian way, introducing it to his country. From now on he would become a "Communist" himself, joining a party of that name which was beginning to grow in China. The party distinguished itself clearly from Sun's Kuomintang, though there was friendship— for the time being—between them. Sun Yat-sen died and his place was taken by Chiang Kai-shek, one of the war lords, who now became, to raise himself above the proliferation of military rank in China, "Generalissimo". But the right wing of Chiang's Kuomintang government was strongly in favour of the age-old system of big landlords and little peasants.

Mao naturally, fired as he was by Marxist fervour, disagreed. In 1927 he submitted to the Chinese Communist Party his "Report on an Investigation into the Peasant Movement in Hunan", his home province. Already he was a force to be reckoned with in the Communist movement. In his Report he recommended no less than bloody revolution to overthrow the landlords and divide their land among poor peasants. No matter that China was still recovering from an earlier revolution: the earlier one would prove to have been tragically pointless unless it were followed up.

The Party decided against revolt at that time, but the news got out. Chiang Kai-shek, hardly surprisingly, set out ruthlessly to destroy the infant Communist movement. There were bloody massacres all over China and by mid-1927 the Communist Party, bruised, bleeding, but very much alive, had gone underground. In August Mao himself organized what he called "The Autumn Crop Uprising", which failed miserably. He was captured by Chiang's forces and was able to escape just before he was due to be beheaded. Now there was nothing for it, for Mao and his ever-increasing band of sworn revolutionaries but to retreat to the hills, build up an army and come back to destroy the Kuomintang. He began to build up an army of peasants in the snow-covered mountains between the provinces of Hunan and Kiangsi. When Chiang sent government troops against them the revolutionaries ambushed them, almost with their bare hands, and captured their arms.

With these, Mao Tse-tung set up his First Red Army.

The speed of recruitment doubled. From all over China peasants rallied to the new red flag, and—at the same time— Chiang's Kuomintang sent expedition after expedition against it. Mao had been joined by another Red Army, under his old colleague Chuh Teh, and between them they flung back four major assaults, over a period of ten blood-soaked months in 1930 and 1931. And with each Red victory, a new haul of arms.

The fifth assault was the one on which Chiang had pinned his hopes. He had imported advisers from the German Army, mobilized a million soldiers. Now he sent them into the Kiangsi Mountains where Mao's forces were in position.

This particular battle was bloody in the extreme. For weeks the forces of Communism and Kuomintang fought each other to a standstill. At one point it looked as if Chiang had been defeated for a fifth time: a day later, it seemed that Communism, as a force, had been destroyed. Eventually the outcome was clear: Chiang's forces had been mauled, but they had forced Mao's to separate into smaller groups. If these groups were ever to coalesce they would have to make their way, licking their wounds, to some other part of China.

But where? Mao decided to lead them, thousands of miles, to the north-west provinces of Kansu and Shensi. From here, with their backs literally against the Great Wall of China, they would be able to resist any Kuomintang attacks. And in their own good time they would be able to move, as Chiang seemed unwilling to do, against the Japanese, now spilling into Manchuria.

But how did one get to the Great Wall of China? There was no question of marching north-west across China, straight at the Kuomintang forces. No, they must head due west, to the Burma border, then sharply north. The trip would be in the neighbourhood of six thousand miles. And it would, of course, be on foot.

This march, which began in October, 1934, is one of the most incredible journeys of all time, making Hannibal's trip across the Alps a schoolboy hike in comparison. It lasted a year (do the arithmetic yourself: 365 days, 6,000 miles), during which time the tattered Communist forces, most of them un-uniformed peasants, in thin cotton clothes, were attacked by cold, by intense heat, by the armies of private war lords scattered about every province, and, above all, by the well-armed Kuomintang. The Long March and its memories united and continues to unite the leadership of China's Communist

Party as nothing else could have done: it was shared adversity on an almost unbelievable scale, lasting twelve months—and it is still the start-point of Chinese political thinking.

For Mao's march had passed through eleven provinces and, as he put it at the time, it was "a manifesto, an agitation corps and a seeding machine", proclaiming to the world that "the Red Army is an army of heroes and that the imperialists and their jackals, Chiang Kai-shek and his like, are perfect non-entities". It also showed to the two hundred million people of those eleven provinces that "only the road of the Red Army leads to their liberation. Without the Long March, how could the broad masses have known so quickly that there are such great ideas in the world?" And it seeded ideas in those provinces which would "sprout, grow leaves, blossom into flowers, bear fruit and yield a harvest in the future".

There were rivals for leadership, but Mao was rapidly gaining ascendancy over them all. And it's interesting to see that, apart from the sound Communist ideas which he was already reproducing in standard Marxist dialectical claptrap of jackals and imperialists, he had begun to have definite ideas about re-shaping the people themselves. Not for nothing a schoolmaster. By 1937, when he was an accepted leader of the new movement, accepted even by Soviet Russia, which had blown hot and cold on Chinese Communism for years, he referred in a lecture at a "Military and Political College" to "the opponents of remoulding who must be remoulded".

Already the idea behind the dreadful "purges" of the fifties had taken shape.

Slowly the area under Mao's control grew. By the end of 1937 he was the absolute ruler of ten million people, had begun delegating power to close associates and spending much time reading. He had never left his native China—the intention, way back in 1919, to go to Paris and study French had been submerged in the rise of the Communist Party—and now he resolved to make up for this by studying the political thought of many nations, but relating it all the while to his own credo. For this credo must be, had to be, absolutely right. He would study the mistakes of others and imbibe, commit to memory, every word of Marxist theory that had ever been written.

But there was more to be done than this. The major Japanese incursion into Manchuria—which had nothing to do with her existing status in other parts of China, for which the western powers can be blamed entirely—began with a dubious "bomb outrage" on the South Manchuria Railway. Damage, so it was claimed, was done to Japanese property, Japanese nationals. The Japanese. who had worked it out in advance, immediately installed the last of the Manchu Emperors, Henry Pu-yi, as "ruler" of what they now styled "Manchukuo". From this date on Japan pressed calmly forward, annexing land and cities, while Chiang Kai-shek occupied himself and his huge forces in trying to stamp out Communism.

As the Japanese advance went on the Kuomintang grew more and more discredited in the eyes of peasants. Apart from the right of way they seemed to be giving to the little men from the east, they had not adhered to Sun Yat-sen's policies and were obviously bent on keeping power among the rich land-lords. As there had been incidents and battles between Communist forces and the invading Japanese, it was easy for Mao to claim that he and his Party were the heirs of Sun Yat-sen.

Then came the "Sian Incident", which like the "Fourth of May" and "The Long March" (everything in Communist history has to have a clear, memorable label) is a major landmark. Generalissimo Chiang Kai-shek, still refusing to allow his forces to engage the Japanese, paid a visit to Sian, the capital of Shensi Province. It was December, 1936. He knew there were Communists about, but he felt safe, for not only was the Governor in Siang a trusted subordinate, but the Governor's palace was full of "Blue Shirts", his own Secret Police.

But Chiang's ear was not close enough to the ground : he can have had no idea how deep the feeling was, right in among his own forces, that the Japanese must be thrown out of China. The forces were on the point of mutiny when Chiang's own deputy commander-in-chief, whose H.Q. was at Sian, arrested him. Had Marshal Chang Hsueh-liang not done this there is little doubt that the Generalissimo would have been assassinated and a wholesale mutiny broken out. As it was, he was taken into custody on 12 December, 1936, and his "Blue Shirts" disarmed.

Marshal Chang Hsueh-liang now told him he would be set free if he ended the futile civil war immediately and led China against the real enemy, Japan. It was at this point that Mao learnt of the arrest. Without a moment's delay he sent one of his colleagues, the now famous Chou En-lai, to Sian to save the Generalissimo's life.

Chou persuaded the Marshal that Chiang's advisers and his wife (believed in many quarters to be his brain) must be sent for, to help the Generalissimo make his decision. It's important to realize that all this was done by Communist pressure, for the troops which had precipitated Chiang's arrest were not Communist: their only interest was in getting the Kuomintang, to which they belonged, fighting against the Japs.

Chiang agreed, reluctantly, to a "United Front" and returned to his H.Q. in Nanking. When he got there he immediately denied having made any promise, ordered the arrest of the unfortunate marshal who, in order to save Chiang's life, had arrested him.

Twenty-four years later, having been taken, in an act of childish vengeance, to Formosa when Chiang's forces were finally driven out of mainland China by Mao's, Marshal Chiang Hsueh-liang was released. He had served two years' imprisonment for each day in which he had held his Generalissimo in protective custody.

And so, thanks to a miscalculation over Pearl Harbour, Japan found herself at war with half the world. China, more or less united now against her, played a part in her defeat. Most of the successes within the borders of China were achieved by Mao's Communists.

But in 1945, with Hiroshima and Nagasaki still smoking, the civil war in China started up again.

And now the fifty-two-year-old ex-schoolmaster was in the saddle, and he pressed on hard with his plans. The Kuomintang would be destroyed and its rank and file won over to Communism. At the same time the outside world would have to be placated—*for the time being*—made to believe that Communism of the variety to be practised by Mao Tse-tung was the only possible solution of China's problems. To this end—a carefully thought out system of duplicity. Public pronouncements were made which were the precise opposites of those made at the Party's secret meetings. Party members were told to differentiate utterly between "the public and the secret work of the Party". Mao had by now built up a private secret police based on the Kuomintang "Blue Shirts", but eclipsing them entirely in both numbers and power. A large branch was organized for the sole purpose of "manipulating the masses". Selected plain-clothes men would go into villages as students or peasants and skilfully whip up indignation against any residents the Party wished to liquidate. Then, at the request of the villagers themselves—many of whom had never heard of the people they were condemning—the victims were led away and shot.

And now, while this was going on, a campaign began, to make of Mao Tse-tung a god. His forces were over-running those of the Kuomintang, despite the active support Chiang was getting not only from the United States but from the Soviet Union. This was a good moment for the Party to point out how quiet, modest, unassuming their Chairman Mao was, against the posturing, bemedalled Chiang. Modest Mao—but also Mao the Prophet. "Each prophecy of Chairman Mao has become a reality." "Today, in the day of Mao Tse-tung, heaven is here on earth."

We need have no doubt: by now Mao was a hero, and a real one. With his strength and his vision he had, almost single-handed, beaten and shaped a large part of China into a willing weapon against any enemy he cared to select. But at the same time, hero though he was, it was vital to *remain* one, simply in order to get his work done. After all, Sun Yat-sen had been a hero—and what happened to him? For the purposes of this book it is a pity Mao was not struck down like Lincoln in the moment of victory: everything he has since done, even though he soars higher and higher in the esteem of much of the world, has been squalid anti-climax.

Victory came in 1949 and the remnants of Chiang Kai-shek's forces, including, as we have seen, his political prisoners, established themselves on the island of Formosa. In October of that year Mao was established in Peking as absolute ruler of the Chinese People's Republic. He held the masses of his people firmly in his hand, thanks largely to the genuine respect and adoration his leadership had inspired. No one else could have assembled a defeated army and marched it six thousand miles to regroup and conquer its enemies, at the same time building up an empire of devoted supporters, millions and millions strong. Mao was a hero. Not content with this designation, he set out to make himself a god. For a god his omniscience was embarrassingly limited. He knew China like the back of his smooth, fleshy hand—and he had an abysmal ignorance of everything that went on outside its borders. He fancied Holland to be part of Scandinavia, had the whereabouts and political systems of other countries hopelessly inverted, had a mental date for the economic recession in America which would plunge that country into bloody revolution. He knew, and said so frequently, with the bland and god-like smile with which his pronouncements began to be made, that Britain would never, never give India its freedom. India, like the United States and one or two others, would dissolve within a year or two in a blood-bath—and then go Communist.

Even gods have to keep an eye on the opposition. Mao was determined to press for the ideal state he had in mind, but he knew only too well that there were those in his vast domain who would object. Without giving this objection time to become vocal he began a series of vast purges in which literally millions of peasants were publicly executed for opposition, real or fancied, to the ideas of Communism—ideas like the wholesale transfer to collective farming—or to the person of Mao himself. Reading of these purges we can easily—and fatally—delude ourselves into thinking that if five million people have to be executed for opposition to the ruling party, then there must be a great deal of opposition, and that, therefore, should we find ourselves at war with Mao's China his first set-back will bring the submerged masses out against him.

But no. It is easier, far easier—particularly if one is god—to wipe out a whole community on the off-chance of there being one family in opposition than to find exactly how much opposition there really is, and deal with that. The totals of Mao's post-war purges give absolutely no idea of the extent of opposition to him in China.

But so the God of the Old Testament did it. And there is much of the Old Testament, with its blood sacrifice, its marches into Promised Lands, and above all its reverence for the Lord and His Sword, in Chairman Mao.

He has made one, unsuccessful, attempt to relax his rule. After the death of Stalin, and Krushchev's first steps to allow a bit more free speech in the U.S.S.R., Mao decided to get in step. He propounded his famous slogan, "Let a hundred flowers bloom, let diverse schools of thought contend", and the result alarmed him. Criticism of his leadership came from many parts of the country; criticism which might probably have been of the greatest use to China and her development, but criticism absolutely against the rules. The flowers bloomed for a short time indeed : then the most rigid control was re-imposed.

But all the time, during what must have been the nerve-racking discovery that opposition did exist, despite the earlier purges, Mao had absolute control. In fact, it has been suggested that the hundred flowers relaxation was only a trick to make dissident elements show their hand and be marked down for future liquidation. Krushchev's abandonment of the cult of personality, of the hero worship of the Stalin days, came as an irritation, just when the cult of Maoism was rising to fantastic heights. This, as much as anything, started the cooling of relations between the two countries. But in China, schoolchildren went right on, as they still do, singing songs which run, to western ears, incredibly, but which are gay and rhythmic and popular. "Always hold up the works of Chairman Mao, if you have any questions seek the answers in these works : the more we study them, the more politically conscious we become." Hard, perhaps, to imagine this in any hit parade, but the same could be said of the 23rd Psalm. As I write a hit play is running in Peking called "The Women Pilots". It is about girls who join the Air Force and then, when a male pilot is killed, lose their nerve. The first act ends with a man striding on to the stage, saying, "All training flights suspended so we may learn the lessons of this accident and study the selected works of Mao Tse-tung."

Smash hit.

And so, though one may have personal reservations, Mao

Tse-tung is a hero, and a real one, on a simply colossal scale. More so than any man in history, far more so than Jesus Christ, he has become a gigantic legend in his lifetime. In Christ's time the population of the world, even had it known of Him, was less than the population of Mao's China, which knows everything—everything it ought to know—about God. The worshippers of Mao, willing and unwilling (for there are those who go through the motions just as there are people who go to church to keep up with the Joneses), at this moment outnumber the worshippers of a Christian God. The disproportion is increasing every second.

The Communist Chinese leadership is a group of old men: Mao, Liu Shao-chi, Chou En-lai, Teng Hsiao-ping. As they go, one by one, will the "hundred flowers" be allowed to bloom again? If not, if the absolute worship, the myth of Mao Tse-tung's infallibility and of the perfection of his ideas, is allowed to run on into another generation—ideas like the desirability of nuclear war which will eliminate three hundred million Chinese but leave more than that behind to rule the world—the outlook for all of us, China included, is grim.

There are signs, hopeful signs, that light is creeping in, that the teachings of the man who should have died in 1949, when he was a hero and not yet a god, are being held up to the window, examined more closely.

But whatever happens to Mao and his memory, history will record that, without him, the giant of Asia, flexing muscles, wondering what to do, where to go next, might well be dead.

171

Chapter 13

Francis Chichester

Solitude is a strange companion. One man knows, I suppose, as much about its effects as anyone living.

He wrote—long, long before his testing weeks of loneliness in a sailing boat on the North Atlantic—words which, since schooldays, I have always remembered:

"If man ever flies alone out of the earth's atmosphere into space—to the moon—though he return safely, he will not live. The awful emptiness of space will change his soul and isolate it. Never again will he be able to make contact with man, beast, plant, or anything. And across the gulf of unutterable loneliness, cutting him off from the world he once knew, he will only see distantly through a film of strange, hard air. Perhaps the soul, belonging to space, will have recognized its home and languish in utter loneliness for it, until, loosening its hold on the body, it floats back again."

When those haunting words were written, in 1933, there seemed little chance of any man, in our lifetime, escaping from our atmosphere; far less reaching the moon. Now, all this has changed—and though no one has yet reached the moon, those words of Francis Chichester may well turn out to be true. For all of us have been alone and some of us would agree we change in the process. We return—almost—to normal. But we have suffered a change.

As space trips get longer, we learn more of solitude. In small doses it may be beneficial, may give a chance to get thoughts and feelings in order. The Church has long recognized the fact, and the same principle is clung to in Buddhism, Hinduism, Islam, and others.

My own, very limited, experience of being alone I have found refreshing and unnerving and, although my situation was entirely different, I found myself remembering Chichester's words.

In 1941 I'd attended an Army course in Burmese at London University. Japan was not yet in the war, but everyone knew she would be, that we would soon be meeting her in what was believed to be the huge wet jungle of South-east Asia. We learnt Burmese extremely fast, and not very well, and we sailed for Rangoon—though this was pure chance—on Pearl Harbour day.

We never got there. An earlier convoy arrived just in time to be taken prisoner as it disembarked and the authorities (with, we felt, some reluctance) spared us the fate. We landed in India instead and it was months before any of us had opportunity to exercise our ability with the Burmese tongue. Then, in answer to a request for Burmese speakers to officer a new, irregular formation of Kachin tribesmen in the hills above Myitkyina, I found myself in Burma.

And the first thing I discovered, as the aeroplane which had dumped me in a field took off and headed back for India, was the interesting fact which had been denied G.H.Q.: Kachins don't speak Burmese.

I took over, somehow, a company from a Kachin-speaking Englishman, took over at the same time his library of two books: one was by Pearl S. Buck, the other by Francis Chichester. The Pearl Buck served its purpose; the Chichester —*Seaplane Solo*—was entirely engrossing.

The company was spread out in penny packets for a great many miles, two or three little men with rifles or shot-guns in one place, the next lot half a mile beyond, at a bend in the river, and so on. At my "H.Q." was a small nucleus of sick and spare, none of whom spoke a word of Burmese, or—obviously —English. There can have been few more futile commanders than I—for my men understood nothing of what I told them, and I not a word of theirs.

I learnt—there was no alternative—the Kachin language. But it took months and for most of that time I was totally incommunicado. Not only was I incapable of understanding them and they me, but I hardly ever saw them. As their officer, I was forced by their custom to reside entirely alone in a tiny bamboo hut. Apart from a puzzled Kachin who brought me food and tried, by sign language, to teach me a few of his words, I saw hardly anyone when I was not visiting one or other of the positions on the river. I would occasionally suggest —by sign language—that a slit trench needed deepening or widening or moving, but it was not until my next visit, stumbling my miserable way through a wet, unfriendly forest, that I knew whether or not my instruction had been understood.

And, apart from Pearl Buck and Francis Chichester, I was completely alone—more alone than at any other time of my life. I found myself having long conversations alone, reading Pearl and Francis out loud, singing madly to myself, like Ophelia. When eventually an Englishman tramped three days to come and see me, I was not, as you might expect, bubbling over with conversation, but absolutely and totally tongue-tied. He thought I was mad.

Then, quite suddenly, I found myself talking, fluently and incredibly, the Kachin language, as if I had been mugging it up at night with earphones in my pillow. It was as if—and Chichester's words echoed round my mind—I had returned with a thud from a visit to outer space.

All of which may seem a wild digression from the tale of Francis Chichester—but to me it is not. Having re-read (for I had read it years before as a child) the startling tale of that flight, its loneliness and its fear, at a time when I was both lonely and frightened, and taken heart, I feel I know the man

—though we have never met. But even had I never read a word of his writing—and I commend particularly his autobiography, *The Lonely Sea and the Sky*—I would still include him in my collection on the basis of what he has done.

He is a remarkable man. Born in North Devon at the turn of the century, he emigrated at the age of eighteen to New Zealand. Before this he had survived, not without protest, a conventional public-school upbringing at Marlborough, which he hated. He admitted later that he had made good friends there, but so distressing was school life to him, with its discipline and its food ("the diet was 150 years out of date", though perhaps a world war may have been responsible), that a term or two before his parents had planned he informed his housemaster he was leaving. Real life was flowing, rushing past; he refused to waste any of it as a schoolboy. Already he had made up his mind to emigrate to Australia. His father, when the boy arrived home, was justifiably furious, but the bridge was already burnt: there was nothing that could be done, except book a passage to Australia. But before this was achieved, young Francis met a New Zealand Army sergeant on leave and was persuaded that the smaller chunk of Empire was the better proposition.

Passages to New Zealand were hard to get. While his name was creeping slowly to the front of the waiting-list he took a job, to toughen himself for his adventures, with a farmer in Leicestershire, who paid him five shillings a week. A few months and he was sacked, having taken part in a disastrous and forbidden race with a flat-bottomed dray carrying milk churns drawn by a stallion. Once again he arrived home unannounced and once again his parents were enraged. But now, to all their reliefs, there was little delay in the passage to New Zealand. Towards the end of 1919 he embarked in the steerage of the *Bremen,* a German ship captured during the war. Halfway to New Zealand he joined the crew as a replacement for a stoker who had deserted in Durban. He arrived in Wellington with nine pounds in his pocket from the three weeks' work.

Here he entered and left a series of jobs: farming, coal-mining, timber, gold-prospecting. He decided early on that he

175

stood a better chance of making his fortune in Australia than New Zealand (he was determined to earn £20,000 and go back to England), but each time he was on the point of embarking for Sydney a new job or situation arose, and he stayed. Now, after three abortive attempts to leave the place, he joined up with a man called Geoffrey Goodwin to start a firm of land agents in Wellington.

His life there was profitable (after seven years of the partnership he was able to go back home on a visit with his £20,000) but otherwise not entirely successful. He found, as others starting off in Australia and New Zealand have done, that society "was in sharply defined layers and I had difficulty in distinguishing their fine differences". (A common problem: of the three years I myself spent in Australia, the first months are a remembered nightmare. I insulted, unintentionally, everyone I met, in what I foolishly believed to be a complete democracy and which turned out to be as highly stratified as a Hindu village.) He married in some haste and repented at not too much leisure (his wife after three years went off to live with her family), but he seems to have devoted most of his time to sailing and to building up the land agency. Soon he and Goodwin decided to stop agency work, to sell only their own property. They bought 1,100 acres ten miles from Wellington, planted it judiciously with pine trees (the first 40,000 of which Chichester raised by himself from pine cones in his back yard), built miles of road and started selling building-plots. By the time Chichester was twenty-six his income had risen to £10,000 a year, and the partnership had spread to embrace a great many strange bed-fellows, including among their number the faintly surprising "Goodwin-Chichester Aviation Company".

It was the failure of the hired pilots to cope with the firm's two Avro Avians that spurred Chichester to learn how to do it himself. And it is here—to my mind—that the first inkling of the real man becomes apparent. He was not a good pupil; he was a rotten pupil. Many others after fifteen hours of dual instruction would have given the whole thing up in despair. By December, 1928, he had logged the very large figure of eighteen hours fifteen minutes without being considered good enough to go solo—but he refused to give up. A few months later, still unfledged, he decided to go to England for a visit. And, incredible as it may seem, *fly* back to New Zealand solo. It would be good publicity for the Goodwin-Chichester partnership.

He went back to England, bought himself a Gipsy I Moth which weighed 880 pounds unloaded. He had at last managed to go solo with a final five-and-a-half hours under instruction at Brooklands and now, as far as Francis Chichester was concerned, the way was clear for him to fly back as far as Sydney. New Zealand, because of the wide Tasman Sea, was unattainable. The fact that only one other person in history had succeeded in getting solo and airborne to Sydney, the Australian pilot Bert Hinkler, was beside the point. He took off for a jaunt around the continent of Europe, to get the feel of his new craft.

The continental trip was encouraging. On 20 December, 1929, he set off on the long trip to Sydney. He found it hard to understand why everyone who waved good-bye looked so glum, why so many had done their best to dissuade him.

We have little time for the details of this remarkable trip but it was satisfactorily completed, to the world's surprise, on 31 January, 1930. The route had been from Brooklands via Pisa, Tripoli, Karachi, Calcutta, Singapore, Batavia and Darwin (and a few other intermediate fuelling stops), and its only delay had been at Tripoli where he broke a propeller landing in the dark. The Italian Air Force, which entertained him while another was fetched from England, suggested, on hearing that this skinny, bespectacled Englishman had already inside four months smashed three of them, that he get them made of rubber. The one that arrived, in the fullness of time, was nevertheless made of wood and with this firmly screwed to the front of his tiny aircraft Francis Chichester took off and arrived at Sydney.

Delighted, but not surprised, over his success, he sat straight down and wrote—or rather dictated, for he needed the money and there was no time to spare—his first book, *Seaplane Solo*. Which is where I, aged ten or eleven, first made his acquaintance. The depression had hit New Zealand as hard as most other places; every penny that could be earned to keep the partnership from collapse was urgently needed. *Solo to Sydney* helped do that.

The book was a success—and most people would have been content to leave long-distance flying at that. But no: Chichester, because no one had yet flown the Tasman Sea, which separates New Zealand from Australia and is two-thirds the width of the Atlantic, decided to make the attempt. This, in fact, was a far more hazardous trip than the one he had completed. There was no question of his getting the little Gipsy Moth across so large an expanse of water, for it could not possibly carry enough fuel. And even if he had felt able to buy the much larger plane needed, no such thing was obtainable in New Zealand.

But there are islands—precious few—in the Tasman Sea, and he worked out that by flying from New Zealand to Norfolk Island, 481 miles north-west, then another 561 miles to Lord Howe Island, which is 480 miles north-east of Sydney, he could, in theory, do it.

There were two snags. Firstly, it was impossible to land an aeroplane on either island. Secondly, the tiny blob of Norfolk Island, attacked from the northern tip of New Zealand, allowed for only half a degree error in navigation. The smallest "target" of this sort which had ever been aimed at was the Hawaii group from San Francisco. And this allowed seven degrees: fourteen times the error.

The problem, men agreed, was totally insurmountable, and it was high time this young businessman, blind without thick glasses—a chap who ought to be back in Wellington selling trees or whatever he did—gave up flying. As far as the Tasman Sea was concerned, he would be taking off on an ill-planned, inartistic suicide: there were no such things as radio aids, and dead reckoning, where an unexpected wind could put a small plane off course by as much as thirty degrees, would be ridiculous. The only way would be, as in a ship, "shooting the sun" by sextant and altering course accordingly. But naturally no one could use a sextant and fly a small aeroplane at the same time.

But, of course, Chichester did. He bought himself a sextant with a built-in horizon in the form of a spirit-level and, to the consternation of many, spent hours shooting the warm New Zealand sun from his speeding motor-car, one hand on the wheel, the other holding a sextant to his eye, while dogs, bicycles and puzzled pedestrians sprang from his path. And this was not all: in between the cross-country drives came long runs, with Chichester pounding through the green of suburban Wellington in shorts and gym-shoes, keeping track of his progress with a sextant.

As for the little problem of not being able to land on either of his islands—even should he find them—that would be solved by fitting a couple of floats to the undercarriage. Gipsy Moth would become a seaplane.

And so, converted into a rather unwieldy flying motor-boat, Chichester's plane took off from the northern tip of New Zealand in a shower of spray and aimed north-west.

He made his landfall and dropped Gipsy Moth into a sheltered cove off Norfolk Island. A little later, flushed with success, he took off, again plotting a course while he flew, so that he reached Lord Howe Island and startled its inhabitants as much as those of Norfolk. Here, though, luck deserted him. While he slept in the house of an hospitable resident, waiting for take-off the next morning, a squall got up and completely wrecked his moored plane. There was nothing to be done but salvage what he could of the wreck and take the pieces on to Sydney in the hope that, some day, a new Gipsy Moth could be assembled, phoenix-like, from the wreckage of the old. Plus, of course, a great many new bits. Like, for a start, four new wings.

But the more Chichester thought of this, the more determined he grew not to arrive by steamer. He would rebuild the plane himself—even to the four thousand separate pieces of wood needed in the wings, and he would damn well fly the thing to Sydney.

He did—with a guts and patience which make Robert Bruce's spider look a coward—(the work took over two months shaping little pieces of wood and metal)—and he was awarded nothing for his patience. He did, though, get the coveted Johnston Memorial Trophy for "The Best Feat of Navigation in the British Empire" for finding his two islands. In fact, the system Chichester developed on this flight was adopted years later by R.A.F. Coastal Command.

This trip across the Tasman had become in his mind only the start of a trip right round the world, and with business bad in New Zealand he would be contributing rather more to the partnership of Goodwin and Chichester by selling the story than he would by trying to sell land in Wellington. The next stage, then, which followed almost immediately, in 1931 and was very nearly his last flight, became the first solo long-distance flight ever made in a seaplane and the first-ever solo flight—in anything—from Australia to Japan. But a spectacular crash into Japanese telephone wires put paid, for ever, to Gipsy Moth and nearly did the same for her master. After a long spell in a Japanese hospital, Francis Chichester travelled on to England by sea.

And perhaps it is now that the truth of his earlier theory of man's loneliness unfitting him for the world he knows, begins to come home to him. He visits his parents in North Devon, stays with them and finds himself an utter misfit: "I was a different person since they had previously seen me." But with cousins who ask him to stay he is on firmer ground. When, eventually, he gets himself lodgings near them, fearful lest his welcome runs out, he is able to start work on the book of the Tasman crossing which is to stave off, a little longer, the financial troubles of the partnership. During this working holiday in England he is presented with his Johnston Prize by the Prince of Wales. By now he has become in many ways a New Zealander and he is bitter and angry at the way English people seem to know and care so little for Australia and New Zealand. Later, he admitted things had changed—"but by then, Britain had missed the bus".

Back to New Zealand and the partnership, slowly recovering from the slump. Chichester was beginning to lose some of the fierce ambition, to enjoy himself reading and sailing and fishing. This doldrum lasted four years: by 1936 he had persuaded a friend, John Herrick, to join him in a trip to England by Puss Moth.

This really *is* his last long-distance flight. They take off light-heartedly and have a savage accident at Baghdad, where

Herrick, in the dark, walks into the spinning airscrew and has his arm nearly severed.

Herrick is an old man, and he makes no progress at all in the Cairo hospital to which the authorities have sent him. Chichester demands his release, loads him up again and flies him, flat out, to England. There he makes a complete recovery.

In England Chichester marries again. But his wife, Sheila, try as she will, cannot learn to love the New Zealand to which he takes her. They return—for keeps—to England. And by this time war is almost on them, and Chichester almost forty. It breaks out and he is refused entry into the R.A.F. on those grounds, but very soon he is Chief Navigation Officer to the Empire Flying Training School. Here he does remarkable work on the difficult problem of low-level fighter navigation.

At the end of the war, determined to be his own boss, he decides to start making toy aeroplanes and, with them, air games, based on his navigational lectures. The idea, still-born through shortage of the right materials, slithers into one for making jigsaw puzzles. He starts to glue the maps he abortively produced for "Pinpoint the Bomber" on to cardboard and cut them up. As the maps are—painfully slowly—used up, he draws others.

Then one day a man walks into his office and says: "This picture map of London is the best I've seen. Take it off this lousy piece of cardboard and I'll order five thousand."

And so Francis Chichester, one of Britain's most successful map publishers, gets into it, by accident, as he nears fifty. At the same time he develops an urge to take up ocean-racing—by boat. He buys a small second-hand yacht, christens it Gipsy Moth II, and begins to spend his spare time racing—from Harwich to Rotterdam, Cowes to Corunna, anywhere where others will race him.

And then, just when his enthusiasm for the sport has joined itself to the new successes of his map business so that he is able to order himself a new boat, *Gipsy Moth III*, he is told he has cancer of the lung.

An operation is prescribed—but Sheila steps in and refuses to allow it. He is weak from worry and overwork, she says; it will kill him. Together they resist the demands of the surgeon.

Now, sick and unhappy, he is buoyed up by Sheila's courage, reinforcing his own, as each grim prognosis is offered and rejected. He forces himself away from England, takes Sheila to the South of France. And here, suddenly ill again, he falls into the hands of a remarkable little man, Dr. Jean Mattei. He undergoes a novel form of treatment with the doctor, goes sailing with his blessing. At the same time all his friends are contacted by Sheila and asked to pray for him.

And this prayer, perhaps more than anything else, Chichester holds responsible for the miraculous fact that, within thirty-two months of being taken ill with a mortal disease, he crossed the starting line for the toughest race ever run.

The idea of a race, solo, across the Atlantic from England to New York, was Colonel "Blondie" Hasler's. He had been a wartime hero, leading canoes up the Garonne to Bordeaux to sink ships in the harbour by attaching limpet mines to them; conducting commando raids of an astonishing audacity up and down the enemy-held coast. Chichester had seen his notice on the board of the Royal Ocean Racing Club just before he was admitted to hospital for what seemed likely to be the last time. But he defeated his disease, as we have seen, and on his return, cured, from the South of France, he decided to enter and pit himself, once again, against loneliness and fear.

With Hasler, he organized the race down to the last detail. There were serious motives behind the idea, motives which appealed to him, overshadowing its sheer impertinence. (For no one had ever sailed the Atlantic alone in either direction, and no one had ever raced a yacht, however large its crew, across that ocean from east to west, the "uphill" way, against current and trade wind.) Hasler's idea, which Chichester shared, was that sailing was still far too complicated: if competitors in such a race were more or less set adrift, alone, they would have to devise ways of making life easier. In a trip which would take considerably more than a month, a competitor would have to find ways of letting his craft steer itself while he slept. And perhaps someone would simplify the various complicated and archaic processes for meeting the different velocities and angles of wind. All this changing of sails, with mainsail, jib, spinnaker, and trysail being substituted for each other; it was rather like approaching the bottom of a steep hill in one's car, getting out, jacking up the rear end and replacing the wheels with smaller ones for greater power.

But perhaps most important of all was the supreme test of man's spirit. For to go right on—for weeks—making all the adjustments needed, adjustments without which a yacht would drop to the rear of any procession, would take guts and tremendous reserves of moral power.

The race had fired Chichester's imagination as nothing before; here at last was a *real* challenge. He arranged for Sheila to take over the map firm while he prepared *Gipsy Moth III*. The number of competitors grew to five: Hasler, Lewis, Howells, the Frenchman Jean Lacombe, and Chichester himself, and in the weeks before the starter's pistol they independently worked out methods of steering their craft while they slept. Chichester based his on the model boats he used to watch on Sunday mornings at the Round Pond in London. If a small boy could so lash and adjust the tiller of his model that it sailed right across the pond instead of floundering about in the middle, Chichester could do the same thing and get a full-size boat across the Atlantic. He devised a sail for the stern which would weathercock with the wind and in the process rotate its own small mast. At the foot of this were two arms which moved with it and could be clamped tight in any position. To these arms he attached ropes, fastened these to the tiller.

With the boat keeping a steady course, the little sail (he called her, with her associated ropes and spars, "Miranda") would stay fixed, and the tiller, once set, would be undisturbed.

But if the boat changed its heading, the wind would blow against Miranda's side and she would move. The tiller would in turn be moved, and the rudder would bring the boat back on its original heading.

A simple idea, remarkably effective. But Miranda needed practice, trial, error and adjustment, before she was ready to sail for New York.

At last, on 11 June, 1960, Chichester and his four opponents set sail. *Gipsy Moth III* was the largest—much too large, as he discovered, to be ideal for such a solo voyage—but it was the only boat he had; and the other, smaller ones got away much quicker. Remembering—the businessman as ever—financial successes of earlier Chichester trips, he started writing a diary almost immediately. For this we must be grateful, for it gives a remarkable, gust by gust, description.

The instructions for all competitors had been simple in the extreme: "Leave the Melampus Buoy to starboard; thence by any route to the Ambrose light vessel, New York." (The Melampus is close to the starting line in Plymouth.) Great circles, which are circles on the surface of the globe whose planes pass through its centre, are the shortest distance between any two points, however curved and interminable they may appear on a flat map, but they have their disadvantages. The one joining Plymouth with New York is beset with fog and icebergs, even in midsummer, for it descends over its last thousand miles or so past the coasts of Newfoundland and Nova Scotia. There is also, as one travels east to west, a head-on Atlantic current to be battled against for two thousand miles before one meets the favourable Labrador Current off Cape Race, Newfoundland. But Chichester decided that the very shortness of his route— three thousand miles—would permit him to heave-to for twelve foggy periods of twelve hours each and still beat a competitor on the longer, warmer southern route, the old windjammer route down to the Canaries, along the trade-wind belt to the West Indies and up to New York.

Gipsy Moth III was nearly forty feet long and fifty-five feet high to the tip of her mast. She had been built for a crew of six, there were six berths, and many doubted whether a solitary man, least of all an ageing, short-sighted one snatched so recently from the jaws of death, could sail it for any distance at all. Francis Chichester had no doubts, but his Miranda worried him. She seemed to need a small gale to operate her, and then, when she worked, the all-important clamp which joined her, via arms, mast, ropes and tiller, to the rudder, came adrift. But gradually she was refined, and by the time the three of them (for so, in the diary, they almost seem, a good-natured trio: Chichester, Gipsy, Miranda) pass the starting point and head along their great circle bearing of 275 degrees, he is happy about them all.

184

Almost immediately, he is flung from side to side, soaked to the skin, pelted with the contents of his cabin, made seasick. A gale gets up and he has to furl his huge 385-square-foot sail of heavy terylene, lash its boom to a deck which is at right angles to the foaming surface of the sea, set the smaller trysail in its place. He injures himself when a door bursts open and a little later he does it again. Thirty-six hours out from Plymouth, at two a.m., he is on deck in a howling gale, congratulating himself on the working of Miranda, when the boat turns round 180 degrees and heads for home. Gently, he puts her back on course. He is unfailingly cheerful, making himself little cups of tea in a wildly plunging cabin, having occasional nips of whisky or Guinness, writing it all down in an exuberant, schoolboy prose in his diary. He is as excited now as when he began that solo flight from England to Australia, but how much more comfortable *this* is, with fish frying in the corner. He may be lonely, and he will be so for a very long time, but there is room to turn round. He is a little tired—most men would have been utterly exhausted—but he thinks of the other competitors in their more manoeuvrable small boats, "cracking on sail", and he makes up his mind to keep awake and change his rig for the maximum advantage.

A day later he has decided this is the slowest race, anywhere, on record. The B.B.C. tells him of the progress of the others (one has returned to Plymouth for a new mast) and he calculates that he himself has travelled a mere 186 miles in three days. The bad weather has hindered him more than the others (though, of course, he still has a mast) because his sails are so heavy that a change takes a long time. There is no mention of his age or his health: his problem, which he faces cheerfully, humorously, is that his boat is just too damn big. At the rate he is going, he doesn't expect to reach New York before autumn.

And so the long, lone journey goes on. He gets to know himself, the problems of dressing when unable to stand up in a storm, of always wearing wet clothes, changing from one set of soaking garments to another, of hanging on to his wildly bucking craft by his finger-nails to change the rigging. He takes a couple of fixes from radio beacons with his receiver, but he is soon out of range and has to rely for his position on the tried and trusted sextant. He consoles himself for the time-wasting business of sail-changing on a big boat when he considers how the others will fare in this weather in boats of five tons and less, when he has nearly broken a rib being flung about his stately thirteen-tonner.

At night it is a queer, queer feeling charging through mist and fog with only a hundred yards or so of visibility. Particularly when one's masthead and navigation lights have been smashed in a storm. He lights a Tilley lamp, keeps watch "like an anxious hen fussing over its chick".

His radio transmitter has a range of a hundred miles, so it is of little use. He hears a Pan-American clipper calling up all yachts from somewhere above him, but he has no luck with his reply. He realizes that Sheila, who is expecting news of him —surely he would be in range of a ship?—will not learn anything of him at all. In fact she learns nothing until the last days of the race, but her faith is undimmed and she travels across the ocean herself to greet him on arrival.

He is talking cheerfully to himself and he considers carefully over a glass of whisky which is suddenly hurled from his hand whether this is in fact talking to oneself or thinking out loud. Alone in the North Atlantic, the problem seems suddenly important. To his delight, he finds a moth on board, takes it carefully into the cabin and makes it comfortable.

By the beginning of July he is nearing Newfoundland and radio signals from there cheer him. But he has no means of replying. Whales appear—four of them only fifteen feet away, one of which he can prod with a boathook—while he is fishing. For these are the Grand Banks, famous fishing corner of the ocean, and he has no intention of passing them without baiting a line. He is also right in the middle of the iceberg zone and although there are less of these monsters in July than in June, the risk is very great. And he is bitterly cold.

The trip—though he doesn't say so—has left its mark on him. He has realized that a single-handed yacht with a self-steering device can never compete with a fully-crewed one. Wind direction, wind speed, are constantly changing, and the trim of sails, the sails themselves and the boat's course all need to be changed constantly to get the maximum benefit from it.

He wonders how "Blondie" Hasler is getting on with his one-sailed neo-Chinese junk. Had he twice the strength, twice the endurance and twice "what it takes", he would have changed sails many more times than he did.

Another frightful storm on the night of 5-6 July and, with belt clipped to a halliard, he is clinging for dear life as he pulls down the mainsail. *Gipsy Moth* is tearing through the darkness, rushing into a black nothing ahead, and his shadow, a giant shadow, is thrown back, by Tilley lamp, to the fog behind.

Suddenly, on 8 July, he contacts Cape Race by radio. The operator—"very patient"—takes down a message for his wife.

At this point he makes a bad mistake which could easily have been fatal. He works out a position from a chart of the wrong scale which happens to be sticking out from under the one he is working on. As a result, he nearly runs aground in bad weather on one of the worst coasts in the world.

Eventually, cheerful, undaunted and, as it turns out, only ten pounds lighter (but with a frame as lean as Chichester's one wonders where the ten came from), he rounds the light vessel, the Ambrose Light outside New York. It is five-thirty in the evening, 21 July. His race is over, forty days, eleven hours and thirty minutes from the time he heard the starter's gun off Plymouth. He has travelled, entirely alone, 4,004½ miles.

The old man—and he is, compared with the others—has won. Blondie Hasler arrives later, after forty-eight days, to be second: the others, day by day, trickle in.

For most of us, this would be the end. A satisfying end to a great achievement.

But not, of course, for Francis Chichester. He had won the first single-handed Transatlantic Race—but his time disappointed him. No sooner had he analysed the lessons, and they were many, of his race than he was preparing to do it again by himself. This second time he would be racing, not against Hasler, Lacombe and the rest, he would be sailing against Francis Chichester. For he knew he could beat that time of forty days, get it down to less than a month. He made changes in *Gipsy*'s rig, altered her from a sloop (with only one foresail) to a cutter (with two), replaced her wooden mast with one made of metal.

187

And on 1 June, 1962, just under two years from the day he sailed out from Plymouth under a wooden mast, he sailed again under a metal one, determined to beat his earlier time—*and* beat thirty days.

He failed to beat the thirty—but his thirty-three days, fifteen hours, seven minutes set an all-time record for a sailing-boat, single-handed *or crewed*, from England to America. Congratulations poured in from all over the world; one was from John Kennedy in the White House, ardent sailor himself.

And in this lone journey Francis Chichester, who had pondered the advantages of finding out day by day just where each competitor was, tested a new system of radio communication which proved able to do just this. For the 1962 trip was only a prelude to the big race of 1964.

In this race, with the eyes of the world now on it, there were fifteen competitors from England, Denmark and France. Two others from the U.S.A. had bad luck in fitting out and had to be scratched.

This time, as before, Chichester was by a long way the oldest man taking part: he was sixty-three. Yet he had more experience of sailing single-handed than any man in the world. Right from the start his position was followed with excitement by the whole world.

But this time the race was won by the young Frenchman, Tabarly, in the time of twenty-seven days, three hours, fifty-six minutes. He was half Chichester's age and his boat had been specifically designed for this sort of race, but it was a remarkable performance, and Chichester, when they radioed him the news, was the first to send his congratulations. By now, with Tabarly over the finishing line, the race had become, again, Chichester against himself. Could he do what he'd set his heart on, make it in thirty days?

And with just three minutes to go before those thirty days were up *Gipsy Moth III* crossed the finishing line.

And so as one pauses to consider time rushing past, and with it age, one has but to think of a slight, elderly figure behind its thick glasses fighting not only time and age but the greatest perils of the North Atlantic in utter loneliness—as it fought and repelled death. And one is ashamed.

Chapter 14

Edgar Christian

It was a dreadful, English seaside, week. It had rained without stop, the leaden sky and water seemed joined together with an horizontal ring of darker glue, and a cold wet wind crept in from the Atlantic. It became more comfortable to immerse oneself in the icy Cornish sea than to sit or stand at the edge.

In fact, the only moderately dry and warm place in our grey seaside resort, in that dismal post-war summer, was the cheerless inside of the wood-and-asbestos cottage we had rented, unseen, for the fortnight. Grimly we resolved never to make the mistake again: all bathing in future would be done in the local public-baths, or on the lawn at home, with a hose. Yet we had paid, and considerably, for our cottage and we used it, in all its horror, with determination. The few books we had brought with us—there would be little time for reading at the seaside—were consumed within forty-eight hours, and we began systematically, like worms, working through the dog-eared volumes on the shelf in the kitchen.

And it was then that I stumbled across him. I picked up the least-well-cared-for book, a slim, scruffy thing about six inches by four with the remains of what had once been a hard cover. Opposite page 142, the last page of narrative which preceded a short appendix—a curt appendix, beginning, "Sir, I have the honour to report"—was a very small snapshot, occupying less than half the page, a snapshot of three crosses, entitled "The Graves of the Victims". Obviously it had not been good enough to enlarge.

Opposite the book's first page was a rather better photograph, looking as if it had been excised from a school cricket group, of Edgar Christian, a good-looking, manly-looking boy of about seventeen with stiff fair hair, plastered down for the photograph, and protruding ears. He was wearing an open-necked white shirt.

Two things strike one immediately about the boy's photograph. Firstly, boys don't look like that any longer. The shirt is a perfectly ordinary cricket shirt, the haircut is a perfectly ordinary haircut of the pre-Beatle type. No—there is something about the face, the expression, the state of mind behind it, which is way, way pre-war. It dates from an era when right was right and wrong was the other and no one had any doubts about it, even when they were mistaken. When young men knew they were just that: young men, junior members of mankind, modestly aware of their lack of seniority in the club, but at the same time aware of their potential, aware that the years would slip by and that they would soon be as good as, probably better than, their elders. They were not teenagers, a separate sex; they were not even adolescents. They were men.

But—and secondly—quite apart from this feeling of an era, stamped on the intelligent, stubby face, a look one might probably have seen on every other face in the Dover College cricket photo, there is something different, quite personal.

It is hard, very hard, to explain, but it is there. If I try to describe it, the best I can do is a look of sensitive ferocity. It is as if he has just been punched hard on the nose by a much bigger boy and is on the verge of tears, but is collecting himself to deliver a right to the point of the jaw.

Sadly, the book, published by John Murray, in London,

under the title *Unflinching, a Diary of Tragic Adventure,* is no longer in print. It is hard to borrow a copy from a public library, but if you possibly can it will reward you immensely. As for me, it is, quite simply, the most moving book I have read. I devoured the first dozen pages standing up in the seaside cottage before I realized I'd done so. Then I lowered myself, still reading, into a chair. I finished the book in that chair, with its broken leg, an hour later, and so spent was I by the experience that I went alone for a long walk in the rain along the sea-front.

Absence, they say, makes the heart grow fonder, and I look back on that corner of Cornwall with something approaching affection: the weather was indescribable, the cottage also, but all this has been mercifully blurred by time: the tale of Edgar Christian is as poignant as the day I read it.

He was born on a day which was to become famous for quite a different reason, many years after he had perished in the frozen north of Canada. His birthday on 6 June would even have a film named after it—but Christian's June was that of 1908, not 1944, and he was six years old when the *First* World War broke out. That was a war in which his father, Lieutenant-Colonel Christian, was to receive the D.S.O. Some hundreds of years before this, a kinsman, Fletcher Christian, led a mutiny on His Majesty's Ship *Bounty*.

So it's hardly surprising that a life of adventure would appeal to the boy. He counted himself lucky to have as a relative—his mother's first cousin—John Hornby, who had made a name for himself as explorer and hunter in the remotest, unexplored parts of northern Canada. He had admired Hornby from a distance since early childhood and so, after leaving Dover College in 1925 and doing work on a farm to fit himself for a future as yet uncertain, he was delighted to meet the man, his own cousin, in the flesh. It was the winter of 1925-26, and Hornby was home on leave from Canada.

The explorer had always prided himself on being a judge of men. Immediately on meeting Christian he realized this was a remarkable youth—one who might benefit from an expedition to the uncharted north and one whose company Hornby would certainly enjoy. One of his theories was that only men with blue eyes are capable of taking the full rigours of northern life: his interest in the boy was clinched by the realization that his eyes were a piercing, icy blue.

Young Edgar Christian was flattered, delighted. The two left England in April of 1926.

They duly landed in Montreal and thence, via Ottawa, Toronto and Winnipeg, they made their way to Edmonton, the base from which they would set out to winter on the Thelon River and then, when spring came, explore a route eastward from Great Slave Lake, just a few miles south of the Arctic Circle, into Hudson Bay. A long trip, as you will see if you look at a map, and over terrain as inhospitable as any in the world. Hornby had promised (and forgotten the promise) to take another man with him, a man of twenty-eight, the next time he went on an expedition. (Hornby was about forty.) Quite by chance and somewhat to his annoyance, they met again at Edmonton. Hornby asked his young cousin if he minded having another with them and the boy was delighted. "I don't mind a bit," he wrote, "because he is a nice chap and will be more company and makes it so I am not the only greenhorn in the camp."

Harold Adlard had been in the Air Force during the war, had met Hornby at some stage and received his promise. When they next met, in Edmonton, Hornby saw at a glance that the other was drifting, making a failure of life. The kindest of men, he offered to fulfil his promise—and was accepted.

The three set off in high spirits and although Edgar Christian's diary does not begin for many months—or if it did the early part has been lost—we get a clear and vivid picture of their trip north from his last posted letter, on 7 June. They are at Fort Smith on the Slave River, nearing Great Slave Lake. We learn that they "left the hotel in an awful rush" and caught the train, in the nick of time, from Edmonton to a place called Waterways. This, on the map, is 300 miles to the north. It is a goods train, with a solitary coach for passengers, and with it they get to Waterways and unload their canoe.

We learn from Edgar's long letter to his parents that they paddle and portage their way, meeting colourful communities of Indians, some of whom remember Hornby with affection from earlier visits as much as a dozen years before. This fascinates Edgar and through all the letter and the subsequent diary runs this note of admiration, hero-worship, for Hornby.

The letter was posted and duly reached Colonel and Mrs. Christian. But Edgar began his diary three months after posting it, so we have no idea how the trio spent the months of July, August, September. We do know from the diary (it begins on 14 October, 1926) that by this time they are living in a small log cabin on the Thelon River, about seventy miles downstream of its junction with the smaller Hanbury. The hut had been built earlier by trappers who spent a time in the area, and it was a hundred yards from the river bank. Whether they had known of its existence or whether they had stumbled on it, we do not know, but the place was in a fair state of repair. Under the leadership of the experienced older man, the two greenhorns get to work laying a floor, building a porch and a wood-shed, and banking up the north side as a defence against winds—winds which, in a few months' time, will be bringing temperatures of fifty and more below zero.

But as soon as the diary opens, one senses all is not well. There can have been no success at all in the business, so dear to Hornby's heart, of living off the land. On 18 October, "Jack returned in the evening with glad news, having seen thirty Caribou on a distant ridge behind camp, so tomorrow we go all out in last effort for winter's grub". All out. Last effort. It sounds bad—and it is.

The temperature is still fairly warm: 24 degrees Fahrenheit. There is little wind.

By the 21st, the temperature has dropped to eight degrees. They have been going round their traps and they have caught nothing. They have managed to lay in a very small supply of meat—ptarmigan, hare—and as they have brought some flour and other essentials they are still optimistic. The temperature fluctuates wildly; sudden blizzards descend on them and they are unable to leave the hut. Then the sun shines, snow and wind cease, and (27 November) it is "a fine day, but we are all taking life easy to economize on grub".

Fine or not, the temperature has already dropped to minus fifteen degrees. And there are no caribou.

193

Five days later it has dropped to minus thirty-seven. Sixty-nine degrees of frost.

By December there is no doubt at all of their predicament. "Now we must throw up trapping and practically den up and get hold of any grub we can without creating big appetite by hunting on short cold days." A day later they work out that they have enough "little fish" for fourteen days, at the rate of two per day. "Then we have a hundred pounds of flour between us till spring when Caribou ought to come again." They make holes in the ice and hopefully lower lines, and in the process Edgar freezes his knee and is unable to use the leg for several days. He is upset, terribly upset, that he is not contributing enough during these days to the struggle for survival and he says so, but by 16 December he is able to move again and goes out in search—yet another futile search—for the elusive Caribou, with the capital C he always gives it, which was to have fed them, by Hornby's disastrous miscalculation, throughout the winter. He sees nothing. But, "having no fish, we had foxes for supper and they certainly seemed exceptionally good". This is one of the foxes they have trapped, earlier, for its skin, one of the skins they had hoped to sell in the spring to pay for their expedition. Its body, undecayed in the sub-zero weather, makes good eating.

They are to find in the next hideous months that their agony, their life, is prolonged, week after week, by the rediscovery of entrails, fish-heads, bones and skins which they have left outside. All three, in their separate ways, are worried, but Edgar manages, unlike the other two, to be completely aware of the situation and its probable outcome, and yet invincibly brave and cheerful. On Xmas Day, his last Xmas, he "enjoyed the feast as much as any, although we have nothing in sight for tomorrow's breakfast". They have eaten "rich Bannock I enjoyed as much as turkey". He hopes "everyone in England has enjoyed today".

Most days they manage to trap or shoot something—something pitifully small, like a ptarmigan—and on 3 January Edgar finds, under a tree, "a very welcome addition to the larder, fourteen white fish we had thrown there for bait if wanted".

194

But on 6 January we at last get some insight into what must be going on: the tension, the fear, in the little log cabin. "Harold went for a walk up the creek—said nothing all morning before going and never spoke for some time after coming in——"

22 January: eighty-six degrees of frost—minus fifty-four degrees Fahrenheit.

On 1 February they have "a great day of feasting". Somehow, they have found and shot a caribou. Morale rises, though Edgar's seems hardly to have dipped, and "now we have grub on hand things are better and gives one a chance to have a good square meal, even if we go shy a little later on".

By the 9th, they are out of meat, even ptarmigan, but Hornby manages to find a little frozen blood, "which makes a great mixture with floor". Harold Adlard has by now frozen his nose and is staying in all the time, until the 19th, when "Harold is at last getting out and cutting wood which relieves the burden considerably". But on the 22nd, Harold refuses, when asked by Jack Hornby, to cut wood at all. They are all feeling, for the first time, the insidious effects of malnutrition, and Edgar stays indoors, smashing bones for grease, "feeling rotten, and Jack is in the same condition, but took a look for ptarmigan, seeing none".

March comes in, miserably. They find a hare in a trap, the occasional fish set aside, months ago, for bait; they shoot the occasional small, thin, meatless ptarmigan. By the 26th they are starting to eat the wolverine skins—just the skins, the meat went long ago—which they had planned, all those incredibly distant months ago, to sell. Edgar is still cheerful. "We can keep on till Caribou come North and then what feasting we can have." They are having two meals a day, of hide.

And now—the beginning of the end. There have been references to Jack Hornby's leg which has been giving trouble. By 2 April, "Jack is suffering agonies".

"4 April. I now write today's diary as far as it goes to make sure of it. Jack during night decided that as the weather seemed milder he should make an effort to get in Caribou guts from Barrens as his leg is getting worse and he feels it is the last day he can move on no more grub than we have without eating

Wolverine. Harold dug up fish scraps and bones from bait pile and cooked them up. Meanwhile I rested and Jack kept on saying he would be all in and absolutely crocked when he eventually got home again and that we would have to carry on. What a mental strain it was. I felt homesick as never before and hope to God they know not what Jack is suffering——"

By 6 April, Harold Adlard, the weakest member of the party, is beginning to go out of his mind. He complains of the weather, refuses to go out, feels ill. "Jack had to curse Harold eventually to stop his carrying on and it was like water on a duck's back. He is very queer at times now——"

He is indeed. He shuffles in and out of the hut, never still, looking—exactly like a chicken—for scraps of food. Jack Hornby meanwhile is on his deathbed, in great pain, and "I rub his legs and body at times to relieve him. Harold is an awful worry continually saying how bad he is. As far as looks go, the fittest of the bunch of us, but he is too damned afraid of himself and consequently plays another person out. I am feeling all right, but weak of course to do heavy work and walking. Tonight we have to cut up the best pelt of all, to eat, a Beautiful Wolverine, and then we have 4 more——"

Jack sinks fast, fighting bravely. They are beginning to suffer agonies in trying to eliminate waste from their bodies, because they have eaten little other than chopped bones and skin for weeks, and the two form hard, absolutely indigestible balls inside, which cannot be dislodged. They start passing blood. Harold, ordered out by Jack to find the caribou gut pile, sees a live caribou in the distance so comes back and says he won't dig for the guts—they are bound to get a caribou soon. They never see another.

Jack Hornby probably never learns of this insubordination. On 16 April he dies. And now Harold Adlard, who has been an ever-increasing burden, comes, for a short time, into his own. Edgar is shattered by the tragedy, but Harold, in a last surge of courage, comforts him, brings him "tea and aspirin to help along" and they weather what is not only a personal tragedy but their own death sentence. For without the knowledge and greater experience of Hornby they stand—even if the weather should miraculously improve—very little chance.

On 21 April, Harold is "very bad, but I don't think any worse, thank God, for he overstrained his whole system in helping me when I was left alone at Jack's death".

And so the pitiful tale goes on. Harold is becoming ever weaker, with Edgar looking after him, scratching for fish scraps and cooking them for him, worried—desperately—that he is out too often, scavenging, not giving Harold enough attention.

Harold dies on the 4 May. Before he dies they have between them devised from a test-tube a primitive and dangerous enema, in an attempt to shift some of the clotted bones and hide within their systems, which is giving them agony. After Harold's death, Edgar writes, "I write all this down as I think it is of importance seeing how suddenly Harold and Jack went ill, but I must stick to my guns and endeavour to cure myself now——"

He exists on fish scraps and hide, writing with amazing cheerfulness of his predicament. Soon he is unable to walk, can only crawl, and perversely enough finds quite a lot of food at this level; pieces of fish-head, chips of flesh frozen hard. But now he is no longer hungry.

Edgar Christian's last entry is on 1 June, just five days before the nineteenth birthday he never attained. "I have grub on hand but weaker than I have ever been in my life and no migration North of birds or animals——"

He had been out crawling the day before and—but it was just too late—found "fish and meat in plenty and greasy gut fat on insides of Foxes and Wolverines, containing liver and hearts, kidneys and lights and one fox carcase. All this I cooked up, leaving the hide as a cache. I ate all I could and got rid of much foul food from my system, apparently been stopping me walking.

"At 2 a.m. went to bed feeling content and bowl full of fish by me to eat in the morning.

"9 a.m. Weaker than ever. Have eaten all I can. Have food on hand but heart peatering (sic). Sunshine is bright now. See if that does any good to me if I get out and bring in wood to make fire tonight.

"Make preparations now.

"Got out, too weak and all in now. Left things late."

The appendix of the book is the Official Report of Inspector Trundle of the Great Slave Lake Sub-Division, Royal Canadian Mounted Police. It is a dry, policeman's report, but it describes in pitiless detail how the Mounties, guided by a trappers' report, found the cabin a little over two years later, at the end of July, 1929. The bodies of Hornby and Adlard had been carefully stitched into blankets and laid outside the hut. The body of Edgar Christian was lying on a bunk. Among the bits and pieces left (and everything inflammable, including floorboards, had been used to light the fire) was a pot-bellied stove. On top of this was a scrap of paper with the almost illegible words:

"Who . . .
    Look in
    Stove."

And inside the stove, tucked away from the rain and the wind which have invaded the hut, was the diary, ending so bravely on that 1 June, 1927. With it was a scribbled will of Hornby's and a few last letters the three had written home.

The diary, stained but still legible in its sturdy schoolboy hand, is on display in the chapel of Dover College and there, with the Headmaster's permission, you may see it and wonder. For here, written as only a young boy could, is an absolutely natural narrative-in-the-first-person-singular, free of that moralizing which creeps into any adult offering, which creeps from time to time even into the pages of Robert Falcon Scott.

Here is a hero, then, who never had a chance to inspire others by his example. He was the youngest, least-important member of a disastrous and ill-fated expedition: the other two died without really knowing him, and he himself had been dead two years, out of sight and out of mind for two years since the Mysterious Disappearance of the Hornby Expedition, before he was remembered. By the time Edgar Christian's skeleton of a body and the two others he had so devotedly stitched up in blankets, with his last few ounces of strength, were found, no one really cared. There was a brief flurry of excitement in the press, rather a lot more when the diary was published, and then—except in Dover, where his memory is kept warm—complete oblivion.

Chapter 15

Brian Hession

He did more good to others in the years when he should have
been dead than most of us do in a lifetime.

I claim no credit for that sentence. Somebody said it at the
time of Brian Hession's death in 1961—and it has stuck in my
mind ever since.

And it is absolutely true.

"The years when he should have been dead" number seven.
Seven, and a month or two. During that time, Brian Hession
did more for cancer sufferers than almost anyone before or
since. For a large part of the horror of cancer lies in the absolute
secrecy—the dishonesty—which surrounds it. The English, it
has been said, are the best liars in the world—so perhaps it is
hardly surprising to find that there is a bigger smokescreen
about the disease in England than almost any other country
in the world. And it is this smokescreen, as Hession pointed out,
which has done as much as anything else to make cancer, for
many people, unendurable as well as incurable.

In his own words, he wanted to "bust wide open the whole subject of cancer in Great Britain". In the seven years allowed him, he did just that. He had found out, the hard way, that there was absolutely no national policy for cancer. Money was scattered foolishly in little scholarships, little grants and—most pathetically of all—on rival campaigns by different organizations. Research, even the unco-ordinated research that went on, was a fine and necessary thing: the Imperial Cancer Research Fund appealed for it, the British Empire Cancer Campaign appealed for it, "but not a penny piece that you give either of these organizations goes to relieve the present-day suffering of the cancer patient of today. This is research for tomorrow." Something had to be done to help people fight—today.

And he did it. Brian Hession by his example of courage, and by his teaching, not only inspired countless others in their fight, but created a new climate of opinion about cancer.

His beginning—like most of our beginnings—was dull. His father died when he was eight, his mother had to struggle to send Brian and a younger brother to school. He had no interest, as a young child, in religion of any sort. Yet somehow, between the ages of fourteen and sixteen, he swung so far in the opposite direction that he decided to become a parson.

And so he did, via a scholarship to Cambridge. He was ordained, became curate to a London vicar who made curates learn all the services by heart—there was no point in keeping your head buried in a book when you should be giving your attention to the bride and groom—and to read the Bible in church as if it were high drama.

He went, via a spell as chaplain to the R.A.F. at Halton in Buckinghamshire, to a church in Aylesbury: Holy Trinity. He had been struck forcibly, dealing with young men in the Air Force, just how important films were in their lives. Not only did they flock to them at every opportunity—in those pre-telly days—but they seemed to absorb, like sponges, from each one they saw. If only, Hession thought, the teachings of Jesus could be put on film. Men and women who had never darkened the interior of a church, who would run in horror from a sermon, would have their attention held, their minds won over, by films.

He decided, quite suddenly, to start making them. He would work up, as funds permitted, from making very short films, just short scenes from the Bible, to full-length ones: by hiring these out to churches and other organizations like the Salvation Army, he could make a profit which would then be ploughed back into the enterprise. Gradually, longer, better, films would be made.

The idea was slow in catching on, but by the outbreak of war in 1939 his "Dawn Trust" was breaking even. As the war went on, he found men and women only too delighted at having film shows in their air-raid shelters. A thoroughly captive audience, as Hession cheerfully admitted, but no less likely to get the message.

Surprisingly, and disappointingly, the resistance to religious films came from the Church itself. But Hession was never a man to sit back and do nothing; he had drive, insistence and charm of manner—and in no time we find Queen Mary, no less, taking an active interest in his work. Against this moral backing, even the most strait-laced committees have to give in.

The movement gathers speed. By 1950, the Dawn Trust is a thriving concern. He blames the aches and pains which have begun to afflict him, the constant tiredness, on over-work. At last, but with heavy heart because he loves his work at Holy Trinity; has built up, with his wife's help, a large and devoted congregation; he resigns his Aylesbury living and settles into a full-time career producing religious films.

In 1954 he is sent, as the leading authority in Britain, to the United States, where Hollywood is making a film of the life of Jesus: *The Day of Triumph*. His fare is paid by a group of British clergy and ministers from all denominations in order that, as "spiritual and technical adviser", he can keep an eye on the production, influence what is feared may be a Hollywood extravaganza into becoming a worthwhile contribution to the religious film movement.

He and his wife arrive at New York on 1 May and he preaches his way, as arranged, right across the continent from east coast to west. He is enchanted by the people and the country—and aghast, when he gets there, at the way *The Day of Triumph* is being put together. He makes suggestions, only a few of which are implemented. The director, on seeing the first "rushes", drops dead of a heart attack.

Somehow the film gets finished. In the meantime, pain has caught up with him. It has been recurring at shorter and shorter intervals and now it suddenly grows unbearable. His wife rushes him to a Los Angeles doctor.

Hession has suffered for years from haemorrhoids and it is this condition which the doctor now examines. It is a long examination.

"I'm afraid it's pretty serious, young feller."

He is told to dress, the doctor gives his wife a card. "Get him there, quick as you can."

They get to the address and there find a small and earnest group of specialists. He is made to lie down on a "V-shaped table, like a dentist's chair in reverse", and they proceed to examine him. He lies upside down, weak with pain, staring dizzily at their shoes underneath the table. They mutter.

A voice, booming from miles away: "Anyone examined you before?"

He explains, blood throbbing in his head from the upside-down position, that, yes, a London doctor has examined him. Only a few months ago. He asked the man at the time if the lumps were cancer, and he just laughed: everyone, at the slightest twinge, thinks they have cancer.

A pregnant pause.

The voice, quite calmly, tells him he has cancer—that he is in the "final stage". There is a growth, "like a cauliflower", in the rectum.

How long will he last?

Three days. It might be four.

Oh.

And an operation is out of the question, it's far too late. "Sorry, kid, we wouldn't touch it. Shall we tell your wife? Can she take it?"

Catrin can and Catrin does. (And it is later, when he has decided to devote his remaining life to cancer sufferers, that he has a chance to compare this tough and honest method with the English one. In England, he realizes, only Catrin would have been told. She would have been virtually sworn to secrecy

—and instantly he would have read the truth on her face. She would, perhaps, have denied it; ever more vehemently, he would have known she was lying, and death would have torn them apart in just about as deplorable a mental and spiritual state as could be imagined.)

They drive back to where they are staying, back along all the familiar film-world names, along Hollywood Boulevard, Sunset Boulevard. . . . They close the door behind them and he kneels and begins to pray. Then he hears Catrin's voice:

"Oh God—help us to find the right man."

And he realizes she is right. God is good—but they must find God's instrument, a surgeon brave enough to operate.

Frantically, for the hours are clicking past, they ring up hospitals: but it is late and no one seems willing to submit, or commit, the names of specialists. They will have to wait until morning.

But Catrin's prayer is answered, for—long before dawn breaks—they find their man. He has a voice on the telephone which makes them feel they have known him all their lives. He promises to check up with the specialists: then he rings back: "We'll have a try."

Hession has a sudden moment of panic in thus committing himself to an operation which is probably doomed to failure. After all, three days, or four, of life are very precious.

And there is the question of the fee. Parsons, even those who make films, are not rich. He stammers and the voice comes back, "Now look here, if you're worried about the money—I never charge a priest——"

The operation is arranged and he and Catrin are determined he will live. To prove it, he sends a cable to England: he had considered buying for his Dawn Trust a house near the sea at Bournemouth, "Greystoke", but has worried that it is expensive. Now he wires, "Determined to survive major cancer operation Monday. Buy Greystoke immediately."

The surgeon, when they meet, explains to him what will be done. He will be opened up from front and back, and everything possible will be cut out—yards of intestine—leaving him just enough digestive system to live. He will be given a colostomy, bringing the digestive tract to the surface just below

203

the waistline, sewing up the back passage permanently.

Then—surprisingly, perhaps—the surgeon tells him: he and all his friends must pray: "We both need help with a job like this."

That was 1954. The cancer had travelled farther than diagnosed: a lot more gut than originally intended had to be removed. The long-term prognosis was not good, even though Dr. Payne did a remarkable job. There was every chance the secondary cancer, leap-frogging its insidious way across the body, would break out in another part.

To be confident this will not happen, one has to go five full years without any form of recurrence.

He would put his trust in God. But that, Hession knew, was not really enough. "Do not," he wrote in his *Determined to Live,* the first of his many writings to encourage, give strength to others, "do not imagine for one moment that being a Christian means that you have not got to face the problems that come to human beings in this world. It does mean that it gives you a greater power and strength to face these things— the knowledge that underneath are His everlasting arms to support you."

However short a time he lasted, he would live and work every minute of it. There was work, endless work, to do for his Dawn Trust and its films—but there was a need as great, perhaps greater, for someone to do something about sufferers from cancer. And, for a start, having survived an "Impossible Operation", he must let people know.

And if *he* survived, there must be others. Their stories, too, must be told.

He thought about this during the four weeks and five days he spent in the Los Angeles hospital.

Back home, "convalescing" in England, he set about doing something. "Greystoke", for a start—the house he had bought by cable—had to be paid for. Somehow, he managed to do this, in a non-stop campaign of appealing to rich men, poor men, bank managers. And at the back of his mind was another idea. He would tell the world his story, to encourage others—and the proceeds of the book he would write about it would be spent on the cancer sufferers for whom he wrote it.

"Greystoke" paid for, he decided to make it serve a three-fold purpose. It was too big, too grand, to run without heavy loss, simply as H.Q. for his films: it would be Dawn Trust H.Q. all right: but it would also, for part of the year, be a straightforward, well-run hotel. That, God willing, would make ends meet.

But most important of all: it would be H.Q. of yet another organization. This was his new brainchild, "Cancer Anonymous".

The title, he admitted, was brazenly pinched from "Alcoholics Anonymous", and in the same way as men and women suffering from the disease of alcoholism had been able to lean on each other, lend each other strength to overcome their weakness, so cancer sufferers would reach each other through this new association. For silence, Hession knew, was bad. Silence breeds lies and fear: silence is wicked. And as far as he personally was concerned, "I thank God again and again for the man who told me he could not operate, and that I would die in three or four days. He gave me the chance to find another answer."

His wife might just have waited for his death, not daring to tell him.

He launched the idea of Cancer Anonymous in a sermon—and it caught on immediately. For, not only were there people who knew they had cancer and felt they had nowhere to turn; there were those who feared they might have, without the courage to find out. With Hession acting as centre point, as post office, people began to take their problems to him. He wrote a series of little booklets, and soon his correspondence became enormous. Some of the letters, he admitted, needed courage just to read. But his philosophy, "Cancer can be Cured or Endured": a Christian does not, must not, give up hope; spread encouragement and strength to sufferers all over the world.

He made a detailed study of the situation for cancer patients in Britain, made it his business to spread the information. He found much that needed improving, but much already done—and this had to be told. Many of his correspondents knew they had the disease (despite assurances from their doctors), were convinced they would die of it: they were resigned to the fact, resigned and bitter in a world of lies. Now at last there was someone with whom they could share their secret, and be given strength. For as Hession pointed out, wonderful, if unco-ordinated, work was being done. The Christie Hospital and Holt Radium Institute in Manchester, for example: this was the most advanced radiotherapy hospital in the world. People went there to be cured—not to die.

Many who wrote him believed, not only that all cancer cases died, but that the disease was infectious: they had been told so, they were shunned. And it was hereditary.

Cancer, Hession replied, is neither hereditary nor catching. And he began to cite examples of cures, quoting chapter and verse on each.

But all this correspondence, and the parcels of comforts which he and Catrin tried to send each needy sufferer, took money. In order to earn the money, Hession had to go on writing—and by now he knew he was living—writing—on borrowed time. Had he, as he now exhorted others to do, gone to a doctor in time—and taken a second opinion—the cancer might not have started to spread. Five years was the period: if he could be free of it for five years——

It came back after four, in a lung.

He had a lobe of lung removed, and immediately after the operation he was back at work. Every day now there was more work, as his fame spread: more work, and less time to do it. The longer he went on cheating death, the more of this work for others he could get done—and as his condition grew worse, so the avenues, the outlets, for doing it grew more numerous. He was now being regularly asked to broadcast, write articles for the press: he did both. To prove to himself and to others that life could, must be, lived, and to the full, he took himself to St. Moritz, was photographed ski-ing down the fastest slope. This, just seven months after his second major operation— when three-quarters of his right lung was removed.

But money—more and more of it—was needed. His time-table had become roughly one major operation a year, one book written. Each book, from the first, *Determined to Live*, to the last, *Bridge to God*, told of his faith, exhorted others to believe and be brave—and at the same time to use their brains, not rely entirely on prayer. God, Hession reminded, must have an instrument to work with. The instrument in his own case had been Dr. Payne of California, without whom he would have been dead, years before, unable to do the work for which God must have chosen him.

Brian Hession's last operation, and his last book, were in 1961. He had only a fraction of one lung left, and now still more was taken away. He had already postponed one operation in order to finish a book he was writing, lest it be too late—and on the very day of that operation, on his way to the hospital, he stopped in at the B.B.C. to record for them a message of comfort for those who were suffering, to be included in a programme called the "Silver Lining". For, right to the end, Hession was conscious there were others in worse situations than himself. He, as he pointed out, could go on earning a living: many others could not.

At the end of September, 1961, he was admitted again to St. Thomas's in London. This time he knew there could be no operation: he had entered the door for the last time.

At one stage it had seemed that Brian Hession, the man who had survived "inoperable cancer", would triumph over death itself. In this he failed—but perhaps his triumph was a greater one than that. Brian Hession triumphed over fear—and in doing so, inspired thousands of others to do the same.

Chapter 16

John F. Kennedy

One of the complications of being half anything, half something else, is that one is constantly being torn apart by one's loyalties.

So, in the autumn of 1960, as I followed, from several thousand miles away, the U.S. Presidential Election, the struggle between Nixon and Kennedy, I was torn between Kennedy's intelligence and charm; and the mentally-paralysing fact that I could never forgive his father's attempts, twenty years before, to sell Britain down the river. There was a slight, but nagging, fear at the back of my mind that this misunderstanding of things English might have been passed from father to son, be lying dormant, ready to spring up, a dragon's tooth.

I follow American political personalities more closely than British ones—partly because I have a definite and practically unshakable party allegiance in Britain, which pays little attention to the personalities on either side, as distinct from the policies—and I have none in American politics.

Perhaps, for many reasons, but mostly because of old Joe Kennedy (whom I had met, as a child, and liked, with his young, gay, uncountable family in London), I would have voted against John Kennedy.

But others voted for him, and for that we must give thanks. For without Kennedy's ice-cold judgement, simple courage, in a war of nerves, our world might well have vanished, several years ago.

He did—and tried to do—many fine things, but for this one, the world—including the Soviet Union—owes him a debt of gratitude which, unhappily, it can never repay.

Let us, briefly, go back to 1962.

A high-flying U2 aircraft, at dawn on the morning of 14 October, brought back pictures of a medium-range ballistic missile site in western Cuba. Kennedy had, in fact, ordered aerial reconnaissance well before this, but the weather had been bad. Now there were, quite distinctly and all in the same field, eight missile transporters, four launchers, plus vehicles for missile fuel. It was a complete unit, a "missile base"—and another, not far off, was being started.

Medium Range: 1,200 miles.

Aerial photos are quick to develop, slow to interpret. It was nine the following morning before the President of the United States was told there were Soviet rockets a few hundred miles away, pointing deep into the heart of America.

A meeting of the Cabinet was called for a quarter to twelve —and as one man put it, "On that first morning, the President gathered the threads together in his hands—and held them."

There were several possibilities open to him: he could invade Cuba immediately; he could attack it from the air, destroy the missiles; he could impose a blockade; he could present an ultimatum to Russia.

He could sit back and do nothing.

More U2s were sent over. Now there were Intermediate Range missiles—range up to 2,500 miles—with four dozen or so IL28 jet bombers. By painstaking analysis, the figures of Russian manpower to go with this hardware crept up to 22,000 men.

A meeting had already been arranged between Kennedy and

Gromyko on the following afternoon. This duly took place. It must have been a tense, nerve-jangling affair for the young American President. He was sitting opposite a blank-faced Russian—and Andrei Gromyko's face is as blank as they come, for all that goes on behind—a man who knew his country had assembled enough nuclear power on the island of Cuba to destroy a sizeable part of the United States. Given a chance, his country would use that power.

The younger man knew he knew this—and had to conceal the fact of his knowing he knew. Impossible sentence— impossible situation. Picture it, if you can, on the stage: just the two men, centre front; the audience, hushed and breathless, in on the secret.

But in 1962 there were few people in on the secret. None of the Press, for a start. Only the United States Cabinet, and a few non-Cabinet advisers. (And—one wonders whether this could have been the same in, say, England—every wife of every man knew: no one talked.)

The meeting between Kennedy and Gromyko (what *can* they have talked of?) ended. In the fullness of time Gromyko and the rest would be told, but the time had not yet come. Reconnaissance was stepped up. Now it was reported that a Russian convoy was approaching the Caribbean, bringing more missiles.

The American public and the U.S.S.R. were told simultaneously that there were Russian rockets in Cuba and that the Americans knew. A total blockade had been declared. No ship, Russian or any other, would get within sight of the island. Any that tried would be sunk. The island would be ceaselessly observed from the air, all entry and exit prevented, until the Russian bases were dismantled.

The world gasped, held its breath. Would Russia, under its volatile, yet oddly hamstrung, little leader, back down? Or would one side or the other pull the trigger? There were shrieks from America's allies: Kennedy had taken far too much on his own shoulders; they should have been consulted. Shrill voices, many of them English, were heard shouting that it didn't matter if Russian missiles were in Cuba: there were Yankee ones in Turkey.

For John Kennedy, there was only one feasible course—but

it would take nerves of steel. If this first incursion of Soviet nuclear strength into Latin America—which made useless the U.S. Early Warning System, tooled as it was against attack from the north, over Canada—were allowed to succeed, America was in real trouble. He had to act: act fast.

The Russians, as they had at the time of Suez, muttered of instant and devastating retaliation; rockets would burst in the western hemisphere, America would cease to exist. Kennedy went straight on, listening hard, weighing each threat as it came, against its alternative. And he tightened his blockade.

Krushchev and his Presidium backed awkwardly, unsteadily, down and agreed to remove the bases. The convoy which had been steaming for Cuba halted, hundreds of miles from land, drifted idly, a herring fleet.

Wisely, Kennedy resisted any temptation to gloat. He imposed no time limit for the removal of weapons, demanded only an assurance that they were going to be removed, an assurance he would verify by aerial reconnaissance.

The bases were dismantled, and within weeks Soviet technicians and troops were on their way home. For the first time, someone had summoned courage to stand up to the Soviet Union. The shrill voices which had been castigating the American President now cooed with relief. Kennedy the ogre was suddenly the man of peace, a hero to boot.

To understand him we must go back a bit over a hundred years, to potato famine in Ireland, when the Kennedy family lived in the small market town of New Ross on the banks of the Barrow. Living, perhaps, was hardly the word: starvation faced the whole community—the whole of Ireland—in the face.

And so young Pat Kennedy left New Ross in 1850 with enough money for his fare to Boston. Twenty dollars. The fact that Boston, not New York, was the western terminus of the Cunard Line in those days, has left its mark on history. Pat Kennedy got off his ship prepared to settle in this new world —even though, on the face of it, it seemed even less attractive than a starving Ireland. There were other immigrants, too— English, Scots, Germans—and each nationality hated all the others. As for the Irish, they were believed to be, according to John Kennedy in a speech a hundred years later, "keeping the Sabbath and everything else they could lay their hands on".

Pat married, produced a multitude of children. The fourth of these was christened Pat. And it is with him that Kennedy history really begins.

The new Pat grew up rapidly. His father died when he was a young child; his mother, in order to feed him and his brothers and sisters, went to work in a shop. But Pat's ambition was to get his mother out of that shop and he went to work for just that reason. He decided to profit by his late father's contacts, for old Pat had been a cooper, a man who makes barrels. What better than to start up a saloon?

The barrels got him behind the bar; the bar got him into politics. Any publican in Boston, particularly an Irish one, knew everybody there was to know. Sooner or later, they all came into the bar. Pat Kennedy ran for and got into the State Senate. Respectability followed, he was made Fire Commissioner, met another Irish politician, John Fitzgerald. "Honey Fitz" they called him, from his smooth, delightful manners.

Pat and Fitz, good friends, progressed, became Middle Class. Hardly surprising that Pat's son Joseph—and now we are into modern times—should marry Fitz's daughter, Rose.

Joe had a good start and he made good in the classic American manner: became, while still a young man, extremely rich. But as affluence mounted, so morale sank: he was coming up, more and more, against class prejudice. Boston's society is as rooted in class as that of any English country town, and in Joe Kennedy's youth Irish Catholic immigrants were about as far down as you could go.

Into this family John Kennedy was born, 29 May, 1917. A little later, dogged by prejudice, they moved to New York and here John went to school. He was the second of his family's nine children, described as "slight, industrious polite, hot-tempered". Like his brothers and sisters he was, above all, a member of the Kennedy "club", a close-knit family relationship, Kennedys against the world. They welcomed outsiders if they obeyed the rules, made no effort to invite them in.

Boarding school at thirteen, but soon appendicitis flung him out of it and into hospital. He went, on recovery, to another one, the non-denominational Choate School in Connecticut.

Adlai Stevenson had been there and, though the two were to develop a deep respect for each other in later years, this can hardly have been responsible for the Kennedy family's choice.

(Joe Kennedy was sending his daughters to Catholic schools, but not his sons. The sons had to make a way in life, must get to know and understand all manner of men, the opposition.)

From Choate John Kennedy graduated 64th of 112. Not particularly good—but he was voted "most likely to succeed". And now, surprisingly, he was sent to the London School of Economics. Once again illness intervened and he missed most of the course. Sickness, in fact, played a large part in John Kennedy's short life. He went to Princeton, fell sick, went to Harvard. Here he seems to have read a lot, swum well. There was an ability, when pushed, to get things done. "Kennedy," wrote a professor, "is surprisingly able, when he gets down to work."

At the end of 1937 Joseph Kennedy, millionaire, ardent Democrat with a capital "D", contributor to party funds, was made United States Ambassador to Britain—the culmination, perhaps, of a boundless social ambition. (And with nine children to launch into the world, he can hardly be blamed for having ambitions.) John stayed at Harvard, came to London for holidays. A year before the outbreak of war he travelled Europe, staying with ambassadors in Warsaw and Paris, descending briskly and briefly, but with charm and good manners, on a number of others. War broke out and now, back in Harvard, he wrote a thesis on appeasement. He was urged to get it published and when the little volume, now called *Why England Slept,* appeared in July, 1940, it was noted and praised. Old Joe, bursting with pride, sent copies to Winston Churchill, the King and Queen, everyone he could think of; we have no record of their reactions. It was a well-written, well-argued thesis by a young man of twenty-three; whether Mr. Churchill paid attention to it we will never know.

Meanwhile Joe Kennedy had convinced himself, was trying unsuccessfully to convince Roosevelt, that England had already lost the war. He failed and resigned at the end of the year. John tried to get into the American forces; health tripped him up. He had an old back injury from football, he was refused.

213

He embarked on a wildly energetic course of exercise to strengthen the back, was finally accepted for the U.S. Navy. By 1943 Lieut. (J. G.) Kennedy was commanding a Motor Torpedo Boat in the Pacific.

Midnight on 2 August, 1943, and the Jap destroyer *Amagiri* cut his boat in half, plunged on into the night. Two of the thirteen on board were killed, the rest were left, as the wreckage of their boat sank beneath the Pacific, floundering in shark-infested waters. They set off, under John Kennedy's leadership, for an island three miles off, Kennedy pulling the most seriously wounded man by his lifebelt, strings between his teeth. When they got there, exhausted, and he had made the wounded comfortable, he swam to another island to intercept the American boat which made a regular run past it. No luck, and he made his little party swim to another, nearer, island. Here they found islanders and coconuts, drank the milk greedily. He carved on a coconut-shell, "11 alive native knows position and reefs Nauru Island", persuaded an islander to take it to an American camp.

They were rescued, and all credit must go to Kennedy's efforts in rallying the crew to save itself, and to an uncanny ability, going back into schooldays, as a swimmer. He was decorated for "courage, endurance, and excellent leadership".

Sickness again: malaria and complications. Back in hospital in the States, he learnt his older brother, Joe, Junior, had been killed in action. Invalided from the Navy in 1945 he became a journalist and covered the San Francisco Conference which hatched out the U.N.; was loudly pessimistic of its future.

And now the family, the club, turned to him. It had been old Joe's ambition, his plan, that young Joe should be a politician, and perhaps, in God's good time, even President of the United States. This is a superbly American ambition: one finds it a little difficult to picture Lord Randolph Churchill, or old Mr. Wilson, or even a 13th Earl of Home, making plans for an eldest hopeful to become Prime Minister of Great Britain, but Joe had his plan and he was determined to push it, railroad it, through. He had, as usual, the complete support of all the family: Joe Jr. was dead; it was John's turn.

John preferred journalism, but after persuasion he agreed

to have a go. After a hard-fought, family-backed, campaign, he took his seat in the United States House of Represenatives in Washington in January of 1947. He was twenty-nine.

Two years later the Chinese Communists had driven Chiang Kai-shek's government off the mainland, to Formosa. In a period when half the world dithered, varied from despair to simple faith that "Chinese Communists aren't like the rest of them, it's just a name, really," John Kennedy made a surprising speech in the House, blaming the White House for this turn in events. From now on, he asserted, America would have to assume "the responsibility of preventing the onrushing tide of Communism from engulfing all Asia".

What *was* the boy talking about?

Six years in the House of Representatives. Then a decision to run for Senator from Massachusetts, against blue-blooded, proper Bostonian, Henry Cabot Lodge. He was helped, as he had been before, by a rich, devoted and madly energetic family, a horde of handsome Kennedys of both sexes which swept over the prim state of Massachusetts by car, train and aeroplane, canvassing for brother Jack—and he made it. It was November, 1952: Eisenhower had just defeated Stevenson.

Two years before, he had met a beautiful and intelligent girl from George Washington University. Her name was Jacqueline Bouvier; she was a Catholic. Now they married.

The next year was miserable. The back he had injured at school, aggravated in the Pacific, became unbearable and he had to go about on crutches. He was busy, he hardly saw his wife. In October he risked a dangerous spinal operation which did something to help the condition, then spent six months lying flat on his back.

The following year, 1956, he decided, again with family backing, to run for Vice-President of the United States. He failed to get the Democratic nomination, but the campaigning was good practice. In 1957, when there was a vacancy on the Senate Foreign Relations Committee, he was chosen for it over the heads of men more experienced and older than himself. The chairman of the committee which considered and finally chose him was Senator Lyndon Johnson.

From now on he was in Foreign Affairs, loving them, up to

the hilt. He was maturing fast and he fought the foreign policy of John Foster Dulles, urged—and this, for Kennedy, was a change of tune—that the United States now concentrate more on economic aid than military. It was grist to his mill when the Eisenhower administration appointed Maxwell Gluck ambassador to Ceylon. Gluck knew remarkably little about the place, not even, men said, just where it was. Kennedy lacerated the Republicans over the issue. He objected, too, to French policy over Algeria, maintained loudly that France should give the African colony independence.

His point of view was often controversial, but such was his skill and his obvious conviction on the platform that by 1958 the junior Senator from Massachusetts was getting a hundred invitations a week to address gatherings. His supporters—and these at last numbered more than the Kennedy family—began to campaign for the 1960 Presidential elections.

There had never been a Catholic President of the United States. The last man who had tried to overcome the prejudice against it had been roundly defeated in 1928—Al Smith. To many Americans, the idea of a Catholic President was every bit as distasteful as colonial status: this time, tied to Rome.

He was returned to the Senate in 1958 with a record-breaking majority. This was hopeful—and as they had prophesied, he was nominated Democratic Presidential Candidate in July of 1960.

At first his chosen running-mate, the older, more experienced Democratic nominee for Vice-President, refused to play second-fiddle to a young man from Massachusetts. Then he changed his mind, and that decision of Senator Lyndon B. Johnson from Texas was to have consequences for the whole world.

The Republican candidate was Richard Nixon, Vice-President under Eisenhower. For the first time in a Presidential campaign there were televised debates between the two men, on a nation-wide hook-up. These helped the young Senator; not only were his arguments sounder than, more convincing than, Nixon's, they made him known to a wider public, made him as well known, from Maine to California, as the Vice-President of the United States.

His Catholicism was always under fire. He was obliged, time

after time, to affirm that he believed in the separation of Church from State, and to assure voters that his religion, if he were returned, would have no effect on his duties.

On 8 November he defeated Nixon by the smallest of margins. But it was shown later by the University of Michigan Research Centre that his faith had cost him a million and a quarter votes. On the real issues, then, John Kennedy was returned by a large majority.

And now, much like Roosevelt nearly thirty years before, he began to make senior appointments of "intellectuals", men like Robert Macnamara and Dean Rusk, and Adlai Stevenson as his Representative to the United Nations. His choice of his brother Robert as United States Attorney General was open to a certain amount of political sniping, suggestions of a "royal family", but the appointment was soon justified on its merits.

His wife, "Jackie", was an immediate success as "First Lady" of the United States. Apart from being beautiful she had the gift of friendship, really liked most of the people her rôle made her meet. She had catholic tastes, with a small "c", and soon (once again, much as things had been there, thirty years before, with the Roosevelts) White House entertainments ceased being simple, "folksy" affairs; an invitation to dinner often included a concert or a recital by some international artist—selected by Jackie. She made fairly extensive changes to White House decor, most of it an improvement, then gave the American people a "television tour" of it, explaining, as the cameras followed her about the building, just what she was doing. Eyebrows were raised, some of them audibly, but the idea was a success; the public were grateful, and said so, for this first glimpse into every American's dream. Log cabin to White House has always been that dream, the White House is as remote and unattainable to the average American as Buckingham Palace to his cousin on this side of the Atlantic. And the First Lady, even if she be thrown out every four years, is the exact equivalent of the Queen. We may yet see Her Majesty conducting us through the state-rooms and apartments of her London House.

The Kennedys had two young children who caught the imagination of the American public, held it hard throughout their stay in Washington. Caroline, born in 1957 and therefore three years old when her father was inaugurated President; John, Jr., the only child ever to be born to a President-elect, who arrived to offer congratulations just three weeks after the defeat of Nixon.

Probably Kennedy would have run for a second term; probably he would have been re-elected. Fate, though, ruled otherwise and he served only thirty-four months—but they were momentous. Within three months of his inauguration in January of 1961, Cuba was invaded by a band of anti-Castroites, supported—morally at least—by the United States, a legacy from his predecessor. The invaders landed at the Bay of Pigs, hoping for a rising within Cuba, and, there being no rising at all, failed ignominiously. Kennedy, who had had practically nothing to do with the escapade, was blamed, on the one hand, for being an aggressor and on the other for having made a mess of a legitimate "defence of democracy". At more or less this moment in time, the Russians got an astronaut, Yuri Gagarin, into orbit round the world, a painful blow to American pride. Four months later they brazenly built a wall through the centre of Berlin and the free world felt itself powerless to intervene.

Perhaps, in the light of all these disasters, these blows to American esteem, John Kennedy's action over the Cuban missile bases was even bolder than it first appeared.

At home he worked hard for the passing of a bill which would guarantee equal status with whites for the American negro. By pushing this "Civil Rights Bill" he alienated the erstwhile "solid south", the states which traditionally vote Democrat, and one of his intentions when setting off, in November, 1963, on a tour of the southern states had been to try and set this right. Equal rights for negroes would have to come, and sooner rather than later, if bloodshed was to be avoided: but could he explain this to the white inhabitants of, say, Alabama?

His life had been threatened no less than 860 times during his first year in office. It was no surprise to him when more threats were made as he announced an intention of visiting Texas. But his arrival at Dallas Airport on 22 November was a cheerful, friendly affair, with bands playing and a large crowd. The President and First Lady got into the first car of a twelve-vehicle "motorcade", with the smiling Governor of Texas, Mr. Connally, headed slowly towards the centre of Dallas. There had been five thousand people at the airport, the sun was shining, everything augured well.

It was within minutes of twelve-thirty as the cars passed along Main Street, past the Nieman Marcus department store, towards the triple underpass.

As they passed the Texas School Book Depository, three shots. Screams from the crowd, four-deep on both sides of the road, a Secret Service man ran forward from his car and leapt on to that of the President. The driver of the Presidential car broke convoy, rammed accelerator pedal to the floor, roared through the centre of Dallas, towards the hospital, three miles off.

The President's head, as they got there, was cradled in his wife's lap, his blood staining her dress: two bullets had struck him, a third had hit Governor Connally.

Within minutes of arriving, being carried into the hospital, John Kennedy was dead. Even before the nation had realized what was happening, Vice-President Lyndon Johnson—the man who so nearly refused that office—was sworn in as 36th President of the United States.

A suspect was arrested, Harvey Lee Oswald. He had been seen leaving the Book Depository from which the shots were fired, had recently purchased—by mail order—a rifle like that found by the window. But while he was under escort, he was murdered by a member of the public ("I did it for Jackie") and no case could be brought against him. The Warren Report, many months later, purporting to explain what had happened, gently closing the book, was condemned in many quarters as merely a whitewashing of inept police security and unconvincing attempts to find the real assassin.

And so John Kennedy, youngest elected President of the United States, perhaps one of the greatest, was gone. In a short life he had overcome a great deal: illness, prejudice, fear, had set a fine example of courage in standing up to aggression, pushing through unpopular legislation.

What else might he have done?

Chapter 17

Leonard Cheshire

"Heavens——" said my mother.

"Oh?"

"I was at dancing class with her——"

"Who?"

"Constance Binney. She was about a year older than me, I remember——"

And this, as far as *I* can remember, was the first I heard of that very-human saint, Leonard Cheshire. I considered the implications of the fact that this gallant bomber pilot, not much older than me, had just married a woman older than my mother, and decided they were supremely unimportant. But now, many years later, when I have followed each stage in his unusual career, I think it has a bearing; it gives a pointer to the sort of man he was and is.

The Victoria Cross is given only for a deed of the utmost gallantry. It is the supreme, the final, accolade of heroism, and I suppose it would have been simple—and interesting—to

assemble twenty holders of it and write about them. Whatever they might be as men, however attractive or the reverse,
they would be heroes, tested and proved in the fire of battle.

Heroes, though, come in many shapes and sizes and an
Edgar Christian or a Pope John may be every bit as interesting
as a holder of this top decoration. So there is only one V.C.
in this book and he is included because he is a complicated and
a fascinating man as well as a hero on two quite different levels.

Cheshire was an ordinary and perhaps not wholly likeable
young man, lacking the looks and the temperament of, say,
Richard Hillary, who was saved, as were countless thousands
like him, from the po-faced mediocrity of a future which
beckoned cheerlessly at him, by the war.

No one would probably ever have discovered the greatness
that lay behind that rather forbidding, defensive, exterior if war
had not brought it out, shown us the man within. They say
that, like the thin man inside each fat one, struggling to get
out, there is a hero, if only a little one, inside each of us.
Cheshire's—not a little one at all—fairly leapt out.

Though there are obvious differences, both Richard Hillary
and Leonard Cheshire bore the stamp of their generation and
their class. Respectable young men from respectable middle-
class families, educated at worthwhile, respectable public
schools. They struggled, both of them, in rather futile, childish
and exhibitionist ways to escape from under this blanket of
respectability: they were conscious of not being quite of the
people and at the same time were frankly and justifiably
envious of those, in the 'tween-war years, who were on a higher
rung, the bland and titled scions of great houses who went to
Eton. With Hillary it became, at one stage, an obsession.

With Cheshire, too, it seems to have had an effect on his
wartime behaviour. Would a Leonard Cheshire from a different
background have produced the same brand of heroism in the
same way? Would his own internal hero have been so scratched
and rubbed by events, like the genie in Aladdin's lamp, that it
burst out? Perhaps not. But what is most interesting about this
man is that he went on from being a hero of one sort—a
tremendous, record-breaking hero—to becoming a hero, almost
a saint, of quite a different order.

To start, then, at the start. Leonard Cheshire was born in Cheshire (confusing to begin with) in the old town of Chester. It was September, 1917, and the bloodiest war in history was beginning to look as if it might never end. His father was a noted legal authority and had written a number of important books. The boy grew up, won a scholarship to Stowe, that magnificent Ducal seat in Buckinghamshire which had only just begun its new life as a public school, and there he is remembered to this day as "short, slim and quiet". He was good at tennis—very good indeed—and he tried his hand bravely at a good many other sports, most of which he disliked.

Like Hillary, he had the opportunity, thanks to reasonably well-to-do and imaginative parents, of a time on the continent. He lodged at one time for a few memorable months with the famous Admiral Von Reuter, who had given the command to scuttle the German Fleet at Scapa Flow rather than let it fall into British hands.

At Merton College, Oxford, where, in father's footsteps, he read law, a pattern seems to emerge. He seems to have done very little study, to have worked off his various frustrations in a fast Alfa-Romeo and by the childish, exhibitionist (but undoubtedly brave) device, on those occasions when he chose to be pedestrian, of standing, observed by his friends, on traffic islands and darting forth just in front of approaching cars. Indifference to danger, boastfulness, unconcern for the feelings —the lives—of others. Not a wholly unfamiliar pattern, as the English nineteen-thirties creaked to a close. He would drive off, night after night, to London, roaring thunderously down the Oxford Road, affecting the little shuddering hand movements on the wheel of the racing driver, spend what was left of the evening at the dogs and scream back again. He went to Stowe on a visit, and in showing off managed to crash the Alfa-Romeo noisily in front of the school.

But in his second year at Oxford he decided to sublimate his tastes for speed, danger and acclaim by joining the University Air Squadron and—partly for his parents' sake— getting rid of the Alfa-Romeo. Twice a week he and his fellow fledglings bounced round circuits and bumps in Avro Tutors and before long he became, while still a student at the university, a pilot-officer in the R.A.F. Volunteer Reserve. At summer camp they went to Ford Aerodrome in Sussex and flew Hawkers and Hinds. He found he had the qualities of a good pilot and he began to consider forsaking the law and choosing a career in the Air Force.

He had one last opportunity to indulge the recklessness, spirit of adventure and exhibitionism (which always seem so unlikely if one merely looks at a photo of the slight, earnest young man with the full, pursed lips). He makes a bet with a working man in a pub. "Paris—no trouble at all. Get there with"—he plunges a hand into his pocket—"with what I've got here. Fifteen bob. *And* back."

And the other, admiration writ large on his honest working face, agrees to a bet of a pint of bitter that he can't.

Needless to say, he does. He hitch-hikes, gets across the Channel, then outside Paris volunteers to dig a Frenchman's garden and tells him the details of the bet. From here, of course, he's home at a walk. Fêted, well paid for the gardening, he is urged to write for a Paris newspaper, to broadcast, give a public lecture. He travels back in a cloud of publicity, first class, to find the British press, alerted by their Paris colleagues, waiting with cameras at the ready to see him collect his bet in the Oxford pub.

In 1938, hardly surprisingly, he gets only a Second in Law, and this clinches the earlier thought of joining the R.A.F. He applies for a Permanent Commission by direct entry from the university and is accepted just as war begins.

And now, just as with Richard Hillary, there is little thought in Cheshire's mind of fighting tyranny and the rest of it. I imagine it figured not at all in the reasoning of young Englishmen of his, and my, generation. To all of us, it was going to be one hell of a lark.

He skipped Elementary Flying School, went on to more advanced training, in Wiltshire. Here, when they asked him, he expressed a preference for, first, fighters, then Army Co-operation. The Services being what they are, he was immediately put into bombers. Six months in Wiltshire, another two at Abingdon where he'd flown with the university, and then his first operational squadron.

It was 102, at Driffield in Yorkshire, and here he found he liked bombers, after all. "I was never a good pilot," he remarked years later. "I could put my aircraft where I wanted it, but I couldn't fly continuously at a set speed and height—so I wouldn't have made a test pilot, or been any good on fighters." This is the older, wiser Cheshire speaking and certainly it is unnecessarily modest: no one would have dreamed of wanting him to be a test pilot and the ability to put an aircraft where he wanted it, which he so justly claims, would have made him, in all probability, an outstanding fighter pilot.

102 were armed with Whitley night-bombers. Practically all R.A.F. bombing at that time was done at night, in single file, in these unwieldy aircraft, and Cheshire soon showed himself to be a remarkable and courageous pilot, always ready to dive down into the hell of German anti-aircraft defence if it meant his bombs stood a better chance of flattening the target.

By November, 1940, he had proved himself one of the best pilots in Bomber Command and the old pre-war recklessness was channelled into the task of bashing the Ruhr. And—for it is all-important in a bomber pilot, as against the lone man in his fighter—Cheshire's personality rose to the challenge. Crew members who might justifiably have felt their lives were being diced with, in an aircraft which was always the lowest, most desperately flown in the Squadron, loved, or at least profoundly respected, him. In that chill November, a raid was called on Cologne and the Squadron took off from Driffield, headed over the North Sea, and hit the German flak like a storm of rain, rain which thickened into porridge about them as they got nearer the target.

When they were almost there, one of Cheshire's crew pulled out a flare, got ready to drop it.

As he did, an anti-aircraft shell hit the bomber, flung it on its back and exploded the flare. This, in a brilliant flash, blew out the side of the fuselage and set fire to what remained. Cheshire, struggling with the controls, was tapped on the shoulder: "Fire, sir—we're on fire!"

"Well—put it out!"

To observers below in Cologne, the flaming Whitley above them, like some wandering comet, a twin-engined, million-

Above: Two sides of—and two names for—the same man. On the left, Colonel T.E. Lawrence, "Lawrence of Arabia", liked to wear the flowing robes of the Arab world, and to be a part of it. After the Versailles Treaty, where he felt the Arabs had been badly treated, he decided to relinquish his army commission, turn his back on the past. Then it was the Royal Air Force, rather than civilian life, which attracted him. As "Aircraftsman Ross" he served happily and well as an aircraft fitter—until a popular newspaper exposed him. *Right:* Francis Chichester, at the age of sixty, chose to pit himself, alone in a small boat, against the Atlantic.

The Reverend Brian Hession addresses a meeting with all the fervent sincerity which he put into the films he produced and into everything he did. Already, when the above picture was taken, he was a very sick man and fighting a deadly disease. *Below:* In 1962, United States reconnaissance planes discovered Soviet missiles in Cuba, aimed at the heart of America. While the world waited and photographers took endless pictures, John F. Kennedy, at his desk in the White House, signed the proclamation for a total blockade of the island.

candle-power comet, was a write-off. The crew—if any were still alive—would have to bail out, and fast. No doubt the thought passed through minds in the Whitley—but not Cheshire's. Not only would they stay with their plane, but they would get the fire under control, ignore the missing side which had made them into an open-sided rubber-necker bus, and go on to bomb the marshalling yards.

Almost unbelievably, they did. And the crew, following their captain's example, behaved with tremendous gallantry. The W.T. operator, Sgt. Davidson, was badly burnt, temporarily blinded. He struggled to work the radio, but even when his burnt hands were put on the controls for him he could do nothing with it. In fact, the set, like most of their equipment, had been almost completely destroyed and they got home without radio help. Cheshire, his job done, wanted to land at the nearest aerodrome and get the wounded Davidson to hospital, but the tough little operator refused to be landed anywhere but Driffield, so they crept in to their home base and, to the consternation and wonder of the ground crews, anxiously awaiting the Squadron's return, made a perfect landing with half an aeroplane. For this Cheshire was awarded the D.S.O., Davidson the D.F.M.

Two months later, in January of 1941, he was posted to 35 Squadron, the first to be equipped with the new Halifaxes. By now he had worked out in his own mind the rules for becoming and staying a first-class bomber pilot. They were rules, he felt, that anyone ought to be able to follow; there was nothing secret about them and he was happy to pass them on. Daily, constant flying practice, so one had complete mastery of the aircraft, didn't have to think about it, could concentrate on other things. And a mental adjustment—using the correct half of "the split mind", so that when one attended briefing one concentrated entirely on the opportunities, not at all on the dangers.

A little later he was awarded the D.F.C., for his "gallantry and devotion to duty in the execution of air operations".

The Halifaxes were all suddenly grounded for modification, after a raid on Kiel. Cheshire was sent across the Atlantic by ship to begin, with a few others, the ferrying of U.S.-built aircraft to Britain. He reported to Atfero, the department which was developing the new, urgently-needed ferry service, and was told to enjoy himself, soak up the bright lights of New York until they wanted him.

Before he had sailed he light-heartedly said to his mother, "I'll come back with a film-star wife." A remark any young man might have made, but it seems he meant it—and we are back in the old Alfa-Romeo, hopping-off-traffic-island days. He marries his "film-star wife", though she is twenty-two years his senior, and though he doesn't exactly bring her back with him, as he has to ferry a Hudson to Britain three days after the wedding, she follows him a few months later.

Cheshire's observations at the time and a little later, on this episode of his life—for it was little more than that—are a little strange. He is deeply distressed that his colleagues, when he tells them of his catch, don't think it remotely clever or wise, and one sees the enthusiasm wilting from this moment. He is proud, very proud, of the fact that Constance is rich and gives him money and he defends his marriage by saying, "I could have got all the money I wanted out of Constance, without marrying her."

But with this episode, the private life and thoughts of Leonard Cheshire fade from the picture, leaving only the incredibly skilled and courageous bomber pilot. When next we meet him as a human being, he is different.

But in the meantime Cheshire spent a year with 35 Squadron, now "modified", bombing regularly and with his usual panache the cities of Cologne, Bremen, Essen, Berlin. By September, 1942, he was a wing-commander, commanding 76 Squadron. For his work with this squadron he got a bar to his D.S.O. He had just been promoted to group captain and at twenty-five was the youngest one in the R.A.F., but they had put him, to his fury, on administrative duties and he was only able to keep up his flying by giving instruction to others. Eventually he got back into operations by volunteering to drop a ring, become wing-commander again, take over the suddenly-famed 617 Squadron.

And now began the most important period of his wartime life. The squadron under its previous commander, Guy Gibson,

226

V.C., had already breached the Mohne and Eder dams in Germany, an almost impossible task. Not only had most of 617's members dropped a rank in order to get into this élite, but they had a casualty rate which was unique, and of which they were proud : six out of sixteen aircraft lost on the dams raid; six out of nine over the Dortmund-Ems Canal.

And now they were getting, with the enforced retirement of Guy Gibson from operations, a new commander from outside. At the same time came instructions from the A.O.C. that low-level bombing would cease forthwith, the casualties were too high.

The question of path-finding for bombers was being heatedly discussed. There was argument as to how the new pathfinders, flying out in front, pinpointing targets, marking them with carefully placed flares, should be deployed within groups and squadrons. There was also frank admission that the technique needed improvement.

And now an Australian, Squadron-Leader Micky Martin of the squadron, chanced by accident on the solution. He was practising over water and felt a wild urge to dive-bomb, in his huge Lancaster, a piece of floating seaweed. They were used to flying low in 617, but dive-bombing was different: the great wings might sheer off, or the airframe might be damaged in some less striking but ultimately lethal way. But Martin did it and, to his surprise, the practice bomb landed square in the middle of the tiny floating target.

He told Cheshire, who went up and tried for himself. It worked—but it was as a method of marking targets that Cheshire saw it, a method exactly suited to his own skill and temperament.

But still low-level work was forbidden. Then one day, after a series of reports that the Germans, just across the Channel, were installing not only rockets but a new and gigantic gun which would pump 500 rounds a minute into the heart of London, the A.O.C. told Cheshire, "Go and bomb that factory —low-level. It's in a built-up area, and they've got five hundred girls on night-shift. You're to destroy the factory and not take a single life."

And there was a rider that if they succeeded, the question of low-level marking would be reconsidered, and with it the provision of the lighter Mosquitoes Cheshire had asked for and been refused.

The Limoges attack—at full-moon in February—went perfectly. At zero-minus-ten one Lancaster dropped an orbiting marker twenty-five miles to the north-east and, while he did it, the rest made three low-level runs over the factory, firing guns into the air, warning the night-shift girls to get out. At zero-minus-two they dropped the first lot of target markers from point-blank range, and at zero the bombing began, with just one 12,000-pounder from each plane. As each struck the target it was checked before permission was given for the next. All hit it—ten 12,000-pounders on a factory two hundred yards by a hundred. Photo recce later on showed the target completely destroyed. Reports from the French Resistance showed that no one was killed, and only one—the girl who refused to go away—was injured.

Still, it seems, the Mosquitoes were not granted them, and the squadron went on attacking pinpoint targets all over France without. On one occasion they destroyed the two main sheds of the Michelin factory without touching the canteen in between. Now they were offered four of the "Mozzies" if they would successfully attack Munich, the most heavily-defended target outside Berlin. They could have the little wooden fighter-bombers for the raid—and keep them if it worked.

Cheshire was delighted, and his squadron's Munich raid was a fantastic, incredible success: it inflicted damage forty times as great as the combined Anglo-American attacks of the previous three years.

Now, with Mosquitoes "on the strength", 617 went from success to success, always led by Cheshire, usually in a Mozzy, sometimes in the American-built Mustang. They flattened rocket sites and gun sites, collapsed bomb-storage caves with the new "Tallboy" bombs. Over Le Havre, Cheshire went into a screaming vertical dive, almost into the sea, and marked for a raid which in a few catastrophic minutes destroyed some 15,000 tons of German naval craft—thirty-six assorted R-boats, E-boats and torpedo-boats—and killed over a thousand German marines.

But a month after this, complaining bitterly that he wanted to go on flying, even though his permitted hundred missions were up, he was transferred. Orders came through, transferring him to South-east Asia Command. It was while he was airborne *en route* that he was gazetted as having been awarded the Victoria Cross—an award covering the whole of an astonishing operational career but mentioning the exploding flare in the Whitley and the raids on Munich and Le Havre.

With war within sight of ending, that career, too, seemed to be over—but there was, did he but know it, a new one ahead. A few months in the East and he was transferred to the R.A.F. delegation in Washington, and from Washington he flew home to greet his young brother Christopher just out of prison camp.

It was late, very late at night, the third night of an "almost non-stop celebration", when Leonard Cheshire began to talk to a girl in the party. Conversation, as it sometimes does late at night, turned, a little incoherently, to religion. The girl leant suddenly over the table and said, "How much do you know about God?"

He begins to explain to her that "God is an inward conscience", but she cuts him off. "Absolute nonsense. God is a person. *A person*——"

And suddenly, there in the crowded night-club, he knows she is right.

But there is little time to muse over it. A few days later he is back in Washington, has been told the startling news that an atomic bomb has been invented and that he and the British scientist William Penney are to be the two British observers.

A few weeks later they take off from the American base of Tinian, in a B29, one of several escorts, and climb rapidly in the blue Pacific sky to 39,000 feet. There is joking in the aircraft which grows gradually less as zero approaches and they realize they have missed their rendezvous.

Just as they are about to return, they see the flash, fifty miles away to starboard.

"How pale by comparison Wilhelmshaven; how insignificant Bergerac! Yes, and with such utter devastation before our very eyes, how imperative to do something to see that it should never happen again."

229

(And I, on leave in a bar in Calcutta, heard the news—just how, I forget—and we cheered the Great Eastern Hotel to the echo. We hadn't seen the burst.)

The man Cheshire had changed—in that one terrible flash. And although he stresses in his *The Face of Victory* that it was the girl in the night-club who made him realize the existence of God as a person, one feels that the real change took place 39,000 feet above the Pacific. He was frantic to go home, refused a posting to the Gulf of Mexico to teach the Americans low-level marking (what was the use of low-level marking now?) and fought tooth-and-nail till they sent him back to England. Here he would do everything—or at least *something* —to make sure that this terrible thing never happened again.

The Prime Minister, Attlee, was anxious for a first-hand report and Cheshire took the opportunity of putting forward his plan, his urgent plan, for world peace, while the P.M. sat in smoke-filled silence, pipe between his teeth. Cheshire's idea was simple: *impose* peace, just as the Romans had done. The Allies now had this atomic secret and they must use it. Mr. Attlee must authorize a company to investigate atomic energy as a means of propulsion into space, for with space stations orbiting above, ready at the flash of a signal to hurl atomic bombs on any part of the globe, there would be no question of failing to impose peace.

Cheshire was before his time. We can only imagine Mr. Attlee's thoughts as, pipe now in hand, he stared at the young man. We know, because Cheshire tells us, that his answer was "no".

Shortly after this, Cheshire was summoned to the Air Ministry for a medical board and told bluntly that he was suffering from psycho-neurosis. After six years' almost non-stop operational flying, culminating in the atom bomb, one is hardly surprised. A year's *complete* rest was the prescription. But now the *Sunday Graphic* came up with an offer of a larger salary than he had ever earned, just to write them a fortnightly article. He agreed, with enthusiasm: now, perhaps, he might win men over to his ideas, through his writing. At the same time—and it would have horrified the members of his R.A.F. medical had they known—he began to seize at the present with both hands, making up for the years of operational flying by living as hard as he knew how, in London. He bought himself a large house in Kensington Gardens—after all, he was a wealthy journalist now and still, even on the "non-effective sick list", had his Air Force pay—and staffed it with a butler, a cook and a charlady. Life was gay and exhausting and exactly the reverse of what the medical board had ordered. He even bought himself a Bentley, acquired on an overdraft which his father obligingly guaranteed.

But all the time something new was growing inside him. The schemes for imposing peace were fading, and in their place was coming a desire, a heartfelt, urgent desire, to do something, *now*, for the world as it was, *now*, and the sick and troubled men and women in it. And, somehow, this question—but it was not a question, it was a fact—of God being a person weighed heavily in his thoughts. He had never been a religious man, but now, "how different it all seemed—no longer a series of instructions to have preached at one; no longer a subject only for clergymen and similarly-minded people, and to be mooted in hushed and pious tones, but the story of a person. Yes, a person——" He read his Bible, sought religious advice.

But it was not until he decided to air these feelings in the *Sunday Graphic* that things began to happen. Suddenly, the response to his printed suggestion that someone should take over a disused aerodrome and found a community on it of ex-servicemen and women, with the strong supporting the weak, the skilled the unskilled and the rich the poor—the response was enormous. He had struck some chord, latent, unsounded, in almost every breast, and within three weeks he was able to summon a public meeting, a packed one, and to make decisions. The community—for now it was a fact, it had to happen, even if no one knew quite where or how—would support itself by farming and other productive activities. Any man with a trade would be urged to set it up, handing in profits to a central pool.

And it failed. Leonard Cheshire and a few others worked themselves to a standstill on the scheme—"V.I.P." they called it, from "Vade in Pacem"—and it did good work, but in the end they became insolvent. Cheshire, who hoped he had got it on its feet and was now trying to snatch a little at least of the "complete rest" so long ago prescribed, was summoned back from British Columbia by an urgent cable. He had been staying with an old family friend, Bishop Embling, leading a healthy outdoor life and slowly building up his strength, his reserves of nervous energy: now he dropped everything and flew back to England. There was nothing he could do, when the facts came out, but close up V.I.P.'s big Hampshire house which they had acquired so cheaply and which had promised so much, and liquidate the scheme. But he stayed on there, at "Le Court", as it was (and is) called, stayed with one or two devoted helpers, trying to think things out.

Then one day someone came to the door and said, "Arthur's very ill—he's in hospital, wants to see you——"

He remembered Arthur, the old man who used to feed the pigs in the ill-fated V.I.P. venture, and he went to see him, clutching a little fruit and some flowers. When he entered the hospital he was told the matron wished to see him in her office.

"You know," she said, "that he is dying of cancer?"

Cheshire had not known. And she went on to point out that their hospital was only a small one, there was a shortage of beds, and Arthur just couldn't stay. What was Group Captain Cheshire going to do about it? After all, Arthur had given his address as Le Court—he had no other, and he had no relatives —and this, unless matron was mistaken, was the group captain's.

There was nothing for it but to take Arthur in: once again Le Court would be a haven for the weak; and strength would have to be found, somewhere, somehow, to support them. For already the idea had taken shape in Cheshire's head: Le Court (it is pronounced Lee Court) would no longer be a community of healthy men and women trying to live a corporate life and be self-sufficient—it would be a home for the chronic, incurably ill.

This idea—as now we all know—really worked, thanks to the non-stop, back-breaking work Cheshire and a few others put into it. The second inmate was old Granny Haynes, ninety-one and completely bed-ridden. Her husband had just had a stroke, been carted off to hospital and she was alone.

232

What, came the inquiry, would Le Court do about it?

There was no question, any more than there had been with Arthur: Granny Haynes must come—and a way would be found to feed and look after her.

And a way was found. Arthur and Granny were only the vanguard of a procession which has continued, ever swelling, ever since. Arthur died—buoyed up in his last hours by his Catholic faith, and Cheshire, who for the past week had been doing everything for the old man, feeding him, washing him, carrying him to his commode, asked the priest if he might stay with them and hear the little bed-side service.

A few months later—Christmas Eve, 1948—he was received into the Catholic Church. Le Court went on filling up with the disabled and the helpless; and the helpers, who had also increased in number, for there are good people as well as sick ones in the world, went scavenging in dustbins and rubbish dumps. To avoid the cost of fitting electric bells they grouped the patients who would need help at night into adjoining rooms and Cheshire himself slept outside the door.

And so they came—not all of them quite helpless, many of them able to help, which they did to the best of their abilities: the epileptics, the lame, schizophrenic and handicapped. Cheshire had by now resigned from the Air Force and his hands were full, looking after not only Le Court but a new home they had acquired and christened St. Teresa's, in Cornwall.

And on 20 August, 1952—just four years after Arthur's death —he learnt, when a visiting priest forced him to go for X-ray, that he had T.B. of the lungs.

Hardly surprising. No man, worn out with years of war— from which he emerged the most-decorated man in the Royal Air Force—who had driven himself to the limit for a further seven years when prescribed "complete rest", could expect much else. He was sent to bed—immediately, no messing about this time—and in bed he stayed for two and a half years, most of it in Midhurst Sanatorium in Sussex.

Here began a series of operations on his lung and he was strengthened for the months of pain that lay ahead by his new faith. On the eve of his first operation, a life-sized reproduction of the Holy Face from the Shroud of Turin was put on the wall at the foot of his bed. For a whole month, recovering from that operation, he did little else but lie and look at it.

The face, the Holy Face, of the dead Christ has been imprinted by some chemical action on the winding sheet in which He was buried—or so it is believed. The sheet is fifteen feet long and of linen. It has been handed down from generation to generation and now it is preserved in Turin.

Here, Cheshire realized, was The Face of Victory. It was the face of Someone who acknowledged—still acknowledges—no defeat. He studied it, week after week, and thought.

Out of hospital—but by no means cured—he wrote of The Face: "Who now could be content to lie back and rest so long as anywhere in the world there remains but one human being in want or distress?"

A daunting thought. But that, ever since, has been the life of Leonard Cheshire. The work he began with Arthur and with Granny Haynes, which he went on working for in hospital, has spread and spread all over the world. There are Cheshire Homes for the sick, the incurable, in India, Africa, Jordan, Hong Kong—and like dragons' teeth they keep on springing up, to do their job of mercy.

Then to one of the Homes, in Bedfordshire, came a girl called Sue Ryder, who was as remarkable in her own way as Leonard Cheshire. She had been a member of the Special Forces in Europe and since then had devoted her life to these forgotten allies.

Immediately, they had much in common—in particular, plans for extending their work, different but *au fond* how similar, into new parts of the world where it was so desperately needed. Cheshire, just out of hospital, still shaky but now on his way to start a new home in India, saw only a little of Sue Ryder, and she too was busy.

They saw little of each other for many months. Then they married.

The work they now do is under the over-all heading of "The Ryder Cheshire Mission for the Relief of Suffering". Probably there has never in history been so inspired, far-reaching and effective a mission, run privately. (And one realizes, with a gasp, how much misery each day is swept underneath the carpet: what did these wretched people do *before* Leonard Cheshire, what is happening, even now, to those for whom homes are yet to be built?) The mission includes an ever-increasing number of separate and autonomous foundations, from "Sue Ryder Forgotten Allies" Homes in England, Germany and Poland, giving comfort to the victims of Nazism, to the large number of Cheshire Foundation Homes for the Sick, caring for sick who are not only incurable but homeless. And most of them are young people. The average number of inmates in a home is thirty.

And behind all this is one man—the Oxford undergraduate with the Alfa-Romeo who went on to become the greatest bomber pilot of the war—of all time.

He was a hero then, no doubt about it. And what is he now? A hero—many would say a greater hero—and cast in a different mould. One can hardly compare the two: in fact, writing about the pre-war, wartime and post-war Cheshires is writing about three different men.

He is a hero. And is he—almost—a saint?

Chapter 18

Richard Hillary

The cockpit cover of a Spitfire was always a cumbersome thing. There are few, very few, Spitfires left, but if you go to Northolt Aerodrome, a little north of London on the A40 road to Oxford, you will see one of these cocky little fighters parked just inside the main gate, a monument to its breed and to the men who flew them. Try, if the guard on the gate will let you, to slide the cockpit cover in its grooves. Pretend to yourself that this Spitfire is yours and that the Tannoy has spoken—absolutely calmly, in a deadpan, upper-class voice, but at an almost incredible volume which has thundered across the tarmac, "Squadron take off. Patrol base. You will receive further orders in the air. Squadron take off. As quickly as you can, please——"

You will find that the cockpit cover, after a quarter of a century of English weather, of the gentle mist, drizzle and sleet which seeps into the bones of men and the grooves of machinery, is locked stiff. Try as you will, you cannot shift it.

Get help and a hammer and a tin of oil and you will do so.

Then, gasping from your exertion, climb in and take off, under the nose of the astonished guard commander, to your imaginary dog-fight, as the fast-moving cars and lorries of the sixties thunder down the Oxford Road in front of you. You will need to close the cockpit before you can take off, and this will consume time and patience and strength, so that when eventually you taxi out the sweat is pouring down your face.

And as you turn into wind for take-off, blinded by the cloud of dust from the leading section which is belting down the runway ahead of you, think for a moment of what may happen if you are hit, catch fire, have to bail out. Will you have the brute strength—and above all, the time—to force the cockpit open?

Or will you spin helplessly earthward, trapped inside, with the ever-thickening air fanning your flames so the cockpit is literally an oven and the barbecue smell which eddies round before you lose consciousness is the stench of your own burning flesh?

If you consider these things, you will be able to enter, for a moment, the mind of Richard Hillary.

It was 3 September, 1940: exactly twelve months of war had rushed, crept and rushed past again, when he took off on his last Spitfire flight, from Hornchurch Aerodrome twelve miles east of London, with a defective cockpit cover. The field had been bombed a day or two earlier, his Spit had been damaged on the ground, and now it had been fitted out with a new cockpit cover. Perversely, this refused to slide along its grooves. For two hours, from eight in the morning when he came out on the tarmac to be near it, until a few minutes past ten when the calm loudspeaker voice ordered all pilots into the air, Hillary and his fitters had wrestled with the new cover. By the time of take-off it was sliding exactly halfway along its grooves.

The squadron took off in a cloud of dust and sand and blue-black fumes, heading south-east, climbing on full boost. At twelve thousand they burst out of cloud: but on and on they climbed, straining for a sign of Messerschmitts.

Suddenly, the Messerschmitts were there. A whole swarm, a thousand feet above.

The Spits tore into them and the next ten minutes was a blur. As Hillary wrote of it, much later, "One Messerschmitt went down in a sheet of flame on my right, and a Spitfire hurled past in a half-roll; I was weaving and turning in a desperate attempt to gain height, with the machine practically hanging on the airscrew. Then, just below me and to my left, I saw what I had been praying for."

What he had been praying for was a Messerschmitt climbing and below him, and now, with a whoop of triumph, he closed in. Four hundred yards, three hundred, two hundred. Then he gave it a burst.

The Messerschmitt seemed to stop dead. Then a trickle of flame, a cloud of smoke. Hillary, determined to make sure of his victim, gave it another burst. As he did, he was hit by a long, long burst from another German fighter. The thing he had most dreaded happened: his cockpit filled, instantly, with flames, the heat mounted terrifyingly so he could neither see nor breathe. He reached up to open the hood, and it refused to budge.

His only chance lay in unstrapping, standing up in the spurting, mounting flames, using all the strength at his disposal to force the thing open. This Hillary did, and the cover, agonizingly slowly, slipped and jerked along its grooves until there was just room for a man to squeeze out. But all the time the heat was growing, and he could smell his burning flesh. Then he lost consciousness.

He cooked slowly—mercifully unconscious—while his Spitfire spiralled like a burning leaf from 25,000 feet to 20,000, 15,000, 10,000—at which he was seen from the ground to fall out, like a small brown stone. He fell like one until he regained consciousness in time to pull the rip-cord of his parachute, check his descent and flop into the sea.

"I was pleasantly surprised to find that my life-jacket kept me afloat. I looked at my watch: it was not there. Then, for the first time, I noticed how burnt my hands were: down to the wrist, the skin was dead white and hung in shreds. I felt faintly sick from the smell of burning flesh."

He was, in fact, hideously, almost unbelievably, burnt and although the genius of Archibald McIndoe restored for him some sort of face, his hands, right up to the time of his death—so inevitable, so unexplained—a little more than two years later, were little more than twisted talons.

Richard Hillary, whose book, *The Last Enemy*, inspired so many of his own "lost" generation—and others, not from his generation, not from England—was, though few people noticed at the time, an Australian. He was born in Sydney, on 20 April, 1919, of Australian parents, but his name became such a legend, so bound up with the "Few" of Churchill's famous phrase, the few who in defending England saved the world, that this quite important fact has often been lost sight of. His father was an Australian Government official, his mother a member of one of the great pioneer families of Western Australia, that huge, barren, challenging, left-hand third of the continent. The family moved to Melbourne and lived there for the first three years of Richard's life. He was a beautiful, startlingly beautiful, child, and this beauty grew and strengthened as the boy grew older. He was at the same time stubborn, sensitive and easily hurt. Yet he recovered, as easily, to flash the broad, friendly grin which was melting hearts before he was four.

But by this time he was in England. Michael Hillary had been transferred to Australia House in London for three years. Then, in the middle of this tour of duty, he was offered an even better post in the Sudan, as Auditor General, a post which would be permanent. He realized he had to take it and at the same time that it would involve more contact with London than with Canberra. He bought, as roots for the family, a holiday house in Beaconsfield, north-west of London. From this house, Richard went to that most English of institutions, the boarding preparatory school (which he hated), thence on to public school, at Shrewsbury. This he enjoyed. He derived pleasure and benefit from a system which, however imperfectly, tried to inculcate team spirit, modesty, sportsmanship. He had always been brave, even reckless, in the Australian tradition. Now he learnt, slowly, painfully at first, that recklessness was little more than boastfulness, that it was better to suppress one's own urge to glitter on the football field or on the river, and make sure the team won.

And it was on the river that he excelled. Rowing seemed to combine team-work with the right degree of individual effort—and Shrewsbury had a good crew; it was an honour to row for it. His family wanted, as families do, to place him gently in his father's footsteps, let him grow into an official in the Sudanese Government. Richard agreed, on the condition that they let him travel, by himself, to the Continent each year at Christmas and at Easter, to learn languages. (His parents only came back to England in the summer.) To this, Mr. and Mrs. Hillary agreed. In Germany, Richard became interested, then enraged, by the bovine admiration of Germans of his own age for their National Socialist government. Picking up the language at speed, he would sit up all night debating with them—and at the back of his mind was the half-understood realization that one day he would fight them. In the meantime, he would row against them, beat them.

His premonition and his wish came true. The wish, to row against Germans, was granted in the summer of 1938. As an undergraduate at Trinity College, Oxford, he collected another nine oarsmen and wrote the German Government, suggesting his "university team" go over and row in their summer regatta. The team was invited, all expenses paid by the Hitler government, and as he later pointed out in *The Last Enemy*, the race was almost a pointer to the course of the war. The English oarsmen were untrained and disorganized; they arrived in Bad Ems very late for the start of the race, to the anger of the five German crews and the noisy disapproval of their hundreds of supporters. The race began, and within seconds they were well behind.

Then, at half-way mark, as they passed under a bridge, someone above them spat.

Something clicked. There was a grunt of rage, and the "English University Team", galvanized by rage, tore up the river—and won. They returned to Oxford with the Hermann Goering trophy.

Earlier, he had joined the University Air Squadron, and so, the next year, when Britain declared war towards the end of the University Long Vacation, he drove up from the house in Beaconsfield and reported for duty.

No one wanted him. Then, reluctantly, he was accepted. Then, after several moves, a great deal of foot-drill and frustration—and no flying—he and his friends were posted to Flying Training School in the north of Scotland. He had already—somewhat to his surprise—been given an Air Force commission, and he travelled north with the one thin ring of the pilot officer on his sleeve. And with his friends. He had a gift for friendship: his book is full of friends—of Frank Waldron, Noel Agazarian, Harry McGrath, Dixie Dean—and above all of Peter Pease. He and Peter met when they were posted to an Army Co-operation Squadron outside Salisbury. For Peter, the quiet, thoughtful, self-possessed Etonian ("I never knew him to lose his temper"), Hillary formed, despite his prejudices, a deep attachment. He would try to anger Peter, laugh at his tradition of land-owning and good-works-among-the-tenantry, laugh at "the sort of people who go to Eton", the fops, the foolish and "the fox-hunting bounders", but he was at heart profoundly impressed by this new friend. His death—all Hillary's friends died in action, before him—nearly broke his heart.

When France fell, the opportunity for which they'd been praying arose. He, Peter, and a few others, left the world of Army Co-op, its slow-moving, string-tied Hectors and Lysanders, and joined a Spitfire squadron. Here they were taken in hand by the battle-seasoned pilots of Number One Squadron, taught the tactics of dog-fighting, the psychology of German pilots, the reasons for attacking from height and sun, for never following a plane down after hitting it—and the absolute importance of working as a squadron. It was the Shrewsbury lesson again, and in earnest.

And above all, they learnt to fly the magic Spitfire.

He, Peter Pease and Colin Pinkney were posted together to 603 Squadron, which had just three vacancies. They took over their Spitfires at Turnhouse outside Edinburgh, then flew them on to Montrose, to the windswept north-east fringe of Scotland. And it was here that one of the pleasanter interludes took place, of a war which was to be far from pleasant. They made friends with little children billeted at Tarfside, the village near their aerodrome—children evacuated from other, more vulnerable, towns than Montrose. There was Betty Davie, aged ten, to whom he lost his heart, and a host of others down to the smallest small boy, "Rat Face".

"How are you, Rat Face?"

"Quite well, thank you. You can pick me up if you like."

Suddenly—everything happened suddenly that summer— the squadron was ordered south: morale soared. They would miss the children (the local adults, if there were any, seemed to make no impression on 603 Squadron), but this, at last, was the real thing. At last, with the Germans beginning their attacks on southern England, they would see action. To all—and none, not a one, was to survive—*this* was what life was for. They were honest: none professed to feel he was fighting tyranny, oppression or even Hitler; they would fight for the love of flying, for the simple thrill of killing.

As they took off for the last time, slipped into line astern and dived in salute to the village, they saw the children had spelt out on the road in big white stones, stones they could only just have lifted, the words, "Good Luck".

A few maddening, unexplained, days at Turnhouse, then— all the way. They landed at Hornchurch on the Thames Estuary on 10 August, 1940.

The next morning Richard Hillary was in action for the first time. He climbed, confident of immortality, impregnability; with a cold feeling inside, that today, for the first time in life, he would kill. He tried to visualize what the man would be like. "Was he young? Was he fat? Would he die with the Fuehrer's name on his lips? Or would he die alone, in that last moment conscious of himself as a man?"

A moment later, it happens. A Messerschmitt 109 at 18,000, one of twenty against the squadron's eight, way, way, above them. Brian Carbury leads the section into a brilliant bit of aerobatics, right over the top, so that, miraculously, the Germans lose, in two short seconds, all their advantage of height. Hillary sees a sitting duck, kicks rudder, lets it have a four-second burst from right angles, full-deflection.

The tracer from all eight guns drills into the Messerschmitt. An agonizing pause and a burst of flame, a pillar of smoke. It spirals away, out of control.

"My first emotion was one of satisfaction—at the final logical conclusion of months of specialized training—then I had a feeling of the essential rightness of it all. He was dead and I was alive: it could so easily have been the other way round; and that would somehow have been right, too."

The few short weeks of strength and beauty—and Spitfires—which remained for Richard Hillary, aged twenty-one, passed by. They were crammed with action and there was scarce time to reflect on friends, who, one by one, did not return.

On 3 September he was shot down. He was picked up, hideously burnt, by the Margate lifeboat which had been searching for three hours and was about to give up. He knew his face was burnt because of the pain which a damp English sun gave as he lay in the bottom of the boat. He got to hospital, blind and in agony, was given a shot of morphia and passed out.

He woke. By now his face, his hands, were covered in tannic acid which had hardened into tar. His body hung helplessly on straps above the bed, just clearing it, he could just see propped up in front of him, fingers like claws. He was in a sea of pain, being given injections of morphia every three hours, unable to eat. Then, later, only liquids, through a tube in the raw, featureless horror of his face.

His parents, whom he worshipped, came down on the second day to see him. They behaved with an almost incredible stoicism, confronted by an unrecognizable son—only the voice remained—a young man, however brilliant any plastic surgery might be (if he lived long enough to submit to it), who would never again look like their son.

He was put under anaesthetic for the ordeal of having the tannic acid chipped from his hands, and while under it he saw Peter, his greatest friend, being shot down from behind in a dogfight. He came to, screaming, "Peter, for God's sake, look out behind!" with two nurses and a doctor holding him down.

Two days later, a letter from Colin Pinkney. It hoped he was getting better; Peter was dead.

He was given devoted treatment. It was largely, he wrote, the efforts of two girls, Sue and Anne, who changed his dressings every two hours—and it took over an hour to do—which saved his hands from being amputated.

Then one day his door was opened and Denise walked in. "I knew at once who she was. It was unnecessary for her to speak—she was the most beautiful person I have ever seen.

" 'I hope you'll excuse me coming to see you like this,' she said. 'But I was going to be married to Peter. He often spoke of you and wanted so much to see you. So I hope you won't mind me coming instead.' "

His friendship with Denise, which did so much to enrich the little time still left to him, must have been one of the great experiences of his life—and she must have been a remarkable person. And soon after she had entered his life and he had implored her, in a hastily dictated letter the moment she left, to come back and often—but to give him warning, so he could adjust himself, prepare his mind for the emotional impact of her arrival—he was transferred to that remarkable workshop in East Grinstead, the plastic surgery clinic of Archibald McIndoe, where men without faces were given them—though painfully, slowly, and inch by inch—where hands and feet which had been burnt to cinder were made to function again.

McIndoe, like Hillary, is dead—though he survived the war and was able to rejoice over his transformations—and might well have been included, were there space, in this book. Anyone who heard, as I did, that Christmas Day broadcast, the annual tour-de-force of the B.B.C., linking the world in a nostalgic memory of when Abroad really was Abroad, the wartime broadcast with those few emotional minutes from Archie's hospital, is unlikely to forget it. The place had been decorated with holly, paper-chains, a tree and even mistletoe, a few bottles of beer had been opened, and the patients began to sing, for the listening world's benefit, their own song. It was set to the rousing tune of "The Church's One Foundation", and it started off, "We *Are* Mac-Indoe's *Children*—We *Are his Gui*nea *Pigs*——" The tears were tumbling helplessly down my cheeks as I listened—and at that very moment men and women all over Britain were seizing pen and paper to protest over the desecration of a hymn tune.

Hillary called it The Beauty Shop. McIndoe, after saying, "Well, you certainly made a thorough job of it, didn't you?" and "Four new eyelids, I'm afraid, but you're not ready for them

yet", was asked by Hillary just how long it would be before he
flew again.

"Next war for you."

The face could be made presentable; the hands would never
again function properly. Hillary inside had known this and now
he felt no emotion at all—though an earlier, snap answer that it
would take six months before he could fly had depressed him
terribly. He was given, in a great hurry lest he go blind, an
enormous pair of upper eyelids, "real horse-blinkers"; he had
to raise his head to look in front of him. Yet in a remarkably
short time they fitted and he found he could raise and lower
them, like natural, non-McIndoe, lids. He was amazed, childishly amazed, and grateful.

With intervals of convalescence outside the hospital he spent
many months in an interminable series of operations. A man
who needs a new face must have it cut from some other part of
his own body, a predicament which gave endless cause for
laughter, mirth which tempered the horrors of the actual process. No other graft, save that from an identical twin, will take;
it goes septic or worse, is rejected as flatly and finally as an
unwelcome suitor, and the process of taking suitable bits off
buttocks, legs, arms, transferring them and then letting both
wounds heal before going on with the next bit, is heart-
rendingly long. And all the while, two determinations were
rising inside him. He would write his story—the story of so
many young men, maimed, mutilated, perhaps destroyed—and
he would somehow get back into the air. The problem in each
case was his hands: twisted, rigid, fleshless claws, which could
no more write a book than fly a Spitfire.

But eventually, between operations which seemed to be
stretching into eternity, he was able, on a borrowed typewriter,
with one bent talon, to write the first chapter of his story. The
problem, which he had never considered, was where to take
it then. This was solved, as so many of Hillary's problems were,
by a pretty girl. A V.A.D. in McIndoe's hospital, a war-time
nurse who had worked for the publishing firm of Macmillan,
gave him an introduction to Mr. Lovat Dickson. Armed with
his precious first chapter, Hillary burst into Dickson's office.
It was February, 1941, dark and damp and miserable, and he

had been in hospitals for most of the five months since being shot down.

"When he said he would like to read me what he had written," says Lovat Dickson, "I urged him to leave the manuscript with me—this he quite firmly refused to do—he fixed me with that blue eye of his and a bright smile and said that he thought I had better listen. I prepared myself for the worst. I did not hear him read the first few lines because I was watching his thin skeleton fingers, horribly raw in colour, without nails and permanently bent, gripping the pages. He did not read well. He was shy, and the nervousness underneath his domineering manner made the skin on his face flush, so that all the marks of the burns stood out like weals. It was really a terrifying sight, but not a horrible one."

Lovat was interested, the book had possibilities, and he urged the young man to write a few more chapters and come back. When he next saw him, ten months later, the young man had been to America, more or less on his own initiative, to tell American munition workers about the war—though the appalled British Information Services in Washington had taken one horrified look at him and said he must go home, and immediately; the people of America, far from being inspired, would resolve never to get involved. Fortunately, Hillary found good friends in the States and did not return until he had been encouraged and helped—by the loan of an office and a secretary —to finish his book. When he reappeared in Dickson's office, the book was finished, the American rights were sold, and he presented the astonished, rather angry, publisher with a complete set of proofs. But it was a good book, and Dickson's firm snapped up the English rights. It was immediately successful, both in America and in England. Richard Hillary had proved that not only did he have a story to tell—a remarkable and in places unbearably moving story—but he could tell it superbly well.

He had always wanted to be a writer, and this literary triumph meant much to him. But there was still Ambition Number Two—to get back into the air. The authorities tried hard to stop him, offered him work on the ground, almost any kind of work he cared to name, and if that did not appeal, he could resign with a large gratuity and a pension for life. Richard Hillary was adamant. In his heart he knew he could never again handle the controls of a Spitfire but there was one possibility open. He could wangle himself into a night-fighter squadron, where there was no dog-fighting, no violent manoeuvre involved; this sort of flying, he hoped and believed, would be within his capabilities, the weak and stiffened fingers would be able to cope.

He bullied Fighter Command—and now, with his new-found fame, he could bully anyone—into sending him on a night-fighter course.

His friends were horrified and all of them tried hard, some desperately, to make him change his mind, but that mind was made up with all the stubbornness of the little Australian boy of twenty years back. He was posted to a training station in Berwickshire at the end of 1942. A little over two years had elapsed since that hideous, flaming descent into the Thames Estuary, and he found, to his utter dismay, that he felt on arrival just as he had found when he arrived, for the first time, at each one of his schools: he knew he was going to hate it. And as he wrote his friend Eric Linklater (one of several writers and artists Lovat Dickson introduced him to, each of whom was to help him in a different way), "this place, a veritable wilderness, has very nearly broken me in two days, and last night I crawled back to my freezing little hut and wept like a child. Not a very auspicious start——"

But his mind was made up.

There is one intensely sobering experience before the end. On a short leave in London he is in a pub during one of the worst German air raids. The volume of noise, as they stand there drinking, shuts out all thought, "there was no lull, no second in which to breathe and follow carefully the note of the oncoming bomber. It was an orchestra of madmen playing in a cupboard."

The house next door is hit, and they are all flung, deafened, bruised and filthy, about the room. Everyone but the barmaid is able to get up, white and shaken. An A.F.S. man comes in and the girl is taken away on a stretcher, with Hillary following along behind to help among the wreckage of the next house

They dig frantically in the ruins—men from the Auxiliary Fire Service, an A.R.P. warden, a soldier, a taxi-driver—working silently, desperately, against the ticking clock of death. At last they come to the feet of a woman and "like prospectors at the first glint of gold" they work frenziedly on. She is in bed, with a small child, and they get the child out first, then they drag out the mother, as gently as they can, blood-streaked in her cotton nightdress, but calm, resigned. She is dying, and she reaches instinctively for the child, while people around her shout instructions, "Give her air—where's the ambulance?—don't move her——"

Hillary takes out his hip flask of brandy, holds it to her lips. The teeth are clenched and very little goes in.

Then she grabs his hand, takes a long, last look at him and says:

"Thank you, sir. I see they got you, too."

I have quoted this episode, which left a scar to the end, a little out of context; it happened before he got back into the air and he describes it in *The Last Enemy*. The face of that dying woman and her frank assessment that he was not, would never again be, like other men, was with him from that moment on.

Just after midnight on 8 January, 1943, he took off from Berwick on a training circuit. He had completed one already that night which had been perfectly normal, perfectly satisfactory. It was a cold, cloudy night and a little sleet was falling.

His instructions were to circle the aerodrome, keeping an inboard eye on its flashing beacon. With cloud about and no moon, this winking light would be all he would see: no horizon, no stars, no land.

There was none of the usual nervous chit-chat over the RT and after a minute the Controller Night Flying called him up on it. "Are you happy?"

"Moderately," was the answer. "I am continuing to orbit."

He was called again a minute later and this time there was no answer. From the ground they could see his navigation lights getting nearer, vanishing in cloud, reappearing, getting brighter as he lost height. Again and again they called him but there was no answer, and the lights, in a brightening, widening circle, got lower.

He crashed, was killed, two miles from the airfield perimeter.

The verdict was: Pilot Lost Control in Cloud. But no one will ever know how or why.

Richard Hillary in his short and vivid life seemed to epitomize his generation. I include him in this book partly for that and partly because his example of quiet courage and determination, coupled with schoolboy high spirits, became a legend, a legend which made, I think, better men of those, like me, who read and marvelled. The legend of the sort of man, crippled, shorn of the strength, the beauty, which had meant so much (for he had been vain and freely admitted it), who could ring up a middle-aged London publisher and tell him in the accents of Hollywood that it had been decided to make a super-colossal epic of *The Last Enemy*—with the proviso that the lead rôle be played by the publisher himself, Mr. Lovat Dickson. When Dickson politely demurs, the Hollywood voice, so precisely caught, collapses in helpless laughter.

Hillary had shot down five enemy aircraft before his brief career ended in the Thames Estuary. Others shot down more, many more. He was hideously maimed—but others were as badly burned as he and others showed an equal stoicism. Others, a few, insisted like Hillary on being allowed back into the air. Others died.

But none had the combination of guts with brains and talent and beauty and—as he was the first to admit—simple luck (but, oh *God*, was that luck?—was Richard Hillary *lucky*?) to make their life a challenge to a generation.

Chapter 19

Edmund Hillary

"Abode of Snows" they call it, in the world's most perfect language; a colossal range of mountains, stretching from the seventy-fourth to the ninety-sixth meridian east of Greenwich. For "Himalaya", in the ancient Sanskrit, means just that. Sanskrit, the most important, most highly organized tongue in the world (the word means "perfectly made"), is very nearly the oldest. It is a literary language now, much the same to Brahmanism as Latin to the Roman Catholic Church; yet a thousand years ago and more men spoke it in their every-day affairs, haggled in the bazaar, made love—in Sanskrit. Life—at least to listen to—was finer, nobler, then.

A digression. But, standing on a hilltop in Mussoorie, north of Delhi, or on another near the northern tip of Burma, watching in wonder, from either end of the Himalaya, watching as clouds whip past those snowy peaks, I have goggled at their very timelessness. A thousand years ago—or was it two or three, or longer?—and the early Aryan invaders looked up at this astonishing sight, named it "Himalaya", "Abode of Snows". And through the ages the Abode has been there, a challenge to men, looming up above them, miles in the sky.

Near the middle of these fourteen hundred miles of ice and snow is a peak, far higher than the rest. Most of the time she is shrouded in mist, invisible. But then, without warning, mists melt away, clouds drift off, and she is there for men to marvel at. Hard and cold and beautiful. "Chomolunga" some call her: Goddess Mother of the World. But the name by which we know her, in our clumsy English tongue, might have been expressly created for her; if ever there were a peak destined for perpetual, endless peace, undisturbed by the depredations of man, the cries of birds and animals, a summit which would Rest for Ever —it was Chomolunga, balanced austerely on that southern scarp of the great plateau of Central Asia.

But, in fact, the so-appropriate name is just the one belonging to the Indian Surveyor-General at the time Chomolunga was surveyed, Sir George Everest. And the enormous, towering height revealed by that survey, worked out painstakingly, trigonometrically, from the nearest points which could be reached, averaged over six readings, was 29,002 feet. Just a few feet short of five and a half miles. Straight up.

There is nothing, not a thing, in the world so high, and Mount Everest became a symbol, a challenge. Yet not until 1921 was a first reconnaissance made of the slopes. The Kingdom of Nepal, in which the southern approach lay, refused flatly to allow any expedition; it was necessary to go via Tibet and have a look from that side. On the results of this northern recce, two climbing expeditions set off in the following year. The first reach 26,700 feet—two thousand three hundred vertical feet short of their target—and the second, using oxygen (for the thinness of the air at that height makes physical effort an agony), reached up another six hundred.

In 1924 came a third, and now Mallory and Irvine were seen by their companions, setting off on a final bid, just the two of them, at 28,000 feet. They were never seen again.

In 1933, a fourth expedition found Mallory's ice-axe.

Fifth, sixth, seventh attempts were made between 1935 and 1938—without success.

Then, in 1951, the combination of Tibet's refusal to allow more expeditions and the sudden compliance of Nepal made a first recce of the *southern* approaches to Everest a possibility.

The Nepalese slope of the mountain had always been regarded as impossibly difficult—apart from being forbidden—but this only encouraged men like Eric Shipton. In that year, 1951, he was granted permission by the Government of Nepal to go on a reconnaissance of the southern slope.

A young New Zealand bee-keeper whose hobby was mountain climbing had already made a name for himself as a fearless climber. Shipton asked him to join the team.

This, for Ed Hillary, was the biggest moment of his life. With his fellow-countryman George Lowe, also invited, he sent off an immediate acceptance. Perhaps, somewhere in his mind, was the thought that some day he might even be standing at the summit of Mount Everest.

Whether he thought it, as he opened the telegram from Shipton, or not, he was, in less than two years, standing on that summit—and the first man in history to do so.

To find out why and how, we must go back a few years in time and deep in distance into the world's southern hemisphere. He was born in New Zealand, 20 July, 1919, more or less into a swarm of bees. His father had hive after hive of them—sixteen hundred hives, and there was so much work to be done that the boy spent all his school holidays helping with it. He liked it, of course. The sun shines all day long for most of New Zealand's days, and he loved the feel of it in his face, the rush of the wind, the constant, warning hum of the bees. It was an adventurous life: all 1,600 hives might swarm at once; the bees could do, and did, unexpected things; the honey crop might be enormous or negligible, and one never knew until it had been harvested.

In the months of southern winter, in June, July and August, he would go for long walks by himself through the hills. It was then that he was happiest. It hadn't occurred to him, yet, to climb a real mountain.

Then, just before his seventeenth birthday, he was able to go on a school trip to Ruapehu, the nine-thousand-foot, snow-covered volcano on New Zealand's North Island, and there try his hand at the strange sport of ski-ing.

He loved it, though, as he remarked later, he never bothered to look up to the summit. He was too happy in the snow, the first he'd touched or even seen—just halfway up.

Three years later, after a spell at university, which convinced him and his parents that bee-keeping, not solid geometry, was his life's work, he settled back into his father's business. He was a bee-keeper, he loved it; he had need of nothing more.

But when he was twenty he had more opportunity for travel. He was able to go with a friend and visit the rugged South Island of his country, with its chain of Southern Alps. They sat one evening, over-awed by two garrulous climbers who were describing in the hotel just how they had climbed Mount Cook. Early the next morning they set out with a guide to climb a mountain—any mountain—themselves.

Late that afternoon they reached the top, could stand with the wind rushing past them and gaze in wonder at glaciers, snow, jagged peaks.

The die was cast: Ed Hillary knew he had to be a mountaineer. When, a week later, he got back to his bees, he bought or borrowed every book he could on the craft. Two of these, *Nanda Devi* by Shipton, telling of his attempt on that Himalayan peak, and *Camp Six*, Frank Smythe's book of an unsuccessful climb up the north face of Everest, became his constant companions.

Came the war, and he was seriously wounded as a navigator with the New Zealand Air Force. He fought back to health, never doubting for a moment that he would go on climbing mountains. By 1946 he was back at it, climbing bigger, more alarming peaks than before, more difficult ones each season, till he had hardened himself to whipcord, made body and mind into a machine for climbing, a machine which took decisions automatically, without conscious thought: there is little time for thought: every correction, every step has to be automatic and correct—automated—when you climb on ice.

An exciting visit to Europe and its Alps, so different to the Southern ones he knew, and a climb each day with friends he made there, climbing every daylight hour of every day, determined not to waste a single minute. And it was towards the end of this holiday that he got a letter from his old friend George

Lowe. The two had been asked to go, next year, on an expedition. It was heading for the world's greatest mountain range, the Himalayas.

There were many, many problems—not the least of them financial—but eventually a four-man team of young New Zealanders got to India, headed north by train to the Himalayas. On the way, they read in a newspaper that the Nepalese Government had decided, after all, to allow climbers to tackle Everest—should they care to—through Nepal. The object of their own expedition was to scale a far lesser peak, Mukut Parbat—a mere 23,760 feet—but each of the young climbers, hardly daring to say it aloud, set his heart on having a crack, some day, at the mother of mountains herself.

They scaled, not only Mukut Parbat, but six other peaks, came back to their hotel, flushed with success, and found a telegram from Shipton. It invited two of them, Hillary and Riddiford, to join an Everest recce the next year.

They accepted—then had to swallow their impatience for a whole year. But Shipton's reconnaissance began, as planned, in September of 1951. By the time Hillary and Riddiford had met up with Shipton and his party of four, in India, they were relieved to find Englishmen much like themselves, not changing for dinner each evening, or passing the port. "My first feeling," Hillary wrote later, "was one of relief. I have rarely seen a more disreputable bunch, and my visions of changing for dinner faded away for ever."

On, through the settlement of Namche Bazar, another three days of footslogging, and the foot of Everest. At Namche they had recruited hill people, the Sherpas, as guides and porters, and now they went on, through steep gorges with ice-cold water foaming through them at incredible speeds, through jungle, up and down wooded foot-hills, with snow-hung top-heavy peaks dangling out above them.

The plan was to establish Base Camp on the massive Khumbu Glacier to the west of the mountain, and this they did, 17,500 feet above sea level, at the end of September.

On the 30th, Shipton and Hillary climbed together, lungs aching in the rarefied air, to 20,000 feet. From here, they could look down into the great ice-filled valley between themselves and the mountain. When they had recovered their breath enough to do so, they stared down at a view no man had seen before. Almost in the same gasp, they both shouted, "A route— there's a route!"

There was—or so it seemed—but it had to be reconnoitred and studied from every possible angle. During that time Hillary, the Himalayan greenhorn, learnt much of Himalayan lore: learnt—and it was presented as fact, solid fact, by the Sherpas—of the Abominable Snowman and his enormous, size-twenty-five, human, feet, padding about the mountain; of the spirits which haunted the Snowman's territory. More valuable, perhaps, he learnt how to deal with the gallant little Sherpas themselves, the men who accompanied and helped them. Most of this, as Ed Hillary cheerfully admitted, he got from the older, wiser, Shipton: "His ability to be calm and comfortable in any circumstance; his insatiable curiosity to know what lay over the next hill or around the next corner, and above all, his remark-able power to transform the discomfort and pain and misery of high-altitude life into a great adventure."

Quite a lesson. Ed Hillary never forgot it.

They ended the recce in November, confident the only way up Everest was through the dangerous ice-fall they had looked into from the glacier. It would be difficult—and dangerous— but if the mountain were to be climbed, those factors would have to be ignored. It would be an adventure, a great adven-ture. Nothing more, and nothing less.

The party separated on its way home, and it was while Hillary and his fellow-New Zealander were being welcomed at the British Embassy in Katmandu that they learnt the galling news that already permission had been granted by the Nepalese for an expedition the following year. A Swiss expedition.

Despite this, Shipton, when he heard about it, decided to push on with plans for a full-scale assault in 1953. In the meantime, there would be a testing, hardening, "dummy run", somewhere in the Himalayas, in 1952. Hillary was invited, then was overjoyed to find his old friend George Lowe invited, too.

Cho Oyu is the seventh highest peak in the world, just 26,867 feet above mean-sea-level. The problems, the emergencies, the crises, which beset mountaineers can never be the same on two different days, even on the same mountain, but high-altitude acclimatization under Himalayan conditions, within sight of the ultimate target, Everest (Cho Oyu is twenty miles away, to the west), was the next best thing to a sortie up Everest itself. They set off to scale it.

Cho Oyu was never climbed: a great deal of valuable experience came out of the attempt, but twin hazards of over-hanging ice which no one had anticipated and the invasion of Tibet by the Chinese, suddenly alarmingly close, caused Shipton to stop short of his objective.

In any case, it was only a "dummy run". What really mattered was: how had the Swiss fared—on Everest?

First report, as they clambered down into the green valley, was from an óld Sherpa, leading a yak. "Oh, yes," the man said. "Seven have reached the summit. Seven."

A stunning blow. By all means let the Swiss—damn them—have every possible ounce of good luck, good weather, success. Up to the last hundred feet. Then, dear God, send them back. That had been the prayer. God, send the Swiss back happy and healthy from their expedition. And let the British get there first—next year.

But a few days later, Shipton's party were overjoyed, completely overjoyed, to find the Swiss had failed. They met the party, learnt from them, while forcing faces into frowns of compassion, sympathy, that their leader Lambert, and the Sherpa climber Tenzing, had got to within a few hundred feet of the almost mythical twenty-nine thousand and two. Then they had been beaten, by the weather.

And so, a British attempt, under Eric Shipton, was planned for 1953. It was an auspicious year, a young Queen would be crowned in June. There was talk, most of it foolish, about a New Elizabethan Era—but there was no doubt, and the team in their hearts knew it, that the scalp of Everest would be a fine Coronation present for a Queen.

As in Scott's expeditions to the South Pole, no one was certain whom the leader would take with him, till almost the last minute. Then Shipton asked, among others, three New Zealanders, Lowe, Ayres and Hillary.

But, even before 1952 was out, came trouble. A difference of

bove, left: Richard Hillary at Oxford was
ikingly handsome. *Above, right:* After he had
en shot down and disfigured, his face was largely
built by plastic surgeon Archibald McIndoe.
ght: Group Captain Cheshire, most decorated
mber pilot of the Second World War, at the
ight of his career. *Below:* The post-war Cheshire
chats with an inmate of one of his Homes.

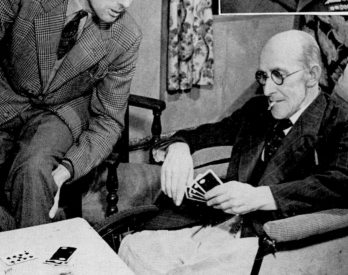

On this snap of herself, An[n]e Frank had written, in Dutc[h] "This is a photo as I wou[ld] wish myself to look all t[he] time. Then maybe I wou[ld] have a chance to get [to] Hollywood. Anne Fran[k, 10th October, 1942." *Left:* [a] more recent picture of t[he] house overlooking the Pri[n]zengracht Canal in Amste[r]dam where she hid un[til] betrayed to the Gestapo[.]

Above: High-altitude men. Left: Edmund Hillary with Sherpa Tenzing at London Airport after their conquest of Everest. Behind Tenzing stands John Hunt. *Right:* John Glenn being loaded into his space capsule.

opinion with the "Himalayan Joint Committee" made Shipton resign and for a while it looked as if the attempt had been tacitly forgotten. Then, in October, Hillary, back with his bees, got a letter from a stranger signing himself "John Hunt". He, Hunt, was now in charge of the expedition, hoped Hillary would still be joining them, and felt it "most unfortunate that it should have happened this way, and very bad luck on Eric Shipton".

No use crying over spilt mountaineers: Hillary agreed to come.

And so the great year dawned. From New Zealand and from England, the team gathered, at Katmandu. As well as Hunt, the England contingent consisted of Evans, Gregory and Bourdillon—who had attempted Cho Oyu against ice and Chinamen—Ward who had been with Shipton and Hillary in the '51 recce, and Noyce, Wylie, Band and Westmacott with a physiologist, Dr. Griffiths Pugh.

Pugh's task was to make tests of how each member fared in conditions of altitude, cold and strain. There was a cine-cameraman, Stobart.

From New Zealand came George Lowe and Ed Hillary.

And, last but the reverse of least, among the Sherpas who would be employed was the tough little climber, the man who, with Lambert the year before, had climbed higher than ever man before: Tenzing.

March tenth: the team began its move to Everest. The weather was wonderful, they were able to sleep under stars, swim in rivers, for each of the seventeen days to the monastery of Thyangboche. There they set up temporary base camp, from which they could go out and get experience with the new equipment, prepare themselves for the rigours of oxygen starvation farther up.

They ran into an unexpected problem. The intense reflection of sunlight from the snow, a whiteness surpassing any washing-powder advertisement ever dreamed up, made all of them without goggles go blind. This for a start meant all the Sherpas. Stobart solved the problem: there were large panoramic goggles with the team, just a few pairs, and these he proceeded to cut into small pieces and issue, two at a time, to all who needed protection. In a short time he had made, helped by Hillary, some thirty pairs of "goggles".

That problem solved, others took its place; but by the end of May, after endless trial and error, the team was ready for a first assault on the summit. They had been moving supplies to a series of camps, each higher than the last: Base Camp was now high on the Khumbu Glacier; Camps Two, Three, Four and Five were, if we are to give the lady Everest a human form, rounding her left breast and heading out to the tip of the left shoulder. Camps Six and Seven were on the approach to the "South Col", or creeping up over the shoulder, with the lady facing west. Camp Eight, halfway along the South Col, was halfway along her shoulder.

The final assault, then, was up the lady's neck, jaw, cheekbone, to the flattening surface of her bald and rocky head, the South Summit. A final struggle to the top of the scalp, the Summit, and the lady would have been overpowered, for the first time in—no one asks a lady's age.

Hunt sent off a first two-man assault team, Evans and Bourdillon, while a second team, Tenzing and Hillary, watched from Camp Eight. The lady's head was wreathed in cloud, swirling, churning cloud that hid her from the jawbone up, but when these miraculously and for a few seconds swept away, Evans and Bourdillon could be seen, struggling under their loads of oxygen, high up on the South Summit, on the lady's scalp.

There was an alarming diversion when the older John Hunt and the Sherpa, Da Namgyal, who had been placing supplies of oxygen above Camp Eight, got into difficulties. Hunt, determined to leave as much oxygen as possible in this advance base, had taken off his own supply, left it there and tried to descend without. The brave attempt nearly cost him his life, and Hillary, forgetting his own mask in the emergency, rushed up the slope from Camp Eight, helped the exhausted pair down.

But without oxygen, Hunt was unlikely, even with Ed Hillary's arm around him, to get back to Camp Eight. Hillary dumped him on a tussock of ice, tore back for his own supply.

By the time Hunt had recovered, the first assault party could be seen descending.

No—they had not achieved it. Evans had had trouble with his oxygen, and both were running short. They decided, wisely, to return—though Bourdillon felt he might have made it alone.

Everything now depended on the second assault. Hunt, protesting, was sent down to the lower camp with Evans, Bourdillon and one of the Sherpas. The remaining six prepared a way for the new assault. This time, no chance could be taken; the monsoon was on its way, and one more hurried try was as much as time would allow. The hopes of the expedition rested on Hillary and the little Sherpa, Tenzing.

Another Sherpa became violently ill, had to be sent down. Now there were five men and three of these set off early in the morning of 28 May to lay supplies for the remaining two. An hour after they had left, the more lightly loaded Hillary and Tenzing started after them. At two-thirty in the afternoon, having caught them up, they stopped at what seemed a suitable Camp Nine—the highest place it would be feasible to provide as a jumping-off spot. Lowe, Gregory, Ang Nymia, left. Hillary and Tenzing were alone.

There was no time to waste; a tent had to be put up, and fast, lest they die of exposure in the whistling, screaming wind. There was no oxygen to waste, even with the supplies which had been carried up, for oxygen needs heavy containers, and it goes fast, so they pitched their tent on the little ledge without its help, their lungs in agony. Then they crept into the tent, turned on the reduced supply of "sleeping oxygen". The tent, a dozen times, seemed on the verge of being lifted bodily and hurled over the side, to crash humiliatingly, occupants inside, on the roof of the monastery seventeen thousand feet below, but they managed to keep it moored.

Six-thirty in the morning of the 29th: they got up, thawed out boots over the little stove, had a quick breakfast and strapped on oxygen equipment.

Tenzing led the way up to twenty-eight thousand, halfway up the lady's cheek. Then, with South Summit directly ahead, the New Zealander took over the lead. The going had become more difficult, it was like mounting the side of a skyscraper, with a fierce, unbelievable wind whistling past, trying its best to hurl one off into the abyss, and a numbing cold which seemed to dig deep into body and mind. They pushed on, loads growing heavier, and then suddenly a piece of solid rock broke in half and Hillary, looking down between his legs, saw a gap—two feet wide and ten thousand feet deep. He scrambled to safety, and now, as they went on, they started to slip back, with each step, almost as far as they went forward. There was only a thin, paper-thin, crust of frozen snow preventing them from avalanching, in an over-sized, two-man, snowball, to the jagged valley beneath.

28,700, and things improved. Hillary found thick, solid ice with his axe, was able to cut steps in it. Now, with a wild exhilaration, he was sure they would succeed.

But not too soon: Tenzing was in difficulties. The little man, who had been moving so deftly, so skilfully, was crawling. Aghast, Hillary watched him, then slithered back and grabbed at the outlet of his mask. It was two inches wide, like his own, but it had frozen over. The ice, as Hillary frantically hammered and twisted, fell out on the snow and Tenzing, with a wild snort of relief, was breathing.

Almost 29,000. At ground level the climb would have taken only a few minutes. At this height, with four hours oxygen left, they might just do it.

And now they were hard up against what Hillary, ever since 1951, had known to be the chief, almost insuperable, obstacle. He and Shipton had seen, through binoculars, the great outcrop of rock hanging into space.

It was impossible. At ground level it might have been scaled —just. Here, at twenty-nine thousand, sheer rock work on a convex, overhanging bulge was out of the question.

There was a chance by going round to the left—but no certainty that they would get back. On the right of the rock bulge was a matching, seemingly endless bulge of ice.

And then, Ed Hillary saw it. A part of the ice bulge was cracking, tearing itself from the mountain. There was a crack between rock and ice, a vertical crack, not much of a space, but big enough—perhaps—to let a man climb up inside, and not trap him inside it.

Back jammed against ice, feet and fingers scratching into rock, Hillary began to force his way up the narrow passage. If the ice, wedged out by his efforts, broke off, he would shoot out with it at the end of his line and catapult Tenzing, forty feet farther down, out into space to join him. They would spin slowly, one on top, then the other, for a mile, two miles and more before they smashed against the rocks below.

But there was no time to consider this. Up and up, inch by inch, Hillary squeezed and wriggled his way, while Tenzing, just outside the lower end of the fissure, felt his rope grow tauter.

Just as the rope went tight, Hillary reached the top, scrambled through, lay gasping like a landed trout. A minute later he began to pull Tenzing through.

Tenzing got through and now they were near—very near. If only strength would hold out. They were desperately tired, lungs bursting; backs and arms, from hacking steps in the ice, dragging themselves up the rock face, were agony. Could they make it? For a moment it seemed most unlikely.

But the slope was easier now, the angle less steep. They got up and went on, Hillary still in the lead, feet slipping out behind each time he put one forward, so he seemed to be going slowly backward.

Despair eddied up inside, as he struggled over a piece of bare shingle, came to another slab of ice and began, almost unconscious with fatigue, to hack out more steps.

And then, when it seemed the long, cold, breathless slog would go on for ever, the ice ended. And in front, miles in the distance, were the highlands of Tibet. He had reached the top, was looking right over the top of the top, he was there, they had done it. . . . Frantically, he waved Tenzing up. The time, as he looked at his watch, was half-past eleven, the sun high in the heaven.

Tenzing had been carrying a few little flags wrapped round his ice-axe, and now Hillary got him to unfurl them and stand, triumphant, on the summit. Then he took three photographs of him. Above, as a background to the little man, were lumps of porridgy cumulus. In between they could see the mountain giants, Kanchenjunga and Makalu, only a few miles away. As fast as frozen fingers could operate the shutter, Hillary took photographs of them; then photos, in a different direction, of the Tibetan hills; photos, to west and east, of the Himalaya; Abode of the Snows.

And in front between them and Tibet lay the north slope, now forbidden, up which so many Everest expeditions had climbed to end in tragedy or frustration. He looked for some sign of Mallory and Irvine. Had they perished—or perhaps just disappeared, into some cavernous, mystic state deep in the guts of Everest, a land of Abominable Snowmen, Tibetan monks— and captured British climbers?

Not a sign.

Tenzing dug a small hole in the snow, placed offerings of food inside it, a thank-offering of sweets, a stick of chocolate, some biscuits. Hillary put beside it a little cross.

Eleven forty-five. Fifteen minutes at the top of the world— and they had to get moving down again. Hillary slithered down to the first rocks, stuffed a handful of tiny stones in his pocket as a souvenir. Then they set off.

Hours later, they saw George Lowe scrambling up toward them with spare oxygen and a thermos of hot lemonade. They gave him their news, strapped on oxygen, gulped the drink. At Camp Four they saw what they had been looking for— a little group of figures coming out of their small tents, moving slowly, uncertainly, in their direction. Charles Evans, Tom Bourdillon were there: they, through no fault of their own, had failed in the first attempt and now, if this second one had done no better, it was all over. The party came out slowly, uncertainly, and Hillary, in a sudden fit of cussedness, resolved not to let them know, by any gesture, what had happened.

Then, as the rest stumbled up, the irrepressible George Lowe could contain himself no longer. Wildly, hysterically, he waved his ice-axe at the summit.

The men approaching stopped dead—then rushed towards them.

And so the impossible had been achieved. The Goddess Mother of the World had been humbled.

It would be difficult—and pointless—to compare the efforts of Evans and Bourdillon, who so nearly made it; of Hunt, without whose leadership it could never have been achieved; of Tenzing, who got there a rope's-length after Hillary. Somebody has to be first. The efforts of all these men were remarkable : but the only name that will be remembered will be Ed Hillary's. Men may soon run a mile in three-and-a-half minutes; yet the only name we remember will be that of the man who first broke the "impossible" barrier, did it in four.

Whatever Ed Hillary does now, whatever he did later—like his energetic deputy-leadership of the British Commonwealth Antarctic Expedition, under Vivian Fuchs in 1957-58, which brought adverse comment on his head—is immaterial. He was the man—and there can never be another—who first did the impossible, and scaled the highest point on earth. To that extent, his "world record", unlike Roger Bannister's, is permanent, unique and unassailable. Men may dive deeper in the seas, run faster, fly faster, go farther into space—and others, later, will beat them. No one will ever again, in a million, million, years, be first at the top of the world.

Chapter 20

Anne Frank

Two of the people in this book are children, unimportant, unsung in their day, and practically their sole record is the diaries they kept. Both died tragically and it was months before the details were known. Apart from these similarities, they could hardly be less alike. Edgar Christian wrote a boyish, immature chronicle, a moving and courageous tale which grabs at one's imagination partly because it *is* so much a very young man's writing: reading it side by side with that of Anne Frank, one finds it hard to believe this boy, dying alone in the north of Canada, is quite a few years older (at time of writing) than the sensitive and literary little girl who was to die even more horribly half a world away.

But apart from having been written by brave young people about to die, these diaries have, can have, little in common. Anne, as she wrote, was buoyed up with the thrill of growing, the tenderness of young love—two emotions which flowered as fully in the stuffy darkness of her "Secret Annexe" as they

264

would have in the air of freedom. She was full of the excitement of living in her prison, determined to live for every minute of every day there; to study, to think, to live—and to improve herself. She had little thought of dying: when she had, she brushed it aside.

For Edgar Christian, death, as soon as he took up pencil, started to write, was staring him in the face. His diary, factual, laconic, is moving because of what one reads, in letters a yard high, between the lines. And it continues, as far as we can tell, to the day of his death. Anne Frank's journal is a prose masterpiece, a masterpiece of self-revelation, the autobiography—for over two years—of a girl, candid, sensitive, intelligent—and quietly, very brave.

Life ended for Anne Frank a little before her sixteenth birthday. She died in March, 1945, seven months after the last entry in her beloved diary, the almost human "Kitty" she had been given two years before, on her thirteenth birthday, and to whom she had confided for those two years all the thoughts she had been unable to share with another human being.

"I hope," she wrote in Dutch, as her first entry in the book, "I hope I shall be able to confide in you completely, as I have never been able to do with anyone before, and I hope that you will be a great support and comfort to me." The previous day, 12 June, 1942, had been her thirteenth birthday, and among the presents waiting for her in the sitting-room of the family's comfortable house in Amsterdam, among the sweets and flowers, was the stiff-covered little book in which she was to keep a diary. She had never kept one before: the prospect was thrilling. At thirteen, the thoughtful child needs friendship, a sympathetic ear into which to pour its thoughts without a returning flood of warning and advice from parents or grown-up friends. For Anne Frank, this friend was "Kitty".

The Diary of Anne Frank, published by Valentine, Mitchell and Co., and in paper-back by Pan Books, has been beautifully translated from the Dutch. And yet, little Anne herself, who spent much of her two years in the Secret Annexe studying French and English, who could read and enjoy Dickens, thrill to the voice of Churchill on the radio, could probably have put her journal into an English no less appealing.

Dutch was not Anne's mother tongue. Her parents were prosperous German Jews who had emigrated, not before time, from Frankfurt-on-Main and settled in Amsterdam. That had been 1933, when she was four years old. Her father, luckier than many—at least at this stage of his exile—became managing director of a firm called Travies NV. He was a kind man who seemed to understand his younger daughter more than did Mrs. Frank—and his kindness, fairness, as an employer of Dutch staff served him well when the time came.

For the first seven years out of Germany, life was pleasant enough—though there were ghastly tales of what was going on behind them, what was happening to people they had known. There was the sudden arrival of Anne's seventy-three-year-old grandmother, fleeing before the Gestapo.

In May, 1940, things changed dramatically for the worse. The Dutch surrendered, the Germans flooded in. Jews were forbidden to go to theatres, cinemas, concert halls; to use tennis-courts, swimming pools, playing-fields. They were forbidden to drive cars, ride bicycles, travel on trams. They must not visit Christians, their children must go to Jewish schools.

And all Jews must wear, prominently displayed, a large yellow six-pointed star.

All this horrifying detail—so much of it forgotten now, a generation later—is sketched in lightly and without malice by this girl, just thirteen, for the benefit of her new, stiff-covered friend, "Kitty". She has decided she must have a close friend, a real friend, to whom she can tell what is going on in her heart. With flesh-and-blood people, whether they be her "darling parents", her older sister Margot, her aunts and uncles or her school friends, "I can never bring myself to talk of anything outside the common round. We don't seem to be able to get any closer, that is the root of the trouble. Perhaps I lack confidence, but anyway, there it is, a stubborn fact and I don't seem to be able to do anything about it.

"Hence this diary. In order to enhance in my mind's eye the picture of the friends for whom I have waited so long, I don't want to set down a series of bald facts in a diary, like most people do, but I want this diary itself to be my friend and I shall call my friend Kitty."

And having told Kitty—it is Saturday, 20 June, 1942—just who she is, where the four of them, Mummy, Daddy, sixteen-year-old Margot and her thirteen-year-old self, have lived and are now living, she adds, "So far everything is all right with the four of us, and here I come to the present day."

The story is, of course, incomparably best told by the diary itself, but that runs into many thousands of words (she soon used up the first exercise book, went on into others) and that we cannot do here. But not a line is dull of the thousands she wrote in her not-too-neat hand-writing, and if by some mischance you have never read *The Diary of Anne Frank,* I urge you to buy, borrow or steal a copy and do so.

The first weeks of the diary are those of a normal young girl at school, not too certain of her maths, pretty confident her other subjects are good enough to move her up, in the Jewish secondary school, to the next class in the next term. She is mildly interested in the boys at school; she is pretty and she knows it and boys stumble over each other to cycle home with her. She is frankly aware that these first infatuations are short-lived: "After a while it cools down, of course, especially as I take little notice of ardent looks and pedal blithely on." There is one boy, Harry Goldberg, who appeals to her; he is shy, good-looking.

Exam results come out, she and Margot have done well, particularly Margot. Margot, Anne notes proudly, is brilliant. There is every reason for them to move up into the next form in September.

But, of course, they do not move up in September; they never again go to school. Her father has known for a long time that one day the S.S. will send for him, give him the euphemistically styled "call-up papers" which mean concentration camp and probably death. So a hiding-place has been prepared, where the four of them, when the time comes, will conceal themselves until the end of the war. They have little doubt of war's outcome. They have listened to Churchill's voice on the BBC; they believe when he tells them Britain will win, will drive the invader from the countries he has occupied.

But there must have been dark moments when they had to face the possibility of German victory—the personal victory of a warped and twisted psychopath, sworn to exterminate each Jew on the earth's surface. For how long, *then*, could one live locked up, never allowed out for even a moment? Even the prisoner with his life-sentence in jail gets into the open air.

The call-up comes: then horrifyingly turns out to be not for Mr. Frank but for sixteen-year-old Margot. The scheme must be put into operation immediately—ten days earlier than planned: but as the older people have been preparing the hide-out for months—the back part of the tall, rickety building which houses Mr. Frank's office—this is not impossible. Anne had asked her father only a few days before about the plan. Yes, says Mr. Frank, " 'we shall disappear of our own accord and not wait until they come and fetch us.'

" 'But, Daddy, when would it be?' He spoke so seriously that I grew very anxious.

" 'Don't you worry about it, we shall arrange for everything. Make the most of your carefree young life while you can.' That was all. Oh, may the fulfilment of these sombre words remain far distant yet!"

It was a matter of hours. That entry in the diary was made on Sunday morning, 5 July. At three o'clock in the afternoon the door-bell rang, the call-up notice was delivered.

Seven-thirty the next morning, after a night of frantic preparation, in which they are helped by a few Christian, Dutch, friends—and very real friends they turn out to be— they set off on foot in the pouring rain for the hide-out. They get sympathetic looks from men and women on their way to work, but no one dares offer a lift, with those yellow stars. As they slosh through the rain, her parents explain a little of the plan to her (Margot has gone on ahead with a Dutch friend, Miep). They are wearing, because of the speed-up of the plan, all the clothes they can get on, for obviously they cannot be seen carrying a suitcase. "I had on two vests, three pairs of knickers, a dress, on top of that a skirt, jacket, summer coat, two pairs of stockings, lace-up shoes, woolly cap, scarf and still more; I was nearly stifled before we started——"

The office building in which they are to spend the next two years overlooks the Prinsengracht Canal in Amsterdam: a four-storeyed, narrow erection, unexpectedly deep from front to back, and typically Dutch, with extra sets of stairs that mount almost vertically from one floor to another, two above, missing the intervening floor altogether. The back rooms can be shut off, making a more or less separate establishment. The four of them, with another Jewish family, Mr. and Mrs. Van Daan and their son Peter, are to share the back parts of the top two storeys, living in this confined space for God knows how long. But Anne is thrilled when she sees the accommodation; writes the whole description out for Kitty, with a numbered map; then ends, "I expect I have thoroughly bored you with my long-winded descriptions of our dwelling. But still, I think you should know where we've landed."

The Van Daans arrive a few days later and Peter turns out to be "a rather soft, shy, gawky youth; can't expect much from his company", who has brought a cat with him. Mr. and Mrs. Van Daan, who are to amuse and infuriate the Franks for the next twenty-four months, arrive, with Mrs. Van Daan's chamber-pot in her hat-box, because, as she brightly tells them, she never feels at home without it. Mr. Van Daan does not bring his, carries a tea-table under his arm. Almost immediately the two of them start quarrelling, in a toe-to-toe, insult-swapping routine, which at first horrifies the two girls—"Mummy and Daddy would never dream of shouting at each other"—and which later, for it seldom stops, they grow used to.

The entrance to the hiding-place, on a landing, is concealed by a book-case, made for them by a Dutch friend, Mr. Vossen. It can be moved away to allow a few Christian friends—Mr. Frank's employees—to bring in rations. The Frank family settles down as if all their lives have led up to this adventure.

It is nearing the end of August when Anne writes, "I'm not working much at present: I'm giving myself holidays till September. Then Daddy is going to give me lessons: it's shocking how much I've forgotten already. There is little change in our life here. Mr. Van Daan and I usually manage to upset each other, it's just the opposite with Margot whom he likes very much. Mummy sometimes treats me just like a baby, which I can't bear. Otherwise things are going better. I still don't like Peter any better, he is so boring; he flops lazily on his bed half the time, does a bit of carpentry and then goes back for another snooze. What a fool!" But, "it is lovely weather, and in spite of everything we make the most we can of it by lying on camp beds in the attic, where the sun shines through an open window. Yours, Anne."

And so these hunted people hide, squashed together in an intimacy no one desires, a painful intimacy impossible to avoid. Anne keeps her diary, telling it everything she would tell a best friend, and we watch her, month by month, growing up, changing from child to young girl, unfolding like a flower before our eyes. After the unpromising start of her friendship with Peter Van Daan, a love begins to grow between these two young captives. At first, we are told, nothing could be duller than lazy Peter upstairs: then the two are drawn together, but with a delicacy, a restraint which, viewed from these freer, coarser days, is surprising—and almost unbelievable when one relates it to the speed at which life is rushing by, disaster growing nearer.

But, of course, for Anne disaster is a thing one hardly ever considers. She knows only too well it is there, not far beyond the locked door and the book-case and the Prinsengracht Canal, but hope, throughout the two years of her journal, is the dominant emotion. Even the arrival of the little dentist, Dussel, on 17 November, who must now share her room while Margot gets an alcove to herself, does not distress her. She is prepared to like him, "He is a very nice man, just as we had all imagined", and she does so throughout and despite his childish, petty and at times insufferable behaviour. He is like a spoilt child, refusing to allow her to use the table in what till now has been her room, ticking her off a hundred times a day for behaviour of which he disapproves, sneaking to her mother. "When I've already just had a dose from him, Mummy goes over it all again, so I get a gale aft as well as forward. Then, if I'm really lucky, I'm called on to give an account of myself to Mrs. Van Daan and then I get a veritable hurricane!"

Mrs. Van Daan, even making allowances for the nerve-rasping intimacy of their confinement, must have been an unpleasant person. She quarrels with everyone except Mr. Frank—with whom she tries embarrassingly to flirt—does her best to make sure it is the Frank family's china, cutlery and, if possible, rations which they use. Anne has rows with her, but seldom writes anything unpleasant. They have been confined for a year when at last she blows her top, tells Kitty that the woman is "very pushing, selfish, cunning, calculating and is never content. I can also add vanity and coquetry to the list. There is no question about it, she is an unspeakably disagreeable person."

But the entry ends, "P.S. Will the reader take into consideration that when this story was written, the writer had not cooled down from her fury!"

By "the reader" she means Kitty, but she has admitted on more than one occasion that she plans to be a writer. And on the evidence of the journal, she not only would have been a fine one: she is already that rarest of birds, "the born writer". Her descriptions of the few bleak rooms they inhabit, the "feel" of them, the life that goes on inside, its friendships, jealousies, joys and stark, staring terrors—as when there are strange knocks in the night, visits from the police, or when the house is sold over their heads—all these are evoked, vivid and fresh, so that one seems almost to be there, in the smell and bustle of those over-crowded rooms above the Prinsengracht.

And all the time there is a running commentary on the events of the day, events from that forbidden outside world, as learnt from the hidden radio. One of the German leaders has made a speech somewhere and she notes that: "All Jews must be out of the German-occupied countries before 1 July (1943). Between 1 April and 1 May, the province of Utrecht must be cleaned out (as if the Jews were cockroaches). Between 1 May and 1 June the provinces of North and South Holland. These wretched people are sent to filthy slaughter-houses like a herd of sick, neglected cattle."

There are cheerful entries: "Mussolini has resigned, the King of Italy has taken over the Government—we jumped for joy!" There are air raids on Amsterdam which terrify and yet delight them, but she is worried about the young Canadian bomber crew—one of them oddly enough speaking perfect Dutch—which she learns has parachuted to safety and then been carted off by the police.

271

And on Thursday, 6 June:

" 'This is D-day,' came the announcement over the British radio, and quite rightly, 'This is *the* day.' The invasion has begun!"

Three days later, "We heard over the BBC that Churchill wanted to land with the troops on D-day. However, Eisenhower and the other generals managed to get the idea out of his head. Just think of it, what pluck he has for an old man, he must be seventy at least——"

There are chatty references to the BBC's Frank Phillips, to the eighteenth birthday of "Her Royal Highness Princess Elizabeth of York", and it is hard to realize that this young girl and her sister, cooped up in squalor, hiding week by week from a fate growing ever nearer, can have minds to encompass "asking ourselves what prince this beauty is going to marry, but cannot think of anyone suitable. Perhaps her sister, Princess Margaret Rose, can have Prince Baudouin of Belgium one day."

But love, stirring dimly, unrecognized at first, is coming to Anne Frank. It begins with a long reminiscence for Kitty's benefit. "What a silly ass I am! I was quite forgetting that I have never told you the history of myself and all my boy friends." She has remembered her days in kindergarten, and clutched at the memory. She liked then a boy called Karel, who had a cousin, Robb, who was good-looking, and "aroused more admiration than the little humorous podge, Karel. But looks did not count with me and I was very fond of Karel for years. We used to be together a lot for quite a long time, but for the rest, my love was unreturned. Then Peter crossed my path, and in my childish way I really fell in love. He liked me very much, too, and we were inseparable for one whole summer. I can still remember our walking hand in hand through the streets together, he in a white cotton suit and me in a short summer dress—Peter was a very good-looking boy, tall, handsome and slim, with an earnest, calm, intelligent face. He had dark hair and wonderful brown eyes, ruddy cheeks and a pointed nose——"

Peter and his parents move away. "There is a saying, 'Time heals all wounds,' and so it was with me. I imagined I had forgotten Peter and that I didn't like him a bit any more—but when Daddy kissed me this morning, I could have cried out, 'Oh, if only you were Peter!' I must live on and pray to God that He will let Peter cross my path when I come out of here, and that when he reads the love in my eyes, he will say, 'Oh, Anne, if I had only known, I would have come to you long before!'"

And slowly this memory of Peter Wessel is transferring itself to the real, and present, Peter Van Daan. She starts to talk with him, help him (though he is three years older) with his lessons, become interested in him. "He talked about the Jews. He would have found it much easier if he'd been a Christian and if he could be one after the war. I asked if he wanted to be baptised, but that wasn't the case either. Who was to know whether he was a Jew when the war was over, he said.

"This gave me rather a pang; it seems such a pity that there's always just a twinge of dishonesty about him——"

But later that evening, "He said something that I thought was nice. We were talking about a picture of a film star that I'd given him once, which has now been hanging in his room for at least a year and a half. He liked it very much and I offered to give him a few more some time. 'No,' he replied, 'I'd rather leave it like this. I look at these every day and they have grown to be my friends.'"

And a little later, Anne tells Kitty, "Don't think I'm in love because I'm not, but I do have the feeling all the time that something fine can grow up between us, something that gives confidence and friendship. If I get half a chance I go up to him now. It's not like it used to be when he didn't know how to begin. It's just the opposite—he's still talking when I'm half out of the room."

Already, "Peter Wessel and Peter Van Daan have grown into one Peter, who is beloved and good, and for whom I long desperately."

Halfway through 1944, one is beginning to wonder just how long this imprisonment can go on. The people who used to let them have extra food coupons have been caught, they have only five ration cards (under false names) for the eight of them, and "supper today consists of a hash made from kale which has been preserved in a barrel—it's incredible how kale can stink when it's a year old! The smell in the room is a mixture of bad plums, strong preservative and rotten eggs—our potatoes are suffering from such peculiar diseases that out of two buckets of *pommes de terre, one* whole one ends up on the stove. We amused ourselves by searching for all the different kinds of diseases and have come to the conclusion that they range from cancer and smallpox to measles . . . quite honestly, I wouldn't care so much about the food, if only it were more pleasant here in other ways. There's the rub: this tedious existence is beginning to make us all touchy."

There are one or two terrifyingly close shaves, with burglars, police, workmen coming to do repairs on the other side of the secret door. After one such horror, Anne sits down and writes a moving entry in her note-book on what it has meant to her, what she thinks of the future—if there is to be one. "If we bear all this suffering and if there are still Jews left, when it is over, then Jews, instead of being doomed, will be held up as an example. Who knows, it might even be our religion from which the world and all peoples learn good, and for that reason and that reason only do we have to suffer now. We can never become just Netherlanders, or just English, or representatives of any country for that matter. We will always remain Jews, but we want to, too.

"Be brave! Let us remain aware of our task and not grumble, a solution will come. God has never deserted our people. Right through the ages there have been Jews, through all the ages they have had to suffer, but it has made them strong, too; the weak fall but the strong will remain and never go under!"

But now—"now I've been saved again, now my first wish after the war is that I may become Dutch! I love the Dutch, I love this country, I love the language and I want to work here. And even if I have to write to the Queen myself, I will not give up until I have reached my goal."

This is not to be.

One wonders how the rest of us would react to this confinement, with its ever-present threat of destruction. For myself, I fear I might think of little else, would brood over present and future, rack my mind for some solution, knowing at the back of it that no solution existed. I doubt if I would want to read smuggled library books, for fear they would, like gloves to a bloodhound, bring nemesis upon me. But, "Dear Kitty, we have had a book from the library with the challenging title of 'What Do You Think of the Modern Young Girl?' I want to talk about this subject today."

She is candid and revealing about the "modern young girl", most of all about herself. She has a better side, but "you must realize that no one knows Anne's better side and that's why most people find me insufferable".

One finds it hard to believe that anyone could find a little girl who writes like this and is as pretty as the photograph which now accompanies her diary, anything but delightful.

That entry, the one for 1 August, 1944, is the last one. In it, she goes on to examine her thoughts and her behaviour, and the entry—the diary—concludes:

". . . if I'm quiet and serious, everyone thinks it's a new comedy and then I have to get out of it by turning it into a joke, not to mention my own family who are sure to think I'm ill, make me swallow pills for headaches and nerves, feel my neck and my head to see whether I'm running a temperature, ask me if I'm constipated and criticize me for being in a bad mood. I can't keep that up: if I'm watched to that extent, I start by getting snappy, then unhappy, and finally I twist my heart round again, so that the bad is on the outside and good is on the inside, and keep on trying to find a way of becoming what I would so like to be, and what I could be if . . . there weren't any other people in the world."

Three days later German Security Police make a raid on the main office and force the good Mr. Kraler, who has worked there daily and kept them supplied with what he could, to show them the entrance to the hiding-place. He and another man called Koophuis who works there, has helped them, are arrested, with all the eight occupants of the annexe: three Van Daans, Mr. Dussel the dentist, Mr. and Mrs. Frank, the two girls Margot and Anne.

Kraler and Koophuis, grilled by the Gestapo, yet manage not to divulge the names of the two girls, Mr. Frank's employees Elli and Miep, who have also faithfully helped the little band of prisoners. After the two Dutchmen have been put in a local concentration camp, these two girls are able to go back to the annexe and find, among other things, the notebooks which are Anne's diary. They keep these safe until the liberation and then hand them over to the only survivor of the secret annexe, Otto Frank, Anne's father.

The Franks, Van Daans and Dussel, packed into cattle trucks, were sent east to Auschwitz. Here Mr. Van Daan was selected for the gas-chamber and died in it. This fate, no doubt, would have overtaken all of them were it not for the advancing Russians who free Mr. Frank and are responsible for the other survivors (the families had been split up) being sent hastily westward to other camps, out of their reach.

Mrs. Frank died. So, at different times, did Mrs. Van Daan, her son Peter, and Mr. Dussel.

Towards the end of 1944 the two girls Margot and Anne had been sent to Bergen-Belsen. Reports of survivors from this other dreadful camp, people who knew them there, say Anne was as courageous and cheerful under these infinitely more appalling conditions as she had been in the secret annexe. But by February of 1945, both girls had caught typhus. Already they were skin and bone: now this dragged them to the edge of death. Somehow, their spirit seemed to triumph above this.

One day, Margot, pitifully weak, fell from her upper bunk, one of the hundreds of bunks in the barrack-room, half now loaded with corpses. The shock killed her.

And now, at the start of March, the death of her beloved sister did finally what two years of hiding, months of concentration camp, had not done. Suddenly, there was no longer a reason to live.

A few days later she was dead. A few weeks after that, Belsen was liberated.

And so this remarkable child, gay and courageous to the end, died, in circumstances so horrible one can hardly bear to think of them. But her name, her story, will never, ever die. The diary was published in the original Dutch in 1947—and since then it has been translated into no less than twenty-eight languages. And it has been made into a film.

There are heroes and heroes. It all depends, of course, on what you mean by the word.

Chapter 21

Yuri Gagarin and John Glenn

In my day it was Lindbergh. He it was who alone, and with remarkably little help from the aircraft industry, first flew across the Atlantic. Alcock and Brown had done it, of course, but there were two of them and they flew not much more than half as far.

But, exactly thirty years after Lindy's flight, something happened which pointed the way to a future in which his flight, indeed, every flight, from the Wright Brothers straight on down, was to become humdrum, ordinary.

For on that day in 1957 the first man-made satellite joined the moon on its journey round the earth, left the gravity which held the air in place, was out on its own, to where there was just sufficient gravity to balance the centrifugal force as it began to orbit the earth. "Sputnik" would travel round the globe—in theory indefinitely—as man's first contribution to the solar system since Copernicus discovered we were not, after all, the centre of the universe.

It was a Russian device, with the pleasing name of "Sputnik", or "Companion". More strictly, "Fellow-traveller", but that awkward English term has such muddled connotations, one prefers the Russian. It was the Russians who had built Sputnik and, even more remarkably, the huge rocket which shot it out into space. Within a week, the word was a part of every language on earth.

And, of course, the first thing that passed through every mind was—how soon a man?

Men followed, but it took time—and there is every reason to believe it took astronauts. More than one dead man is now probably orbiting the globe for ever, like a lost and shrunken moon, or crashed to death on the earth's surface. Guesses as to the number of unsuccessful attempts the Soviet Union made between 1957 and 1961 to put a man into orbit run up into two figures. As the Soviet Government never releases details of a "space shot" until it has been successful, we are unlikely ever to know. Nor are we likely to know the precise nature of the Soviet space programme, for the purpose of each shot is described, in retrospect, by what it has actually achieved.

So there might well be a case for choosing, as space hero, the first unfortunate citizen of the Soviet Union who bravely allowed himself to be shot into space on the nose of a rocket tested only for a lifeless Sputnik. But as we will never know his name, we must turn instead to the likeable young man who eventually did go into orbit with a practised, tested rocket—and came back to tell the tale.

His adventure—and in many ways it was man's greatest adventure since our fishy ancestors struggled from the still-warm slime and took a look at the world—took place over a period of rather less than two hours on the morning of 12 April, 1961. He was blasted off in a capsule fixed to the end of an enormous solid-fuel rocket, from somewhere in the eastern Soviet Union, at precisely seven minutes past nine in the morning, Moscow Time. Fifteen minutes later, a quarter of an hour after leaving the launching-pad, his first words came back, distorted, faint, intelligible: "Flight proceeding normally."

That message came from somewhere over South America— a message from a snub-nosed, cheery young man who had

278

been on the ground a few minutes before, where it had been morning. Here over the middle of Argentina it was late evening of the night before, of 11 April.

At 10.55 he was back in his proper day, and he landed, so reports say, in a "prearranged spot". Certainly, as the world was to see within a few days, he was back, in good health and tremendous spirits. He was fine, it had all been exciting, tremendous fun. "My legs," he announced, "they weighed nothing. Objects floated round the cabin, and I didn't sit in my chair, I hung in space."

Of this astonishing feat, there could be no doubt in even the most sceptical quarters. The rocket's nose capsule, the "satellite" as it became when it separated, with Gagarin inside, was tracked from several different stations, including Jodrell Bank in England. His voice had been heard calling control from it; the pictures of his arrival, his own accounts to the world's press, dispelled any doubt there might have been. Man at last had escaped from his earth, taken a look at what went on outside and come back, under his own volition, unharmed. He was immediately, understandably, the biggest hero man's imagination could encompass. His was a heroism transcending national boundaries as easily as he had transcended the earth's. Not every Russian or German can be expected to admire John Kennedy or Richard Hillary; the parts of Africa and Asia resigned to blindness and purdah are hardly likely to go overboard over Helen Keller or Emmeline Pankhurst: there are cynics to decry each name in this and every book.

But by the evening of 12 April, 1961, when the whole world knew it had been girdled, spied upon, remarked about, by a grinning twenty-seven-year-old officer in the Soviet Air Force, that world broke out into spontaneous praise, from Saudi Arabia to Salt Lake City.

Ten months after Gagarin's flight, John Glenn followed. The date was 20 February, 1962, and instead of Gagarin's single orbit, the American achieved no less than three. But as the Russian Titov had come in between, with a total of seventeen, this was not, in itself, of much moment.

But Glenn's flight is of greater historical importance than the longer one of Titov, for the simple reason that he was the first man from the west to go into orbit: *and* he had started as much from scratch as Gagarin the year before. No worthwhile information about space travel had been handed over by the Russians (and none had been expected), so that Glenn went into the unknown with less practical experience behind those who projected him than behind those, four thousand miles away, who in all probability were loading up a third, fourth or later attempt in the cherubic form of Yuri Gagarin.

John Glenn was forty, thirteen years older than Gagarin, when he made his own particular bid for immortality. He might have had, if it occurred to him, one comforting thought: whether he came back alive or not, he was already, thanks to the glare of New World publicity, a hero in either present or past tense. Gagarin would have entered his own capsule knowing (if he, too, stopped to think of it) that if he failed to get into orbit, disappeared in the direction of Mars, no one would know. He would be, in George Orwell's happy phrase, an un-person.

It is difficult to say, on reflection, which is the preferable of these states of mind.

Of Gagarin's flight we know little more than I have already told. Of Glenn's, thanks to the blinding and in many ways deplorable glare of publicity in which the American Government saw fit to conduct it, we know just about everything there is to know. We know that in Glenn's case the delay, the postponements of the flight, were enough to have shattered all confidence in the breast of a lesser man. Two of the seven selected for training, Alan Shepard and Virgil Grissom, had already made sub-orbital flights into space (leaving the earth's atmosphere, but not its gravity and therefore not going into orbit) in May and July of 1961, and Glenn's flight had first been scheduled for December of that year.

It was then postponed no fewer than ten times as weather conditions and technical hitches delayed the programme, and each postponement was in the full blaze of publicity. He must have sensed the disappointment, easing gently towards boredom, of the American public, swamped with every detail of each abortive count-down. On several occasions he was strapped into his capsule on the launching pad at Cape

Canaveral on the Florida coast (now re-christened Cape Kennedy) before having his rocket almost literally pulled out from under him.

He had been closed into his capsule for an eleventh time when he was at last blasted off.

The capsule, to the television audience watching, was a tiny pimple on the nose of the Atlas-D rocket when it was fired at 09.47. At first it seemed as if something had gone wrong: there was a rush of flame, a cloud of vapour, from the tail of the thing and it wobbled, pitifully, I thought, as if it had no idea of what was expected of it. The words "Friendship Seven" (each capsule in the programme would carry a reference to the seven astronauts) were clearly visible on the TV screen, circling in large letters the dumpy shape of Glenn's capsule, soon to sever connexion with its rocket, become a satellite drifting silently in orbit round the earth.

Then, with a sickening slowness, the name, centre of a million telly screens, wobbled away to the top right-hand corner, obscured by clouds of what seemed steam.

There was a shrill, mounting, whine as it fought its way up into the sky. It was so unlike the Guy Fawkes, Fourth of July, rockets most people knew: surely—something that started off so slowly would hardly get out of the atmosphere at all, to say nothing of going into orbit?

But the speed rose every second; it cleared its gantry, the huge scaffolding which had held it in place on the pad, and **disappeared.**

Moments later it was visible again, a white-hot flare in the sky, growing smaller and fainter.

It was at almost exactly a hundred miles above the earth when an electrical relay triggered the mechanism which leant the rocket, and with it the capsule, towards the horizontal. Then a second mechanism pushed rocket and capsule apart.

Friendship Seven was on its own, in orbit; the rocket, its duty done, and no longer with altitude control, would drift lower into the earth's atmosphere, burn up.

From now on, Glenn was in continuous contact with the ground, reporting, rather less laconically than Gagarin, exactly how he felt, how the capsule was behaving. It made pleasant, folksy listening down below; from time to time one had to remember that this man was doing something few others before him had even tried, something involving, even as he spoke, the greatest danger. Much of his detailed reporting was done for him, as Gagarin's had been: his blood pressure, respiration rate, temperature, all were radioed continuously to earth in a complex code which included as well exact details of the behaviour of Friendship Seven, her attitude, position, temperature.

John Glenn's flight lasted 4 hours and 56 minutes, during which he covered 81,000 miles at altitudes of between 99 and 162 miles. It was a little before three in the afternoon of a sunny Caribbean day when the capsule dropped gently, slowed by retro-rockets and parachute, into the sea off Puerto Rico. A little later it had been picked up by a destroyer and John Glenn, first American in orbit, was out on the deck, grinning and exhausted, listening to the cheers of his countrymen.

Once again, for lack of adequate information about Gagarin's trip, we must study Glenn's and conjecture that the Russian's may well have been similar in its hazards and its set-backs. Two things went wrong with Friendship Seven and were rectified: the hydrogen-peroxide jets for controlling the capsule behaved erratically and Glenn was forced to take over manual control to finish his third orbit; and a faulty signals device radioed to earth that the heat-shield, designed to prevent the capsule over-heating on its return to the earth's atmosphere (for even with retro-rockets, the speed of re-entry would be fantastic), had come off. The information, fortunately for John Glenn, was wrong, and he returned, uncooked, to earth.

It would be pointless and impossible to give marks to these two exploits. They have, of course, been eclipsed many times since. Longer and longer trips have been made, astronauts have travelled together in the same capsule, or side by side in different ones. Men have walked in space. Women have been in space—and one, lately space-borne, gives birth to a healthy child. Children will be conceived, born, above our heads, in the interest of science—though probably not in the course of one trip.

The moon beckons and there is little doubt that brave men will be on its surface in a few years' time.

But their feat, when it comes, like that of the pioneering lady who was first, they say, to drive along the top of the Great Wall of China in a Ford car, backwards, is unlikely to require more courage than that already shown by the nuggety, smiling little Russian or the big raw-boned American. Nor are they likely to bring back more startling information. With Yuri Gagarin and John Glenn the world reached a new, forbidden frontier and jumped.

We can never get back.

Index

284